*"Those who dream by night in the
dusty recesses of their minds
wake in the day to find that all
was vanity;*

*but the dreamers of the day are
dangerous men, for they may act
their dream with open eyes and
make it possible."*

T.E. Lawrence

Astro-Logos
Language of Life

*The true story of a man
and the people and planets around him.*

© 1989 by James T. Braha

Hermetician Press/Hollywood, Florida

Hermetician Press
P.O. Box 22-1961
Hollywood, Florida 33022-1961

ISBN 0-935895-01-9

Library of Congress Catalog Card Number: 88-081938

Printed in Hong Kong

1   2   3   4   5   6   7   8   9   10

For Lilly Braha
who taught me to dream.

Table of Contents

Acknowledgments

I would like to express my gratitude to the following individuals. They have all made significant contributions. Without their influence this book would not be as it is.

To Lisa Mullenneaux my editor, for all her efforts and invaluable suggestions. To Judy Marsh for her beautiful artwork and illustrations. To Harold Benjamin, Sam Zimmerman, Kerry Breitbart, Emmett and Maria Walz, Dennis Young, Marcos and Jane Tobal, Bob Riley, Alan Collins, Jerry and Kisan Greiff, Fred Morganstern, Sandy Mesics, Pug Pugliesi, Thor Thorgeirsson and Patrick Bosold. And to all who have allowed me to astrologize for them over the years. Thanks.

Prologue

What you are about to read is the story of one man's journey into the world of a peculiar and fascinating language; the star language, the language of life, or what is now, unfavorably, called astrology. One of the results of my journey is a concept called *Astro-Logos*™. Astro-Logos™ is essentially two things. First, it is an evolutionary and enlightening process individuals may wish to engage in. Specifically, it is an analysis of one's birth-chart—nature's communication about a person's character, destiny, and existence—as deciphered through the contrasting but complementary Hindu and Western interpretive systems. The whys and wherefores of this particular way of working are explained in this book. Secondly, Astro-Logos is a proposed organization. An organization whose purpose is to make available high-quality birthchart work and to promote the understanding and practice of the universal, natural language of life. It is a creation to fulfill a need of our times regarding the marvelous, but currently stifled, star language discipline.

An intense discrepancy presently exists between the real meaning and benefit of the star language and what the common person perceives it to be. The difference is so vast—the misconceptions and misunderstandings so prevalent and deeply rooted—that unless laypeople endeavor to practice (interpret) the language there is, realistically, no way to bridge the gap. An educational reconditioning would take several hundred years. However, according to nature's schedule for humanity (according to the stars) the time for public acceptance and common usage of the discipline is very nearly upon us. Therefore, we do not have hundreds of years to solve the problem. We need to address the matter now. Hence the creation of Astro-Logos.

Astro-Logos is an educational "starting over." It is a "re-beginning" in the sense of its presentation to the public. And for practitioners it represents a challenge to discover the greatest, most purposeful objectives and intentions of the language, as well as a comprehension of the implications and reasons for the nearly diametrically opposed Hindu and Western interpretive methods. In addition to the differences between astrology and Astro-Logos (in technique, manner of interpretation, quality control, etc.) these are the considerations that warrant a new name. While such action may seem unnecessary, especially to the nonastrologer, it will make greater sense as a deeper, more accurate understanding of the subject is realized by reading this book.

Astro-Logos could, no doubt, be considered a radical and audacious endeavor for it is clearly a renaming and redefining of an age-old paradigm. And yet it is more than a renaming. Astro-Logos is an assertion of responsibility; a means of claiming our right, as dedicated and discerning practitioners, to present the language in the way we — not the media, historians, or dictionary writers — see fit. It is a way of disassociating the genuine, beneficial, and profoundly healing birthchart and counseling work of so many experienced astrologers from the nonsense in the newspapers, overly general Sun-sign books, and carnival gypsies — all of whom confuse (and destroy) the issue. Astro-Logos represents the position that the star language is a practical discipline, the understanding of which is every bit as accessible to the nonpractitioner as to the seasoned astrologer. The commitment of this undertaking is to provide the common person with everything he or she needs to know in order to determine whether there is anything about the divine language, particularly one's own birthchart, worth pursuing.

Above all else, Astro-Logos is a system of values.

Spiritual values, astrological values, presentational values. This will be understood gradually, page by page. Do not, however, be deceived. Astro-Logos is controversial. It is the creation of one person and therefore does not constitute a democracy. Not everyone may agree with the proposal of Astro-Logos or its theories. Readers are advised to think for themselves. The purpose of this work is to revitalize a great body of knowledge presently suffering under the weight of centuries of misunderstanding and misrepresentation. Astro-Logos is not astrology. It is a different game. The task of the reader is to determine whether or not to play. And if so, in what capacity.

The first half of this text, Book 1, is autobiographical. It provides the background—the basis and reasoning—for Astro-Logos. The second part, Book ll, is a workbook divided into two sections: one for those interested in having their own blueprint interpreted and the other for persons desiring to practice Astro-Logos. Take your pick.

One final note. Astro, in Greek, means star. Logos means word or language. Astro-Logos = star language. Sounds strange, Astro-Logos, but what better name to represent a new beginning?

Introduction

Since the beginning of time there has existed a miraculous universal language, practiced by few, mysterious to most, and applicable to all. The time has arrived for this language to receive the attention and acclaim it deserves. The language, Astro-Logos™, taking its new name at this very instant, is a language in the usual sense of the word. It is an expression and communication of ideas. But Astro-Logos™ is different from other languages. Astro-Logos™ is "extra-ordinary."

Human languages are created by people for the purpose of communicating with other people. Astro-Logos is not man made. It may be "man learned," but operates regardless of man's learning. In other words, Astro-Logos is continuously being spoken whether any human being knows the language or not. This is because Astro-Logos is a language of life; a language belonging to and created by life itself. Astro-Logos is, basically, creation announcing the purpose and intentions of the progeny it has created. It is direct communication from the existing universe to the newly born. The philosophy of Astro-Logos is simple:

Creation speaks.

Stars are its language.

Decipher the language and creation becomes audible.

At the exact moment of one's entry into the world, the destiny, potential, and direction of the human soul are mapped out in detail and openly proclaimed to any and all who wish to listen. The proclamation, given out through the positions and interrelationships of the planets and stars, provides a "mirror" of one's human destiny. It is not that the heavenly bodies are involved in, or connected to, the causing of human destiny. They are not. Although such a possibility is not inconceivable, it has yet to be determined. According to Astro-Logos, the planets and stars merely convey nature's expression. Even Biblical references intimate the stars to be a communication, and not a cause; "And God said let there be lights in the firmament of the heaven to divide between the day and the night. And let them be *for signs and for seasons and for days and years.*" (Genesis).

As words and sounds are the representations used in human languages, the symbols of Astro-Logos are the planets and stars placed within a square or circular-shaped map. The map, a representation of the positions of heavenly bodies at the moment of birth, is called a blueprint (or birthchart). It is appropriately named because it is, to the trained eye, a detailed outline of a person's life. So informative is the blueprint that it reveals not simply one's overall possibility and fate, but even certain specific "inevitable necessities" pre-timed to the year, month, and day. In order to draw a particular blueprint what is needed is the date, place, and time (near exact) of one's birth.

Although Astro-Logos and astrology appear to be identical, they are not. First, it must be clearly understood that there are two entirely independent, autonomous systems of interpretation used to decipher the language of creation. Only when both methods of interpretation are used alongside each other does Astro-Logos exist. At this point nature's communication about a human soul is complete. Of the two interpretive systems, one belongs to the fate oriented Hindu culture of the Far East. This method decodes creation speaking the probable events and circumstances destined to occur in one's life. The other system, born of the Western world, delineates a person's character, disposition, personality, psychology, etc. Regarding the different information gained from the two systems, it is not that nature has given out conflicting knowledge or data. Rather it is that the practitioners of the two cultures, with their contrasting viewpoints, have developed systems of interpretation appropriate to their philosophies. Quite simply, Hindu philosophy teaches that the circumstances of one's life are predestined as a result of actions and efforts made in previous lives. Westerners maintain that our lives depend upon our free will to develop and nurture what talents and potential we have. The result is two distinctly different methods of interpretation, each producing its own special result.

Until now the two systems have remained as distinctly separate as the cultures from which they arose. In Astro-Logos these systems come together in a highly significant quantum leap. The first aspect of this advance is far greater interpretive accuracy. The second advance is the ability to produce an especially complete description of an individual's life, accounting not only for actual events, occurrences, and circumstances, but also the personal and psychological experience of those events. Furthermore, an opening is created to newly proclaim the true meaning and possibility of this natural language.

Contrary to astrology, which carries along with it a heritage of ill-reputed baggage ranging from public ignorance and misconception to fraudulent use and newspaper mumbo jumbo, Astro-Logos has no history. It has no ties nor connections to past experiences that could obscure or distort its definition and reception. Astro-Logos is born at the verge of the Twenty-First Century amidst one of the greatest spiritual and philosophical expansions ever. Indeed, it is only through the open-mindedness that welcomes such an expansion that Astro-Logos could be born. For this new language is, in fact, the bridging of two cultures, the merging of two interpretive systems nearly diametrically opposed in philosophy, which in combination form a complete and profound whole.

Such a fusion is now possible only because our collective consciousness and attitudes have so significantly evolved. Westerners are beginning to accept the notion of predestiny with no threat to their experience of free will and ability to create the future. Easterners are asserting their individual wills more than before with no detriment to their philosophy of predestiny. Astro-Logos is simply the natural and progressive outcome. Moreover, Astro-Logos will be considered in its own light much the same way many new age philosophies (whose origins are rooted in the past) have been. Such disciplines have been given new and powerful life through highly conscious and intelligent presentation and a strict interpretation of their message. Likewise Astro-Logos, though comprised of the elements of astrology, will stand on its own, attract a new generation of enthusiasts, and find its niche amidst a modern world willing to genuinely consider a language of life.

BOOK I

Astro-Logos
Language of Life

CHAPTER I

BACKGROUND;
WESTERN ASTROLOGY

My First Encounter with the
Language of the Stars

At the age of twenty-seven—some seven or eight years into my involvement with meditation and mysticism—I first encountered the unique language that would change my life. I had heard of a woman who practiced the art of astrology and practiced it well. I was skeptical, for at this time I knew "what everyone knows about astrology," but I was told "no seriously, the woman knows what she's doing. She studies lots and lots of books, and she's not weird!" Coming from my practical, down-to-earth wife such words were not to be ignored. Indeed they seemed more significant since my wife had just spent a weekend working on a theatrical project with the astrologer. Her next statement, "You wouldn't believe it, she tells people about their past and future and she's really good," was all my mystical ears needed to hear.

Our consultation took place in the astrologer's apartment on a breezy Boston afternoon. It cost $60, lasted two hours, and left me in a near-euphoric state of mind. This effect was not at all due to having heard any wonderful prophecies of my future existence. It was not that at all. It was that my brain, with its wondrous affinity for concepts and theories, was whirling from the implications of what had just occurred. Based solely on the planetary positions at the time and place of my birth, a total stranger had just described with uncommon accuracy my personal and psychological life experiences as well as certain highly significant circumstances of my childhood. I was awed and felt, in a different way than I had ever felt before, fulfilled. To find out that my life, which I had always so vehemently considered my own, was in fact unfolding according to a schedule unaffected by my passing fancies and idiosyncrasies produced a sense of peacefulness. I felt lighter, as if I had, in a way, come home.

Regarding what had just occurred, the only inference I could make was that the same vast intelligence directing nature, the animals, plants, and seasons also extends, more profoundly than we realize, to human existence. My experience was *not* the result of a mind reader or psychic. For as interesting as those experiences may be, they are the subject of quite a different vision, belonging to a different class. The information just given me was ascertained from a blueprint, a piece of paper filled with symbols and numbers, interpreted by a skilled practitioner. The chart was complicated and clearly Greek to me but was, anyway, now mine to keep should I ever desire to learn the art of interpretation. That desire was already tossing back and forth in my mind, but I was readily aware of the complexity of the work. I knew my astrologer had spent years studying the subject and that she had labored for hours analyzing my chart even before our meeting. Personally, never having been a Rhodes scholar, I opted to let this desire slide.

I rushed home to my wife, Anna, to confirm her accurate assessment of the astrologer's ability. She listened to the details of how my turbulent childhood and intense shyness appeared so clearly as outstanding features in the blueprint. She also heard how accurately the astrologer had described my mother's character and our relationship. Finally I related the astrologer's account of my present and near future indications as she interpreted them. Incidentally, it may be mentioned here that blueprints are only as useful as the interpreter's ability to interpret. At any rate, I was informed that for the past several months I had been feeling powerfully "pressured" to deal with my deep shyness stemming from childhood. In three months (specific dates were actually given) I should expect to experience the "greatest changes of my life." What would occur, she said, would be of an all-encompassing intensity and would affect especially my body, health, and sense of vitality. Once begun, the changes would last a full year. Once complete, I would be quite a different person. My experiences, she said, would be cathartic, emotional, and intense. Though a highly positive experience, extreme pain was possible, depending upon my ability to flow with change and let go of old and worn out behavioral patterns. During the same time I should also expect certain of my relationships to end and a probable "re-testing of my marriage." Nothing to worry about, I was told, but something to be aware of and not to ignore.

I found the marriage news unsettling, especially since I was at the mercy of the astrologer's knowledge. There was no way to know whether what she said was true or not and further whether it was perhaps a sugar coating of what she may have actually determined. But after four years of, what I considered, smooth married life I decided to take her words at face value. When her prediction occurred right on schedule three months later, I remember making a mental note to nominate her "re-testing" expression for the understatement of the year award.

The astrologer's account about my present state of being, especially the pressure I was feeling to deal with the issue of my deep shyness, was an incredibly incisive articulation of what was indeed happening. For approximately five months I had been practicing a remarkable dietary regimen which was restoring my body and physical vitality to a state of acute health. Interestingly, however, I had not learned of the diet out of a search for better health. I learned of it as I was trying to deal with a persistent speech problem, a stutter, which had plagued me since childhood. For some reason it had suddenly reared its ugly head in a most powerful way. The macrobiotic diet, I was told, healed all sorts of ailments, however strange, and I was now eating myself into a new being. My shyness and the speech problem, absolutely the most fundamental (and mostly ignored) issue from my childhood was, as the astrologer predicted, now being focused upon. Further, as I restored my body, the basis was being laid for the physical changes of vitality she said would occur in the following year. No slouch for accuracy this astrologer.

The Astrologer's Predictions Come True

Three months later. January 1980. Black Sunday as I came to call it. As I am attempting to enjoy my macrobiotic breakfast, Anna enters to report that in the past month and a half she has fallen deeply in love with her co-worker. First thought rage. Second thought re-testing. "Re-testing? How the hell could this be called re-testing? Clearly this is called OVER!" Needless to say the year of changes, catharsis, pain, and letting go had now begun. The shock of it, for divorce was truly the last possibility I had ever considered for my life, had a tremendously evolutionary effect. I was forced to open my eyes in a way they had not yet been opened. Painful though it was, rather than fall into depression or resignation, my mind took on a heightened state of consciousness. It was as if I had summoned up all of my greatest resources to deal with what I considered the most important part of my life. I felt tremendous vitality and aliveness. I was wide awake, and it was now all I could do to decipher my responsibility in causing the situation at hand. And if possible to turn things around.

I was already won over by Pamela Raff's astrology before Black Sunday so it was not terribly startling that yet another of her predictions had come true. Even though I was amazed by the intensity of what was happening, the distinction "predestiny" was by now just another reality to ponder. My approach to life has always been through my intellect, but I had been heavily into mysticism and meditation for years, and astrology fit in perfectly with those philosophies. It would soon become clear that the constellation of issues being dealt with—the diet, facing my shyness and speech problem, divorce, and the new enormous vitality were all inextricably interwoven and interdependent. They were all integral facets of a powerful process, all necessary to facilitate the greatest growth and evolutionary period of my life as had been predicted. It was not clear what role astrology, which would soon capture my fascination stronger with each passing day, was going to play. I considered astrology to be a wonderful, thrilling, new means of entertainment but little more than that. Not that it wasn't profound and valuable, but for one bent on mysticism and God realisation, what was the lure of a discipline dealing with relative existence? Not until I studied ancient Hindu astrology in India years later would this piece finally fall into place.

Meanwhile back at the melodrama I spent the next month or two trying to remedy my splintered marriage and understand the dynamics that would have allowed such a terrible thing to happen to such an obviously nice person as myself. With my appreciably heightened awareness the understanding part was relatively easy. Saving the marriage was not. I seemed to be validating the philosophical anecdote, "Understanding is the booby prize." Try as I might—kick, scream, demand, struggle, or plead—nothing appeared to have any effect on my wife. Finally there emerged a highly charged, emotional, Gestalt-type purging experience in which I truly spilled my guts. My soul was laid bare as I expressed the deepest and most sensitive thoughts, fears, and secrets I had fully expected to carry to my death bed.

All this happened quite naturally, but never for a moment was I unaware that my underlying intent was to affect Anna into a course of action that would preserve our union. Such a possibility seemed quite plausible since it was obvious to most everyone, even her friends, that the love affair was likely to burn out as quickly as it had ignited. This, even she admitted, made sense. Further, her feelings for me, by her own words, had not at all diminished. It was, then, a logical conclusion, so I thought, that if she could only be made to know what everyone else knew, as well as recognizing my immense and undying love, then she could put this matter to rest and avoid what was to be one of the most painful years of her life. Thus convinced, I pleaded my case supported by sufficient passion, tears, and sensitivity to impress Sir Laurence Olivier. There was no question that in those three concentrated hours I had been heard. All points had been well taken, well received, and, praise God, even agreed with. Clearly I was only inches away from being home free.

But strangely in the final outcome there was simply no cigar. There was no cigar, no movement, indeed no effect at all. Whether the love affair would last two years or two weeks it would have to be seen through to the end. This, I thought, was not good. Not good at all! Having just experienced the most cleansing purge of my days, having created the most intimate contact with another human being I had ever felt and finding that not one iota of difference had been made sent me into panic. Now I knew for sure I had no control whatever in the matter I considered (along with my quest for God) most meaningful to my existence. Now, for the first time, I was scared. Pain was one thing. Pain I could tolerate. Lack of control was another matter. I was clearly in scary territory and the smart move would be to get help.

Since all that was happening was running according to the schedule of my astrological blueprint, my first thought was to go see Pam Raff. But she was by now a good friend of my wife, who could use Pam's help herself, so that idea seemed inappropriate. Then I remembered a conversation with Pam about a talented and very famous astrologer named Isabel Hickey who lived outside of Boston. Isabel was in her sixties or seventies and had written what I now consider to be one of the best basic textbooks on Western astrology. She was said to be in a very high state of consciousness and was blatantly psychic to boot. Directory Assistance produced her phone number and our conversation began. I explained my plight, and Isabel retorted that she was in the middle of writing her third book and was not seeing anyone. I said that my marriage was hanging in the balance, and she replied that maybe what we needed was "just a nice marital vacation for a while." Jesus, enough is enough I thought as I shouted in the phone, "My wife is in love with another man!" Isabel got the message and replied, "Ok, ok, I was just testing you. I don't have time for curiosity seekers. Bring yourself and your wife and both of your charts to my house tomorrow."

The next day I was driven to Isabel's by some friends I felt fortunate to have. I was quite cognizant of the difference in seeing an astrologer out of curiosity, as I had done months earlier, and what was happening now. Now astrology was being used as a means of counseling, something truly worthwhile I thought. However, being counseled, in the sense of taking advice, I have always considered a delicate matter at best. As far as I can tell, five billion different souls equal five billion different opinions. Nevertheless, I felt I needed advice; objective, outside advice. My own evaluation, based on the lackluster results of my absolute best efforts, was that there was nothing left to do but cut my losses, suffer for God knows how long, and see what came next. But before going through with what is infinitely easier said than done, I wanted to hear someone I could respect say, "Well done James. You've got it straight, carry on." On the way over, I told friends in the car that if I sensed that Isabel was what she was cracked up to be I was ready to follow her advice. To myself I was thinking: if Isabel says to let go then the decision is made. There's an end on the matter, and there will be the freedom—somehow.

Meeting Isabel Hickey; A Great Astrologer

I entered Issie's house in a state of both excitement and apprehension. It was a thrill to be having a reading, as it is called, from a person famous in her field, one from whom it was even difficult to obtain an appointment. The apprehension, on the other hand, came from the fact that such a critical issue was at stake. There was no doubt in my mind that my task at hand was to determine whether this woman, respected though she be, was to be trusted. And for that matter astrology too. Or perhaps what I mean to say is the combination of Issie and astrology for that was the experience I was about to encounter. Fortunately or unfortunately, astrology, when judged by the inexperienced, cannot be separated from the person doing the interpreting. And this was where I sat at the time, despite my belief in the heavenly language.

In any case, I now summoned up the best sense of alertness I could for I knew I was about to tread that very thin line every would-be mystic must; that of maintaining an attitude of absolute openess to *any* and *all* possibility, and the skepticism necessary to merely survive in this world, let alone find the truth. I have always considered myself a skeptic in the sense of being experience oriented. One of the few benefits of my difficult childhood was developing an ability to sort things out and get to the facts. To survive I needed to be able to discern the difference between belief and fact, between spoken promises and tangible action. I learned well before my teens to especially give credence to my own feelings and perceptions above those of others. At the same time I knew that without a sense of trust and a willingness to be touched by others that life would be futile.

As Issie greeted me I was at once aware of a powerful presence. There was that unmistakable sense of a person proficient in her work and confident in her ability. There was also the distinct impression of a no-nonsense, brass tacks human being. After only a few short sentences I knew she would shoot straight from the hip. I had no "re-testing" statements to fear in this session! Instant comfort. Here was a woman of my style and I felt I was in my element. I stared impatiently at Issie as she pondered my blueprint for about five or ten minutes. Then she reached for a book called *The American Ephemeris* to find out the position of the planets on the day at hand. This she was doing to see the relationship between present positions and those of October 16, 1951—my birthday.

The first words out of her mouth I will never forget: "Oh my, Uranus just entered your seventh house. You have no control over this; you must let go. It's all in your wife's hands; it's up to her." Bravo. Here was astrology in its full power and glory. I explained that what she had just expressed was what I found so incredibly scary and why I wanted an outside opinion in the first place. She said that Uranus was a planet whose function was to effect change in a person's life. And that it was extremely peculiar in that it always revealed changes over which no control was possible. The only way out of the frustration of such an experience was to surrender to whatever influence it was bringing and adopt a nonresistant attitude. This did not mean to blow like a leaf in the wind at the whims of others, but just not to get attached to my own particular agenda for the time being. What she was implying was that nature, God, my subconscious, superconscious, or call it what you will had definite plans for my life during this Uranus influence. She made it clear that if control was what I wanted that I could have it by simply letting go of my desires in the matter. And that, she said, was the only practical option.

Now Issie asked for Anna's blueprint and things became clearer still, although her view of the future I had to accept on faith the same as I had months earlier with Pam. About my wife, she surprisingly said to me, "Get her out of your house. She's not going to be happy right now with whomever she's with. Let her be miserable outside of your presence." All of this information was the result of her interpretation of Saturn's present position in the sky forming a relationship with the Sun in Anna's birthchart. Now Issie, as already mentioned, was also psychic and her following statements may have been so influenced. She said, in a manner of confidence that bordered on arrogance, "It will not work out between her and this new boyfriend. She's going to suffer. I'm going to tell her that but she won't listen. I've seen it a thousand times. I want you to stay here and hear me tell her (Anna had by now arrived and was waiting in another room) when she comes in." Then Issie analyzed my blueprint in the usual fashion telling me everything she could see about my life in general and for the future. At one point in the midst of probing my chart her intuition got the best of her and she looked up at me and said emphatically, "You're a very nice person." I remember laughing out loud to hear that in the middle of such serious business.

Issie's final advice on the matter was that Anna should get her own apartment, keep busy, and try as best as possible to bide her time. The point was to postpone any decisions until August, when the Saturn influence would be over. She would then be able to see more clearly which actions would bring the most happiness. I was asked whether Anna's affair had progressed to the point of being "consummated." I said by her account it had not, which I believed. Although that may appear laughable, these were truly innocent days in our lives. We were both involved in a spiritual movement, on the path towards higher consciousness, and purity was the order of the day. So uncompromising were we about worldly matters that even on our wedding day we touched the ceremonial wine to our lips but did not swallow. "Well if she hasn't slept with him then the bond hasn't been broken," Issie said. "But if she does, it will be. Does she love you?" "Yes," I replied. "Then she'll be back because it won't work with the other man. Don't divorce now, and in August she'll be back and then it will be your decision." I believed her and felt relieved.

What she said made perfect sense considering all the circumstances. Indeed, even in the already described intense discussion with Anna, I had said exactly what Issie was now predicting. Only now there were dates. Now, there was a goal which made life bearable. All I needed to do was to wait it out till August. Then the cards would be reversed. Then I would have both Anna and a sense of justice. Assuming that I could handle all this emotionally, with forgiveness, there was only one complication and Issie made that perfectly clear. She had, in delineating my blueprint, said nearly the exact same things as Pam had regarding the enormous changes that would take place throughout the year. She went into detail about the changes and then said that what was occurring was of such an all-encompassing nature that in no way would I be the same person when the process was over. There was, therefore, no way to know whether I would still want to go back to the marriage when the opportunity arose. I was thus advised that in allowing Anna to leave the marriage I should make no commitment to ever take her back.

Unlike Pam, who was young and more of the world, Issie was spiritually oriented and her consultation reflected that. In analyzing my blueprint she was immediately aware of my spiritual interests and addressed herself to those issues. She pointed out that there were great differences between my chart and Anna's in that respect. Anna indeed had far greater desires to participate in society than myself, who would have been generally comfortable to sit at the feet of a guru and meditate. Issie spoke about spiritual matters and described the effects I should expect in the coming months. I then explained that much of what she was expressing had already begun happening. It was an incongruous fact that during this painfully emotional time I was feeling more alert, more alive, and more powerful than ever. I looked great and felt more love for people than I ever imagined possible. As time passed, putting myself to bed at night became difficult because I could not bear missing out on the excitement of life. I don't mean the excitement of parties, people, and places. I mean the excitement of being alive, of just plain *being*.

As my physical energies shifted and my presence took on a radically different vibration (my power and vitality were becoming extremely intense), I found myself being unrecognizable to many casual aquaintances. I eventually made a game of the situation. Occasionally when I happened upon certain friends I had not seen for a month or two, I would wait to see how long it took them to realize who I was. I remember bumping into one friend on a weekend afternoon in the park. He and I had, at one time, both owned retail outlets in a local mall and saw each other every day for about a half a year. This day he was selling his jewelry on a portable table to passersby. I stood in front of his wares for a few minutes, deliberately saying nothing, waiting to see how long the recognition would take. After a long minute or two of several glances he finally looked me directly in the eyes and asked if I needed help. "Hi David," I said. "How've you been?" "Oh, James," he replied, "I didn't recognize you." "Really," I thought, "I wouldn't have guessed." Other times I would pass old friends on the way to work, too much in a hurry to talk. Without any acknowledgment whatsoever I could stare straight at them and walk by unrecognized. It was quite interesting.

There were also numerous episodes of blatant intuition. I often took walks at night and on one occasion, while locking the front door, I wondered whether or not to bring my wallet. Just then a voice in my head, which seemed as loud as a ghetto blaster, said "BRING TEN DOLLARS." I ignored the thought but again heard "BRING TEN DOLLARS." Twice was enough to make me fetch my money. Some minutes later while passing the neighborhood bookstore I noticed in the window the arrival of a book by my favorite spiritual author. The price was $9.95.

The most significant effect of my heightened awareness was that I was at once becoming aware of myself in a deep way. Not just in the spiritual sense of higher self, spirit, soul, etc., although that was certainly also happening. But I was becoming aware of a sense of purpose for my life other than working on my own enlightenment. There was an acute sense of destiny, although I admit great specifics there were not. But I knew as surely as the light of day that I must teach what knowledge I had, and would continue to learn, of spiritual subjects. And I knew I would be known.

This to me was thrilling. The thought of fame as a reality was something quite new. It is true that I was an actor in college and naturally gave as much thought to popularity as any other performer. But there was now a distinct difference in my consideration of the subject. As an actor the thought of fame was an ideal, a fantasy to pursue. If the right circumstances occurred and I did my job very well, and with a little bit of luck, well who knows! But what was happening now was simply not the same. There was no reason I should be known and there was neither any evidence for it. But I knew. The only odd thing, to my mind, was that for twenty eight years I had not known! It felt wonderful and as if my entire life had built up to this point. Incidentally, my sense of destiny was not at all corroborated by Western astrologers. It was only the Hindu astrologers in India that could see this, but that is another story. I will say though that Issie asserted that I had not found my "true" profession when I told her of the retail business I owned. She could not distinguish what my final profession would be but thought I should be serving people, either through teaching or some form of healing.

In any event, as my self awareness increased much of my timidity and shyness abated. I would say disappeared but in fact what happened was that it found a more proper place in my life. Deep shyness will always be part of my personality, but it no longer greatly interferes with my actions. To this day people I meet in certain settings, especially those attending my lectures or workshops, aggressively accuse me of lying when I mention my inordinate sensitivity and introversion.

To my surprise the more time passed the clearer my mind, and all intellectual functions, became. I found it increasingly easier and more joyful to communicate my thoughts, feelings, and perceptions. This was especially pleasing since self expression had been so difficult for me while growing up. That was a large part of the reason for my life on the stage where, by hiding behind a character, I could achieve a form of expression otherwise impossible. My newly discovered intellectual dexterity was also rather fascinating since it so contradicted my background. My high school English grades were so low I was refused admittance to one college because of them. During college there was only one required English course and that lasted one measly semester much to my delight. So I was enjoying my new mental and communicative abilities quite a bit.

Issie predicted that this would be a year of the most intense spiritual evolution I would ever know. As she spoke about higher states of consciousness I was all ears. I explained that pursuing enlightenment was what I had been doing for the past eight years. I also said that aside from my daily spiritual practice I had been flying back and forth to Europe to be with my guru and to meditate for several hours a day for months at a time. I had also practiced *hatha yoga*, twisting my body around and breathing in strange ways. My *tapas*, the Indian word for austerity, she said was now paying off. According to the schedule of my astrological blueprint, I could expect a full year of very high experiences. Actually her exact statement was, "You are going to be in a different state of consciousness when this is over." I assumed by different that she meant higher! I didn't ask. All I could think was the old anecdote, "From her mouth to God's ears!"

Now, Issie was ready to see Anna and as she spoke her final private words to me, I was more aware than ever how special was her ability, wisdom, and compassion for my well being. In fact at this point I wondered how it was possible that Anna was going to ignore her advice but if Issie said she was going to then that was where I was placing my bets. Her final words were: "Remember, let her go but don't promise you'll take her back because you will be in a different state of consciousness when this is all over."

Now as regards the matter of the planetary influences of Uranus and Saturn there is much that needs to be said. I had no difficulty in accepting the veracity of the whole affair, for every time either Pam or Issie gave an important assessment or prediction they spoke intelligently and accurately. It followed then that if they were presenting their findings as the results of "planetary influences," they must have known whereof they spoke. After all, their results were quite impressive. Anyway, there was no reason then to question their statements and references to planets. I had experienced astrology and was, quite simply, thrilled that it worked so well. I was also well aware that in those two words—planetary influence—an entire philosophy was being implied and conveyed. And I chose to accept that philosophy based on my experience. In other words I had by then had two very powerful experiences verifying that astrology worked, and I also had a *belief* about how it did so. I believed that my life was being somehow affected by the planets. However, I obviously never heard, smelled, tasted, saw, or touched these planets; this so-called Uranus or Pluto which was the other planet said to be affecting my life.

As the years passed and I began to practice astrology I naturally gave a great deal more thought to this implied philosophy. While it may or may not be true that planets and stars actually directly affect human lives, there has as yet been no proof of the fact. Not by astronomers and not by astrologers. And though it could still certainly be the case that they do, it is not absolutely crucial to prove it. Mankind has always been capable of enjoying aspects of creation it has not fully understood. What is important, however, is that if astrologers can provide accurate and useful information, then their practice—the language they interpret to arrive at their findings—is worth pursuing. This is especially true since, unless one intends to do an intense scientific study, determining astrology's merit is so simple.

But now on to the issue of belief which becomes important since there is no proof of planets affecting people. Personally I have nothing against beliefs. Indeed, I believe I have more beliefs than most people (but that is just my belief!). What is important, in fact critical, is that beliefs are recognized as beliefs. Thus confusion is avoided and we know whereof we stand. This is easy enough and certainly not a difficult problem. However, in both astrological sessions there were constant references to these planetary influences of which there was no proof, only belief. As I accepted these beliefs I had not the slightest inkling to ask, "Do planets really *cause* effects on our lives?" Now, this is important because had I asked there would have been only one intelligent answer. And these were intelligent women. The answer (and it is one I give out in all my lectures despite the fact that no one asks) should have been something to the effect of "we do not know that planets cause anything. Some believe they do but there is no proof." *But like most people, I didn't think to ask. I didn't have to—it was implied!*

I now realize that whether or not Pam or Issie believed that planets cause effects, they would have used the same terminology in any case. This is because the easiest (and perhaps best) way to help a client understand what is being interpreted is to explain bits of the interpretive process relevant to the person's experience. In my case I was experiencing marital changes over which I had no control. Since Uranus represents change about which there is no control, it would definitely be enlightening to understand that I was "under the influence of Uranus." If I was simply told that I had no control and must let go I would have been left terribly in the dark. Why was there no control? How long would this go on and whose will was this anyway? But because of her explanation, simple though it was, I had a sense of reason and purpose. I could understand that there was a process under way, and that when it was over it would be for the better. Mainly, the references to planetary influences provide a context in which to hold experiences that may otherwise be confusing or alarming.

It is clear when analyzing the language used to teach astrology that there is an underlying belief that planets cause effects and influence human lives. Now while this issue of planetary influence appears absurdly insignificant to anyone who has experienced the accuracy of astrology it is in fact quite crucial. Consider that representing astrology to be the study of "planetary influence on human life" may just be one of the greatest reasons for the malignment of astrology by society. It just may be that for the public, the vast majority of which do not even *know* a professional astrologer, not to mention ever experiencing the subject, that the idea of planets influencing people is simply alien to their innate common sense! Mind you, they may have no problem particularly in believing in predestiny, direction, or purpose, but any kind of physical connection between people and planets may just seem ludicrous.

It is most fascinating that we astrologers, who have no proof that planets cause effects and in many cases do not necessarily believe that that is how it works, continue to express our knowledge in a way conveying cause. It is even more curious that this has gone on for centuries in view of the fact that the public has made clear its lack of acceptance of such a philosophy. While this presentation business may seem curious to some, consider this as a reason for conveying the subject as a language. Imagine what a Russian might say if asked what he or she thought of the Portuguese language. There would be no mention of belief or nonbelief. The question could only be answered in the context of understanding or not understanding the language. Further, whether there was any love or disdain for the language could only be ascertained as a result of familiarity. Yet it is not at all so with astrology. Ask anyone what they "think" of astrology and they will answer in the context of belief. Whether or not they have ever studied or even known a professional astrologer they will voice an opinion about their *belief* in its reality or lack thereof! This is not a fault of public perception but of astrological presentation. Astrologers take heed, the fault lies not in our stars but in ourselves!

At any rate, after her final words to me Issie ushered Anna into the room and began the next astrological session. She spoke in her usual manner, only now her words were ruthlessly direct as she attempted to save Anna from a course of action Issie felt would simply bring more pain. Most of what she said was wonderfully soothing to my bruised ego, though it must have been brutal to my already hurting wife. I recall wondering just how much of this Anna would be willing to take, but Issie's concern was so evident that there was little Anna could do but listen. What Issie said essentially was that Anna was embarking on a misguided course of action. The ardent love affair, Issie stated emphatically, would not work. Indeed it would cause a great deal more harm than it was worth, and therefore the entire matter should be postponed until August when the "planetary influences" would abate.

Now Issie stated, "There is a spiritual difference between the two of you," intimating that in this area we were perhaps not compatible. "I know you feel that you are in terrible pain in this predicament," she said to Anna, "but it is even worse for your husband. It is not you, but he, who is being tested." "What you do now," she said, "is your own decision. But I'm going to say it over and over again. It will not work with this new boyfriend. It will only cause more suffering. If you decide to go with him, it will be a mistake. And if your husband takes you back you will be the luckiest woman in the world."

Issie's latter statement, I believe, was more the result of a person of a different generation than anything else. Anna would not necessarily have been lucky to have me back. There were, clearly, powerful reasons for our marital disruption. For one thing, during all our married life I had been critical, judgmental, and self-righteous. Further, I had never accepted or respected many of Anna's friends. Worse than this, I did not care about perhaps the greatest passion of Anna's life—her art. In this sense I had no commitment to her happiness. So Anna was not simply a jerk or an unfeeling clod. For four years she had been a wonderful and devoted wife dealing with a complicated situation.

At any rate, throughout the conversation Issie made references to the "planetary influences" from which she was making her interpretation. This she did not do for the purpose of proof (after forty years of practicing, Issie had no need to prove astrology to anybody) but so that Anna could relate her present experiences to the astrological descriptions and thereby trust the veracity of Issie's prognosis.

Issie kept her word about reiterating to Anna that the love affair was doomed from the start. As I listened I hoped she would be wrong in her prediction that her words would fall on deaf ears. I had at least the right to hope, for even Isabel Hickey was not infallible. She, like all other astrologers I have known, had made certain statements, descriptions of personality or some such, which were to my perception incorrect. I was, more and more, amazed to think that her advice—so intelligent, practical, and concise—would go unheeded. It was especially disconcerting since I knew that Anna had, over the past several months, experienced the accuracy of astrology both in my life and her own based on a reading with Pamela Raff. So of course I hoped.

Unfortunately, however, on this account I did not win. Anna heard the words and respected their source as far as I could tell, but still needed to finish out her process in the best way she saw fit. What had changed however, was that she now at least had some intellectual understanding of the whys and wherefores of what she was going through. Anna now understood that she was "being affected by" Saturn, the planet symbolizing discipline, responsibility, and maturity. Through the situation at hand she was now in a position to squarely face those issues. According to Issie the love affair was a test but how she handled the matter was her own business. Although Issie had her own opinion of the outcome, she also said that Anna had the free will to prove her wrong. This certainly made sense else why bother with astrology at all? Issie was not in the business of being "right" but in serving people through counseling using the heavenly language as her medium.

One of the most profound aspects of astrology is its ability to provide an understanding of the individual process. Just as there are billions of different souls on the earth so there are as many different birthcharts all unique in their own right. Each one thus indicates specific goals, lessons, paths, and experiences for the person at hand. Nowhere is it more apparent that what is medicine to one is poison to another than in astrology. And nowhere is it more evident that life is but a series of obstacles, tasks, and opportunities placed before us as a path towards greater evolution. To me Anna's actions were monumentally important. To Issie they were irrelevant. To Issie, Anna was simply another person in the process of learning certain lessons, which through astrology Issie could perceive and illuminate. Furthermore, since the lessons were occurring through the Saturn experience they would be learned, according to Issie, the hard way. That is merely the Saturn experience as understood in the language of the stars.

In Anna's case the lessons were indeed being learned the hard way. There was, in short, no easy way out. If she were to follow her present desires, things were definitely not going to work in her favor. If she denied her feelings and needs, needs which had gone unfulfilled far too long, she would feel an acute sense of loss. In her newfound relationship Anna was experiencing a level of fulfillment she had, I am convinced, never known. She was thus, in typical "Saturnian" fashion, between a rock and a hard place. In any case, because the birthchart provided knowledge of Anna's psychology, inner workings, and purpose, there could be no moralizing, finger pointing, or passing judgment. There was instead a keen understanding and description of her unfolding process. There was, in the words of the *I Ching*, no blame.

Finally, I left Issie and Anna to continue their consultation alone. Before I left, Issie recommended certain spiritual books and gave me instructions in a technique designed to stimulate past life remembrances. As I walked towards a local bus stop I was quite aware that I had accomplished what I wanted. I thus felt tremendous relief. I was also quite excited. Issie was more than I expected and of greater assistance than I had hoped for. I recall thinking that what had just occurred was one of the greatest experiences of my life. This I do not say lightly because in seven or eight years of pursuing enlightenment I had had my share of significant adventures. I had in those years plenty of experiences with the supernatural, both with enlightened gurus and in my own spiritual practices. What had just happened had none of the flair or glitter of the paranormal. Indeed, upon reflection the profundity of the consultation will surely be difficult to comprehend without a genuine empathy for the matter at hand as well as a sense of what really occurred. And though it may seem obvious to the reader what occurred I suspect it is not.

Fortunately or unfortunately, astrology is, as Issie stated in the title of her first book, a *cosmic* science. And being cosmic, or in harmony with the universe, it renders itself useful to a variety of tasks, depending upon the situation at hand. What happens in a session with a talented professional astrologer cannot be easily categorized or pigeon-holed, though it is tempting to do so. Although in nearly every case much information is imparted about character, destiny, and purpose, that is almost never what the meeting is truly about. In modern society astrology is, more than anything, a means of healing. It is a means of healing that uses knowledge and awareness as its tools. To those who wonder how "fortune telling" can be healing I would say quite simply, and from experience, that people consult astrologers not for information per se, but for greater perspective on situations they consider outside of their control.

Aside from curiosity-seekers, people consulting astrologers do so out of need. And while their questions almost always center around some such desire they wish to fulfill, it is insignificant whether or not they will realize their goal. What is significant is the relief of the burden of not knowing. More importantly, the consultation provides a wider, and therefore more balanced perspective, and a context in which to hold their experience. That is what makes the difference and puts the mind at rest. Food and shelter notwithstanding, we suffer far greater from what we are unsure of and thus cannot harmonize and integrate than from any material need. When spiritual needs are satiated, it eases the mind, relieves tension, and heals the organism. Healing and harmonizing are thus, in the end, what astrology is all about.

Further, the import and value of the consultation, depends to the largest extent upon the intention and agenda of the client as well as the quality and consciousness of the practitioner of the heavenly language. I have by now astrologized for several years' worth of clients, and nothing is clearer than the fact that, despite my deep commitment to make a difference in all their lives, the clients who entered their sessions with a powerful intent to gain value for themselves are the ones for whom astrology has been the most profound service. There is no doubt that many curiosity-seekers have also gained value. Many such people, who were either non-believers or simply uninitiated in astrology, have had their lives dramatically altered—at least intellectually. But even they were open and willing to create value in their lives. Others, less willing to be responsible for their own growth, may enjoy a "peak" experience which they soon deny or forget.

Over the years I have personally enjoyed numerous astrological readings with many different astrologers under a variety of circumstances. Some have occurred in the West, while at least as many have taken place in the Far East through the more event-oriented Hindu system. Many readings I remember vividly and with fondness. Others I can recall only with effort, and persistence. Still others I have completely forgotten. The distinguishing factor has always been the consciousness and awareness of the practitioner. It has also been the care, concern, and compassion the astrologer has been willing and able to bring forth.

In truth I do not know that such appreciation should be the same for all. And neither do I know that I can properly express my meaning, but I am reminded of a session in Northern India with an astrological guru, Gopi Nath Shastri. Sri Shastri answered only two or three questions for me early in 1983, one of which, I realize in retrospect, was inaccurate. Yet I shall never forget our meeting together. Nor will I forget the happiness and healing created that day or the inspiration I received to spend so many of my days practicing the language of the stars. Though very little was said, meeting Shastri had a profound effect on my life.

I was directed to Sri Shastri by an Indian meditation instructor whom I had asked to recommend a capable astrologer. A young boy was sent to accompany me and function as interpreter. Before entering Shastri's abode, I asked what fee I could expect to pay for services rendered. The boy laughed loudly and said Gopi Nath was a guru and if I offered money I was likely to be thrown out of the room! The proper procedure, I was advised, was to find a local street vendor selling fruits, buy a few, and offer them as humbly as possible. I did as instructed and finally found myself in a crowded room filled with local villagers. All waited patiently for the guru who spent most of the day meditating and doing *pujas* (an Indian devotional ceremony) before coming out to astrologize. Gopi Nath Shastri was quite old and at this point in his life his work centered around a branch of astrology called *prasna* (pronounced prushna), not around analyzing personal birthcharts. *Prasna*, known as horary astrology in the West, is a method of problem solving or answering specific questions based on planetary blueprints drawn for the actual time a question is put to the astrologer. It is a simple procedure but allows only for an answer to the specific question asked rather then a description of one's entire life.

As the allotted time approached a tiny smiling Gopi Nath Shastri arrived on the scene and all rose in reverence. Quickly he directed us to sit, and then one by one he conferred with each individual beginning with the men first. Not speaking Hindi I understood none of the specifics of people's questions or the answers given, some of which were private in any case. I could not help but perceive, however, the warmth and humor of Sri Shastri. Outbursts of laughter greeted his occasional jokes to the group. Most questions were, of course, quite serious as would be expected since these people were typically poor with more important things to do than spend their time idly. According to my young interpreter many asked questions concerning sickly relatives or about pressing financial matters. And some had come simply to bring fruit and flowers in thanks for previous advice or curing methods which had been successful.

Eventually, Gopi Nath ministered to the last man in the room as I gathered up my coconut and bananas in anticipation. However, my presence was ignored as Sri Shastri turned to the women and gracefully took their questions one at a time. Now I was puzzled and tried to decide whether I was being punished for being a *mllecha* (non-Hindu) or honored for being Western and, therefore, savored for the last. In any case I waited and watched. And the more I watched the more enraptured I became by what I found to be a wonderfully intimate and humane form of service. I was, I knew, quite fortunate to be in the presence of this guru of gentleness, compassion, and humor. And the more time passed the more tensions I saw dissipate and the more burdens lifted. People were clearly being deeply touched through Gopi Nath Shastri's astrological ability and humanistic counseling. I was myself, on a level I was unaware of, being profoundly moved. For three years I had been indulging an unending fascination with astrology (the Western system, of course) without any idea towards what end. Possibility was now powerfully revealing itself.

Finally, my turn came and Sri Shastri answered my questions. Two of them concerned my future activities in the field of mysticism and astrology. His responses were favorable and proved later to be correct. The other issue was related to my personal life and in the end his judgment was found to be inaccurate. The reason for this (there is no way to be sure) may be that I had handed Shastri some calculations of my natal Hindu birthchart which another astrologer, an amateur, had computed incorrectly. Or the faulty answer may have occurred because the question I asked was not at all pressing. That is important because in *prasna* astrology the urgency of the question is crucial. For, it is at the moment that a person is compelled to take action (consulting an astrologer) that the heavens reflect the life of the issue in mind. At any rate, all of Shastri's responses were of a positive nature and so I felt quite happy. But in truth, I felt far happier for having met Gopi Nath Shastri than for the particulars of what he said. In reality I had waited over two hours to ask this guru questions which had little to do with my present state of existence. And though I was quite aware of this I would have waited longer still had it been necessary. For somehow I sensed that the medium was, in fact, the message. And this was one medium I definitely intended to experience.

Somewhere in my thoughts that afternoon I resolved to learn the 6,000-year-old Hindu system of astrology. I had, after having my questions answered by Shastri, put forth one more. I instructed my interpreter to ask Gopi Nath, who could not have been a day less than seventy, if he would teach me what he knew of the heavenly language. As I awaited his answer no words were forthcoming. There was only an expression of such angst on his face that I literally could not bear to push for a reply. I thanked him humbly, clasped my hands together in the Indian greeting fashion, and left.

As I was rickshawed back to my lodging amidst the Benares crowds, I marveled over three perceptions I had that afternoon which I intended never to forget. One was that I had just met a very special man. The second was that knowledge of astrology was a wonderful privilege not to be profaned by its use for the purpose of gaining riches. And the third was that in the practice of the heavenly language it was neither the information nor interpretation but the consciousness and humanity of the practitioner which was of the greatest import. In the same way my meeting with Isabel Hickey was infinitely more beneficial because of her way of being, so my association with Gopi Nath Shastri was more dramatic because of his incredible vibrations and *sattwa* (purity). Of all this I was clear.

Upon reflection, it was no miracle that my marital consultation with Issie produced such a profound result. All the forces were in place, all the ingredients present to have that happen. My intention to create a valuable experience could hardly have been stronger. Issie's counseling technique, coupled with her astrological ability, powerfully reflected her many years of practice. Her consciousness was uniquely high and her caring was remarkable. I was lucky to have sought her assistance. As I waited for a bus back to Boston I felt healed and whole and had already begun to let go of my four-year marriage. And along with the pangs of separation, I felt a sense of freedom and grace. Little had changed between morning and afternoon that day save that my perceptions were validated, and I now had a context and perspective with which to understand the changes I was going through. From these simple revelations my emotions were becoming my own again, and I felt my world heading slowly in the direction of normality for the first time in a long while.

Not long after our meeting with Isabel Hickey Anna found herself an apartment and moved out. Issie's prediction that Anna would go ahead with her relationship proved correct. When that happened we broke off communication completely, and I prepared myself to wait out some of the longest months of my life. I literally counted the days till August and maintained faith in Issie's prognosis. Meanwhile my energy and vitality increased as my spiritual experiences grew stronger by the day. More love and awareness was unfolding than ever occurred during the several years I had spent practicing the tedious austerities of meditation, fasts, and the like. The more this happened the more I found myself dwelling on Issie's statement that I would be in a different state of consciousness when the year was over. Now curiosity of this heavenly language was beginning to get the better of me. Weighed against how terribly difficult astrology seemed to me, I could easily bear not knowing how Issie knew so much of my character and destiny. And I cared relatively little how she could predict the affairs of my marriage. But higher states of consciousness was just too serious an issue to let slide.

Learning to Interpret: The Journey Begins

So one sunny day I decided to make my way over to Redwing spiritual bookstore to canvass the astrology section. I knew not the slightest of what to look for but as I perused the shelves I saw two books on the planet Pluto, one of which was written by Issie. It was not her authorship that interested me but the fact that every time Pamela Raff or Issie spoke of my sweeping changes they did so with a statement about Pluto. So, I excitedly read excerpts from the book until a saleswoman offered her assistance. She immediately asked if I was an astrologer and then explained that the book I was holding was absolutely inappropriate for a beginner. I was, however, already transfixed by the little I had read and wanted the book. When I told her why—because Pluto was doing its work on my life—she asked my date of birth. She was herself an astrologer and without looking in any technical books said that Pluto was conjuncting (forming a relationship with) the Sun in my birthchart. She said I need only read the one page describing that effect and let matters go at that. She suggested other books for beginners, which I felt no affinity for. I wanted the book in my hand. She, however, made it crystal clear that it was of no use to a beginner and I finally left. As I walked home each step became harder to take. Finally diplomacy gave way to desire and I decided "the hell with the saleswoman, I want that book!" I turned around, headed back, and bought it.

When I arrived home I immediately called Pamela Raff to ask just what it was that Pluto was doing so I might study the descriptions from Issie's written pages. As it turned out Pluto was involved in all sorts of powerful relationships in my birthchart. I spent hours that night reading, re-reading, indeed practically meditating on what I read. It was the start of a beautiful friendship.

As time passed and I awaited my wife's predicted return most of my free time was spent studying astrology. Difficult as the practice seemed in the beginning, I found I possessed not only a kinship for the work but also a sense of patience, love, and reverence for it. Being of a compulsive nature I bought many more books on the subject than I needed and stayed up until early hours in the morning indulging my passion. Never having enjoyed academics, homework, and the like, I approached the work in my own peculiar way. I bought none of the introductory Sun sign astrology books. I had little interest in studying anything so general as to apply to one-twelfth of the world. Further, if newspaper astrology was based on Sun signs I wanted no part of it. It did not take much to realize the absurdity, even fraudulence, of predictions meant to affect literally hundreds of millions of individuals in the same way on a particular day. I began, actually, with professional astrological textbooks which I applied to my own birthchart. Following that I gathered birth data of all of my relatives and close friends, whose lives I knew intimately, and had their blueprints calculated. I thus had a basis from which to begin my studies.

The way one learns to interpret the language of the stars is through practical experience. Faith in the heavenly language, despite what most think, is not an essential ingredient. In fact not only is it not an essential ingredient, but it could in the early days constitute a great handicap. This is because in order to interpret birthcharts one must be terribly objective just to deal accurately with an inordinate amount of detail. Such detail must be analyzed separately, in isolation as it were. Although it is, no doubt, through understanding the whole blueprint that one truly gains the power to describe a client, it is only by an analysis of the isolated parts that the whole can be perceived. Hence each individual factor must be analyzed and understood.

One studies the meanings of the different factors and

33

their various combinations in the blueprint through the use of detailed reference texts written by experienced astrologers. However, *empirical* meaning is not revealed through these explanations. Textbook delineations in a discipline as vast and complex literally as life itself can only function as guidelines. One actually learns the practice by connecting the particular factors of a specific blueprint to the person involved and ascertaining the results. Thus, practical experience is the ultimate teacher. The purpose of textbook descriptions is to aid the astrologer in isolating each particular factor and understanding its principle and meaning. Therefore, the ability to decipher and understand the language of the stars is a function of one's willingness to be responsible for his or her own experience and perceptions.

In any event, the way to gain experience in the beginning days, when so little is known, is through a process of retrospective analysis. In other words the student begins with a birthchart in hand, of a person whose life he or she is familiar with, and works backwards. For example, in analyzing a chart, the student establishes certain factors present and then studies textbook interpretations of those factors. The next step is to determine whether the interpretations given fit in the person's life. The ultimate test of astrological knowledge lies in its ability to render accurate interpretations. If the descriptions of a particular factor fit consistently (or relatively, since astrology due to its complexity has never been one hundred percent accurate) one tends to remember that meaning as a truth, becomes responsible for it, and finally commits it to memory. The next time the same factor in a birthchart is encountered its meaning is known, experientially so. If, however, the textbook description does not fit, as is sometimes the case, one does not accept its veracity but considers it a possibility as yet personally unproven. Therefore having great faith or belief in astrological wisdom could be detrimental in the beginning when a state of open-mindedness and objectivity would be far more helpful.

Because of my intense curiosity, love for the work, and compulsive studying I learned to practice astrology in a very short time. In fact there is perhaps no other discipline in my life I grasped so quickly. I was, without a doubt, aided by a strong intuition and special awareness. I could also, and would to my astrologer friends and students, attribute the rapid learning taking place to particular planetary influences at the time. But since, with the advent of Astro-Logos, it is time to begin disassociating planets and stars with *causes* in our lives, I will not make that assertion. In truth the planetary effects cannot be (and are not meant to be) separated from other reasons and interpretations given for the purpose of understanding. All reasons and explanations have their validity (or lack of) irrespective of each other. That one explanation of cause is found to be accurate has no bearing on another separate, but also accurate, explanation.

Unfortunately, many people tend to match psychology against determinism, or heredity against conditioning, thinking that the two are distinctly separate and without connection. It is a limited and indeed inaccurate point of view. Even from a narrow perspective, cause of any specific issue is generally complex and able to be explained differently from different paradigms. Cause is generally a result of several interdependent and/or interwoven effects. Most importantly, cause will have to be accepted as a product of itself. In other words, we must inevitably accept that things are the way they are because they simply are that way! Let us take psychology, one perspective out of thousands, as an example. If we question why a person is a certain way, we understand that he or she is that way because of parental or other circumstantial influences. Fine so far, but then why are that person's parents or circumstances the way

35

they are! The answer is that they are that way as a result of *their* parents and circumstances. And those parents are the way they are because of their parental and circumstantial influences.

This logical process continues on and on and on *ad nauseum*. In the quest of determining cause all boils down to previous effects, which ultimately began at the start of creation. Cause therefore is the result of itself, or of the creator if you wish. But even then one asks why of the creator? And to the creator's answer one again asks why. Finally, even if the cause belongs to the creator one must accept the creator's cause as the cause of itself. In other words the creator caused things to be the way they are because the creator caused it that way. This line of reasoning in philosophical circles is known as "false cause." When people offer their logic as an explanation for cause, they are merely playing in the field of false cause—even astrologers, especially astrologers.

So I learned astrology fast, very fast. And I learned it fast because I learned it fast. I also began attending local classes given by experienced teachers, Isabel Hickey being one. There was no lack of people to practice on as word spread quickly of my newfound interest. Since I had virtually no experience I was especially conscientious to explain to those I astrologized for that I was relying heavily on textbook delineations and principles. And though I was nervous about doing so, I did the best I could to provide as much insight for people as possible. As I practiced, I asked for as much feedback as people were willing to give, which was plenty. The more I practiced, the more I inquired and the more I learned.

The process was, fortunately, an exceptionally natural one for me due to certain innate tendencies surfacing more powerfully now than ever before. Serving others through the spiritual and uplifting discipline of astrology happened to fit in profoundly with the direction my birthchart indicated as a path to fulfillment.

Perhaps the most beneficial feature of the heavenly language is its ability to provide direction and purpose. Finding one's niche in life is, to be sure, a delicate, difficult, and time-consuming matter. And while astrology is clearly no panacea to all problems, it is definitely one of the finest aids in helping one discover the areas of life likely to bring utmost fulfillment, growth, and satisfaction. How such information is ascertained is essentially through analysis of the blueprint as a whole. However, there are some few simple and basic elements that communicate the essence of the matter.

There are, in the blueprint, two representations known as the Moon's nodes, specifically called the North Node and South Node. The nodes are actually mathematically calculated points, rather than planets or stars. They are, because of the nature of the information they reveal, considered by many (including this author) to be two of the most important parts of the blueprint. The nodes occupy exactly opposite positions from each other in the chart, and their meanings reflect that fact. The South Node represents an area of life or a way of functioning that the person is innately familiar with. The North Node, on the other hand, symbolizes actions and operations the person may be unfamilar with but must develop during the course of life. The talents indicated by the South Node are ingrained from birth and appear very shortly thereafter as natural abilities. The activities relating to the North Node, being completely undeveloped and untested from the start, are considered the "new territory" for the soul to explore. It is through activities indicated by the North Node that the soul makes the greatest progress and growth. It is also through such actions that the soul experiences its greatest satisfaction and fulfillment. However, whether or not an individual embraces and participates in these activities is a matter of many factors, free choice assumedly being one. Such activities being new, undeveloped, and untested frequently evoke fear or impassivity, at least early on. Certain individuals move very gradually towards their natural direction in life while others seem to advance like arrows to their target. Some may avoid working on their path to fulfillment like the plague. Still others are shocked or jolted onto their course, and so it was for me.

It happens in my own case that South Node activities relate to very personal interests. Home, domesticity, and unfoldment of soul powers have always been easy, natural, and vital interests for as long as I can remember. North Node activities in my chart mean public ambition and dealing with the masses, and prior to the marital shakeup remained dormant, unrecognized, and commingled with great fear. But this was now rapidly changing as were other South Node functions. Specifically there was a nagging behavioral pattern of analyzing, criticizing, and passing judgment on everyone I knew save the perfect! The North Node invitation was a way of life based upon compassion, service, and love. Through the pain and shock of what was now occurring in my life I was, in one fell swoop, propelled into living North Node activities.

It happened most blatantly through astrology. The more I practiced, the more intimate contact I had with the public. And the more contact I had the more I perceived people as intricate and complicated individuals worthy of appreciation and understanding rather than condemnation. I was, make no mistake about it, unclear at the time of the depth and scope of what was possible through the heavenly language. I had no idea then that the fascination it held in my life would continue to grow stronger with each passing year. As I have already stated, the interest in such a mundane discipline provided great perplexity to one dedicated to enlightenment and teaching meditation. But what I did know, what I could feel quite plainly was that my new way of behaving, my desire to teach and be known, and my astrologizing—amateurish though it may have been—together gave life meaning. Finally I had a purpose and a course of action which, when followed, produced a sense of contribution and contentment.

Even in the very early days of practice I discovered the joy of predictive accuracy. I recall a humorous instance of a friend in Kansas City calling to ask how the outlook was for a specific date he was set to appear in court. After analyzing his blueprint in relation to the positions of the planets on that day I saw little of any significance either for better or for worse. This was odd since it was he who was being sued. The following Thursday, however, looked ominous, and I thus advised caution on that particular day. Some days later he called to say that the judge had actually postponed the court appearance until the Thursday I had mentioned! Such occurrences so early on brought much inspiration.

This same friend was, at the time, at a low point in his life, especially regarding love matters. He was living in an unhappy relationship with a woman he had little feeling for. His blueprint, however, revealed the likelihood of an extremely strong and positive love interest entering his life in just a few weeks. When I told him this, his reaction was exceptionally pessimistic. He could not imagine falling deeply in love at a time when nothing else in his life was working properly. I explained that much of the reason I was confident in the prognosis, since I had so little experience, was that the same planetary aspect had occurred some twelve years earlier at a time when he was involved in the greatest romance of his life. Nevertheless, logic told him the prediction must be wrong.

A few days after the dates I had specified he would fall in love, I received a phone call from this friend. He had just met the woman of his dreams on a Greyhound bus of all places. He thanked me for my prediction and commented that this astrology business seemed to be definitely worth pursuing. Having once been involved in Eastern mysticism, which embraces the heavenly language, he had pondered the reality of the discipline with an open mind. But now that he had experienced its accuracy first-hand, his relationship with the language was powerfully altered. The couple later married, and I was honored to be Best Man.

Some weeks before August, as I hoped for Issie's prediction to bear fruit, I analyzed Anna's blueprint to try and determine how her life was progressing. Doubts were creeping into my mind as to the likelihood of her reappearance in my life. Less than six months ago she had fallen intensely in love, had given up her marriage, and turned her life upside down in one quick stroke. Now she was to return because the great Isabel Hickey had pronounced it so? Faith was easy when August was a date long in the future. Now it was just around the corner, and I was having second, third, and fourth thoughts on the matter! Astrology has never been an absolute science. Though there are often judgments an astrologer is tremendously confident about making, there is always room for error. Further, who is willing to ignore the element of free will? And finally, when astrological predictions fall flat, there is no one to blame and no authority to appeal to.

As I studied Anna's birthchart I compared the current planetary positions in the sky with the positions they occupied at the time of her birth to see the relationships formed between the two. This in Western astrology is basically the way things work (there are other methods but they are similar in nature). If Anna was scheduled to return in August, I thought, there should be some hardships or difficulties spoiling her romantic life which might show up in the blueprint. There were, however, no major or important aspects that I could find so I finally gave up, closed my eyes, and went to sleep with the issue still whirling in my brain.

At some point during my sleep I heard a clear message to "see what is happening in Sagittarius." One of the spiritual effects occurring throughout the year of 1980 was a subtle but encompassing level of awareness pervading my being. During the sleep state it was most obvious as I seemed to witness my thoughts and dreams as they happened. As such I woke myself up to go back to Anna's birthchart and follow the instructions I had just heard. I thus found an aspect indicative of disturbances and arguments in the home space. It was a minor aspect, one which could indicate perhaps two or three days of problems, but sometimes such aspects serve as an impetus to action which has been waiting to happen for some time. In any event, I was happy for having had the slightly mystical experience and for the faith it raised in seeing Anna soon. Now I began to ponder how nature would arrange our meeting. It had been months since we had spoken and I had no intention of doing anything but waiting.

Our meeting began with a short note I found in my apartment during the first week in August. A simple request to talk. Relief. Huge relief. Months had passed without a word between us. Now, right on schedule—just as Issie had predicted—Anna was back. It was now time to talk. Neither Anna nor I were ready for divorce despite all that had occurred. Our love was still somehow, God knows how, intact. We both wanted a fulfilling and workable marriage if the possibility still existed.

However, Isabel Hickey's interpretation of the schedule of our lives had not only been incredibly accurate, but her advice was quite astute. I was, very simply, not at all the same person who walked into her house only half a year ago. The changes which had already occurred were massive with yet another six months of "planetary influences" still to come. The essence of change, so far, was in the assimilation or embodiment of my spirituality. My consciousness was raised to a distinctly different level, though not to the state of enlightenment traditional philosophy refers to and that I desired. But it was not consciousness that was significant in my attempt to restore my marriage. It was the choice between a spiritual life and one dedicated to worldly objectives I had to deal with. I had finally reasoned that aside from all our personal needs, desires, and behavioral patterns responsible for the marital breakup, there was a deeper underlying division between Anna and I.

Spiritual life, in reality, does not mean thinking holy thoughts, living a secluded existence, or practicing arduous austerities. It is neither a matter of evolutionary techniques nor even purity of lifestyle though these are, in most paths, the means to the goal. Spiritual life is simply a way of being based upon broad or cosmic vision, and an all-encompassing or all-inclusive philosophy. But it is not philosophy or point of view that generates spirituality. Rather, spirituality, or the innate and ingrained tendency of wholeness within, gives rise to a special perspective and way of being. Spirituality, or spiritual life, is a function of one's intention or will (not desire) to be complete, in harmony, and at oneness with all of life. It comprises a willingness to own up to values or a way of being consistent with that purpose. This was, I now knew, the way of being I wanted for my life. And this was not, I felt, what Anna was up to when she made her decision to break her marriage vows for the fulfillment of a greater, but clearly relative, desire. There was the rub and there was the issue to deal with.

Anna was an actress. She had been on the stage for at least half of her life. It was in her blood. I, on the other hand, could be found on any given day complaining that I missed being with my guru and wanted more time to meditate and pursue God. Anna was becoming more active in the world while I was headed in the opposite direction. During my months alone I was preoccupied with two thoughts. How had I, a mystically-oriented person given to fits of seclusion and occasional monkhood wound up with a career woman committed to one of the most demanding careers? The second thought on my mind was a statement my guru had made years earlier that I had always done my damnest to ignore. It was an answer to a disciple's concern about marrying someone whose goals were different from his own. The answer was something to the effect of: "If the two of you are on different paths, if you are headed in different directions, it probably won't work." Probably —an understatement at best.

Different directions, different paths, different people. When Anna and I finally spoke Anna wanted to know if it was possible for us to work things out. Her recent relationship had been short-lived just as her birthchart had, months earlier, indicated. I made some comments about her decision to ignore the information revealed through astrology. Had she not seen that it was accurate from the very start? But that was silly. I was the mystic, basing my life on things unknown and unseen like astrology, not Anna. Anyway, the process she had been through was an emotional, not an intellectual one. Nothing, in my opinion, could have stopped Anna's course of action. On some level certain actions, even the seemingly bad ones, are meant to be. They are predestined from birth. Anna's was. That was one reason Isabel Hickey knew Anna would not follow her advice. She had seen the workings of fate day after day, week after week, and year after year. Issie was no fool.

I told Anna that I wanted her in my life as much, in fact more, than I had before. I now felt far greater capacity to love. I also saw exactly how I had driven my wife away. I would not make those same mistakes again. Things were quite clear. However, and this was one big however, I was not going to stay married to an actress. Period. I would not attempt to make a life together with anyone who was genuinely immersed in worldly matters. It was simply unrealistic. So it was now up to

Anna. Whether she wished to remain in the marriage simply depended upon her choice between a spiritual versus worldly life, i.e. whether she wished to keep her professional activities in place or not. In my mind there was only one answer that would do. And that answer was, for better or worse, just not to be. When all was said and done my marriage had been, in the words of Pamela Raff, "re-tested." And it had failed.

It was not for some years that I encountered what is called "the composite chart." The composite chart is an astrological technique combining the birthcharts of two individuals in order to produce one blueprint representing the essentials of the relationship. Composites can be done to analyze business relationships, friendships, family relationships, etc. But mostly it is used for love relationships. In the case of Anna and I, our composite revealed no mystery. Ours was a relationship of growth. Lessons and growth. It could not have been plainer. Out of ten planets, ten indicators of different life functions, six were in the sign of Libra—the sign governing relationships. More than this, two of the most "personal planets," planets representing the most intimate and essential features of life (the Sun and Mercury) were conjunct, *within the same degree*, with Saturn! Saturn—the planet of discipline, responsibility, sacrifice, and lessons learned the hard way. In life there are, as they say, no mistakes. Anna and I had played our parts well. We learned our lessons. The hard way.

James & Anna

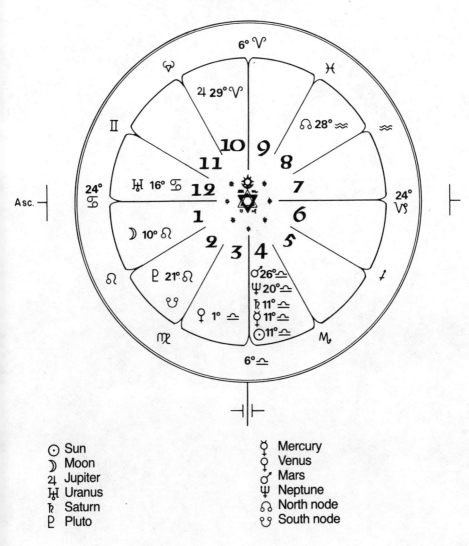

- ☉ Sun
- ☽ Moon
- ♃ Jupiter
- ♅ Uranus
- ♄ Saturn
- ♇ Pluto

- ☿ Mercury
- ♀ Venus
- ♂ Mars
- ♆ Neptune
- ☊ North node
- ☋ South node

CHAPTER II

HINDU ASTROLOGY; THE MISSING HALF

T here is a story about the founder of the Hare Krishna movement, A.C. Bhaktivedanta Swami. One day while sitting on a New York park bench he was approached by a subway conductor. This occurred during his early days in America when he was yet unknown and extremely poor. The conductor inquired as to who he was and what he was doing. Prabhupada, as the swami is called, explained that he was very wealthy and had temples all over the world filled with spiritual disciples. The man looked puzzled at what appeared an obvious fib whereupon Prabhupada replied, *"It is only separated by time!"*

In accord with the Indian Bengali tradition, Prabhupada's parents had consulted an Hindu astrologer immediately after the child's birth. They were especially pleased at one rather spectacular prediction. This boy, they were told, would cross the ocean at the age of seventy as a proponent of a particular religion. He would minister to followers worldwide and would construct 108 temples. The way it happened Prabhupada left India at the age of sixty-nine and the rest, as they say, is history.

Although such a specific and accurate astrological

prediction is extraordinary and would certainly amaze anyone, it would be less startling to one familiar with the 6,000-year-old Hindu system. For, Hindu astrology is simply an event-oriented practice. Unlike its Western counterpart, which excels in character analysis, personality, and the individual's psychology of experience, Hindu astrology focuses almost exclusively on events destined to occur. As mentioned in the Introduction, creation always expresses its intention for the life of its progeny. It does so through its own language—the planets and stars and their interrelationships. But methods of interpretation differ dramatically.

The reason for the difference of approach is obviously a debatable point. But logic strongly suggests the matter is a function of cultural philosophies and their resultant lifestyles. Put simply, Western culture is steeped in the philosophy of free will which dictates that man can accomplish anything with effort, drive, and ingenuity. Therefore, a Western approach to decoding nature's language would quite naturally assume the expression to be a directive of internal psychology and behavior rather than actual occurrences. If not so in the beginning, certainly over time interpretive methods would have developed in this direction. For in a culture where society experiences such free will, where a peanut farmer can grow up to become president, what would be the impetus or rationale to consider nature's communication one of preordained events and circumstances?

Hindu culture, however, is another matter. Its philosophy of karma and reincarnation teaches that every action produces a reaction and, therefore, one's current existence is largely a result of actions from previous lifetimes. Thus, a degree of absolutely fated circumstances is a certainty. And even if Eastern interpretive techniques were not fate-oriented from the start they would naturally have developed that way in order to fulfill society's requirements. The fact that it is, for all intents and purposes, impossible for an Indian to raise his or her station in life creates the need for such a system. India has for so long lived under a caste system, which determines that the offspring of one line shall remain in that line. Children of merchants remain merchants and descendants of servants remain servants and so forth. Further, the country itself is so impoverished that unless one is born wealthy, there is, as perhaps only one who has seen India firsthand knows, almost no way to rise above the circumstances one is born under; unless, that is, destiny as revealed through the stars determines otherwise.

And so it is that Hindu astrology is perhaps ninety-five percent concerned with a person's wealth, fame, and fortune and five percent with personality, psychology, and motivation. It is typical for the Hindu astrologer to predict, for example, how many children a person will have, what sex they will be, and even the years when conception may take place. The person visiting the astrologer expects to be told in no-nonsense terms how great or limited are his or her possibilities for success, happy married life, longevity, obtaining land, etc., etc. And expects to be told what type of career or careers to choose. This is, therefore, the reason traditional Indians consult an astrologer immediately following the births of their children.

However, it should be understood that while the Hindu system, having evolved over 6,000 years, is generally remarkably accurate, it is not a simplistic, all-magical, crystal ball. It may have a reputation as such to the novice due to the commonplace accounts of authentic and dramatic experiences many have had with the subject (the likes of which apppear in this book). But the work of interpretation cannot be one iota less complex than life itself. The number of subtleties and intricacies involved in astrological analysis are as varied as the number of positive or negative possibilities to any concern in life. Few people are either so blessed or so cursed in any one area that their experience of that issue does not include a significant range of highs and lows. Naturally such scope and variety appear in their blueprints. As a result certain communications in nearly every birthchart fall in a somewhat gray, rather than black or white, area. And so the information given, though proclaimed freely and openly through the heavenly language, is at times difficult to pinpoint in the way most desirable. It is actually when the astrological indications for an issue are either extremely favorable or unfavorable that startling predictions are made. In such instances the predictive process is, not only simple but, as only one practicing the system could know, almost child's play. In summation, Hindu astrology excels in delineating events and circumstances in a person's life. It does this exceedingly well but not always simply, clearly, and dramatically. And like anything else the system is neither a panacea nor, as practiced thus far, an absolute full-proof means without error.

♓	♈	♉	♊
♒			♋
♑			♌
♐	♏	♎	♍

My First Taste of the Predictive Astrology of the Ancients

My first encounter with Hindu astrology came in 1982 and was humorously brief but still enough to whet my appetite. It was not an actual appointment with a *Jyotishi* (Hindu astrologer). In fact I do not know the extent of the man's experience or whether he was a practicing professional. The meeting came about through an Indian gentleman I met during my travels in India, who upon hearing of my astrological interests, insisted that I see his friend Rakesh. I accepted the offer and eventually found myself in a casual discussion with a man who shared the same love for the heavenly language. Eventually he asked for my birthchart and I explained that I had one drawn in the Western method but not the Hindu method. He said there was no problem and began transposing my round Western chart into the square-shaped Indian *chakra* as it is called. The main difference in the blueprints lies in the fact that the Hindus use a real zodiac (called sidereal) while Westerners use a somewhat symbolic zodiac (called tropical).

Without belaboring technicalities, a brief explanation may be given. A zodiac is an imaginary sphere encircling the heavens, inside of which the Sun, Moon, and planets travel in their orbits. The sphere is 360 degrees in circumference and is divided into twelve equal parts called zodiac signs. When people speak of these zodiac signs (i.e., Libra, Gemini, Leo, etc.) what they really mean is a particular cluster of stars. The cluster is stationary and forms a kind of backdrop to the orbiting planets, the Sun, and Moon. Each sign or group of stars encompasses thirty degrees of the zodiac. Thus, statements such as "my Sun is in Taurus" or "my Sun sign is Taurus" mean that the group of stars called Taurus formed the backdrop of the Sun on the day of that person's birth. When one says "my Moon is in Pisces" it means that the group of stars named Pisces formed the backdrop of the Moon on the day of that person's birth. Such statements are, however, unspecific since each sign comprises thirty degrees of space while the planet or luminary occupies only one particular degree of a sign. In other words a heavenly body may be anywhere in the beginning, middle, or end of a sign. The Sun, for example, moves approximately one degree per day. Therefore, a person born on October first may have his or her Sun in the beginning of Libra, say the seventh degree, while someone born on October twenty-second may have the Sun in the thirtieth degree just preceding Scorpio, the following sign.

Now the difference between the sidereal and tropical zodiacs is that one takes into account what is known as the precession of the equinox while the other does not. The "precession of the equinox" is a slight movement of the earth's axis. The movement is so small that it amounts to only about one degree every seventy-two years. However, over hundreds or thousands of years the figure adds up and significantly affects the zodiac. Specifically what is affected is the determination of the beginning point of the zodiac—the first degree of Aries. In other words, the point in space called one degree of Aries say 500 years ago is not to be located in the exact same place today because of the gradual precession taking place. That starting point would now actually be found in a different constellation. Of the two zodiacs it is the sidereal that considers the precession crucial and takes the calculations of the movement into account. The sidereal zodiac is therefore a more accurate, or scientifically correct, or "real" zodiac. And this is the method used in Hindu astrology. The Western system, on the other hand, employs the tropical zodiac which ignores the movement of the precession as if it did not exist. The tropical zodiac is therefore considered more symbolic in nature.

Though many wonder how two astrological methods could be so different and still produce accurate results, the problem is not complex. The answer is that the sidereal or real zodiac reveals the actual events and circumstances of one's destiny while the Western symbolic method represents the psychology, potentials, and behavioral patterns of the person. To be fair it must be acknowledged that both systems are capable of delineating both events and psychology. But the Hindu system so greatly exceeds the Western one in predictive accuracy and the Western method so excels in revealing the internal state of the person that, realistically, the two systems fulfill two different purposes.

Having transposed my Western birthchart to the Hindu *chakra* by a few simple calculations Rakesh spoke to me. He saw that my life had gone through great changes just a few years earlier. He said that between 1973 and 1980 I had been extremely spiritually oriented, and yet quite absorbed in married life. But since 1980 my direction had been different. He explained that from then on I was more concerned with career, which he said was dedicated to dealing with society and influencing the public. These years would also bring a great deal of accomplishment in worldly activities but not so much peace of mind. Indeed, the years between 1980 and 1998 he said would be characterized by "insatiable worldly desires." And that the first and last few years of the period were likely to be painful due to the loss of loved ones as well as other general hardships.

Now Rakesh was getting somewhere. He was certainly describing the dynamics of this part of my life. It was a fact that my spiritual activities and the relationshsip with my wife began in 1973 as he had noted. His simple analysis of the immediate past few years was also on target. Not only was it true that the beginning of the period mentioned brought on great changes and divorce. But those events were followed, only a few months later, by my father's death—a very painful affair.

Further, it was during that same year that I awoke to a sense of destiny about my life as a teacher. Since that time I had left Boston and my retail business in search of a spiritually-directed career that could affect society in a more meaningful way. So Hindu astrology was clearly a body of knowledge to be reckoned with. Nowhere in my studies of the Western system had I come across a way of uncovering the specific focus of a person's life for such long periods of time. Rakesh had dissected my life into about six or seven distinctly different periods, although he only told me about two of them, the ones relevant for now. I was intrigued.

In distinguishing the seven-year period from 1973 to 1980 and the eighteen year period from 1980 to 1998 Rakesh was using an astrological technique of the Hindu system called the *dasa* (pronounced dasha). A *dasa* is a duration of time during which one's life is said to be governed by a particular planet. Naturally then, one who understands the symbolism or meaning of the planet according to the language of the creation, is able to predict and describe the tendencies of the person's life during the years that particular *dasa* is in effect. For example in my case the eighteen-year-period beginning in 1980 that Rakesh described as giving insatiable worldly desires and less peace of mind, was that of *Rahu*. *Rahu* (pronounced ra-hoo and known as the North Node in Western astrology) is not an actual planet but a calculated point in the birthchart. In the Hindu method of interpretation *Rahu* signifies worldly desires and accomplishment and disturbance of one's peace of mind. And in its period it almost never fails to bring hardships and emotionally painful experiences (usually loss of loved ones) in the first and last few years of its period. In my particular blueprint Rahu occupies the tenth space which, in the language of astrology symbolizes career, society, and the public. Thus when Rakesh noticed that I had entered a *Rahu* period in 1980 he easily deduced what my life was now about. And in this way he proceeded.

The Hindu method of *dasas*, or planetary periods, incidentally is entirely different from Western predictive techniques. In the one Western method so far mentioned in this book (called transits) what is of significance is the relationship of the current planetary positions in the sky to the positions of the planets on the day of one's birth. Specifically, whenever any planet in its current heavenly position forms a special spacial relationship to the position of a natal planet an effect is indicated. In this scheme whatever the planet at birth symbolizes or represents in the person's life is influenced or colored by whatever the meaning or symbolism of the current (or transiting) planet making the relationship. The effects indicated may last anywhere from a few days to a year or two depending on the movement of the transiting planet and how long it continues to form a relationship with the natal planet.

In the Hindu system the *dasas*, or planetary periods, a person will experience in his or her lifetime are set at birth depending upon the Moon's position in the blueprint. These periods are very long (the shortest being six years and the longest being twenty) and as such provide a kind of life schedule. Although a person may be born into any one of the planetary periods, from that point on the *dasas* commence in a consistent order. The order is as follows: Sun—six years, Moon—ten years, Mars—seven years, Rahu—eighteen years, Jupiter—sixteen years, Saturn—nineteen years, Mercury—seventeen years, Ketu—seven years, Venus—twenty years. But one may be born into the beginning, middle, or end of any one of these periods. After that the set order continues. The periods, incidentally, being so long are further broken up into nine subperiods, called *bhuktis*, which reveal more specific information about each particular time frame within the *dasa*.

After I was given the basic information regarding the meaning of *dasas* and their effects in my life, Rakesh asked me what he evidently considered a highly personal question. "Young man, was there not a woman in your life who did a terrible thing to you?" "What do you mean?" I replied. "Was there some woman who left you for divorce?" "Yes, as a matter of fact there was something just like that," I said, rather disgruntled. At that Rakesh grinned from ear to ear, thrilled with his predictive ability. In fact he then called his young son over in order to reveal his great accomplishment and to teach the ways of the heavenly language. They spoke in Hindi for a minute or two as I pondered this man's strange bedside manner. Finally I broke in to ask whether I would marry again. He replied, "You are lucky, there is a very good woman coming to you." Being relationship oriented (my Sun is in Libra in Western astrology), I was excited and demanded to know when. As fate would have it, Rakesh then noticed the clock and jumped from his seat yelling, "My God, I'm late. Come back Friday." Since Friday was four days away and I was leaving the city the next day there was an end on that matter.

My next experience with Hindu astrology I did not consider terribly significant at the time. I have since learned better as part of our conversation came to form the prologue of my first book four years later. The meeting occurred a week or two after my visit with Rakesh and involved a local Benares astrologer who practiced his art in a small shop hidden from the city crowds. At first I asked several questions about Hindu astrology, and we discussed the differences between the Eastern and Western systems. It is often perplexing for astrologers learned in one system to approach the interpretive techniques of the other. One reason for this is the fact that although the techniques are radically different the tools are essentially the same. Thus, the systems appear on one level to be quite similar when in fact they each have their own complete and separate ways. The tools of astrology, of course, are the birthchart (or blueprint) and the positions of the planets placed within. Although most of the meanings and interpretations attributed to the heavenly bodies are the same in both systems, there are occasional variances, which I was curious about. So I had my questions answered and then sat back eagerly awaiting the reading.

Shastri, the astrologer, calculated my birthchart through the use of certain technical books not unlike the ones used in the West. Once drawn, he silently analyzed the chart and then began to describe my life. There was little drama for the most part as much of what he said I was already aware of. He said he knew from the blueprint that mine was the life of a spiritual truth seeker and a teacher. My endeavors within the field of spirituality and mysticism, he said, would change dramatically from time to time. He said emphatically that I would have several careers and that in this area I should not be too intent on one particular *dharma* (life purpose or worldly activity) or there would be disappointment. While some people find one simple mission in life others are meant to experience many different paths. Still others are less fortunate and never come to understand their course. My career and worldy activities were not, unfortunately, the essence of simplicity. Shastri likened my life to that of a research student in the field of metaphysics. What was most fascinating was that he knew that whenever my experience in any subject reached a peak, whenever I felt my full capacity to appreciate a discipline was exausted, I would simply move on to another challenge rather than stay in the field and reap the benefits which experience normally brings. Research student, indeed; this was a theme in my life for as long as I could remember and still continues as of this writing!

Regarding this *dharma* business, Shastri's interpretation reached into the depths of my being. It was now three years since I had come to a clear understanding of my life as a teacher. But, despite a wealth of experience in mystical subjects—meditation, healing techniques, new age counseling methods, and an endless fascination with astrology—somehow something was not yet happening. At the age of thirty-one, at least four significant professions having successfully come and gone, my life purpose still was unclear. From the psychological and free-will-oriented system of Western astrology, I had learned and "re-cognized" wherein my direction lay. As already described, my life calling, what would bring about fulfillment and the most rapid growth of the soul would be activities involving the masses and compassionate service-oriented endeavors. But despite my understanding and acceptance of this knowledge, I had yet to find my way. The most obvious and fitting activity worthy of my commitment was astrology but this I absolutely could not yet do. The problem was that I was experienced only in the Western system. And the more I practiced and studied, the more clear it became that something was missing.

The Western system is no doubt profound in its ability to reveal people's behavior and internal makeup. But it falls terribly short in providing a genuine picture of their *actual* destiny, their life schedule. Although the Western system does in fact reveal the tendencies, talents, desires, and psychology, all of which are indeed the *basis* for a person's actual destiny, some people ascribe greater importance to their inner stirrings than others. For this and a host of other reasons some readily actualize their visions, dreams, and desires while others may never do so. Thus, knowing one's motivation and behavior is not enough to determine, confidently and consistently, the events and circumstances of one's life. Indeed, for all the truly powerful and profound insights gained in the past two years of intensely analyzing and scrutinizing my own blueprint, here I sat in Benares, India, still seeking answers to the *form and structure* of my life. And it would still be another two years before I could disentangle my own attachments enough to pose the proper question to the proper Hindu astrologer to get the proper answer!

As the reading progressed Shastri spoke of my divorce. He explained that my birthchart contained an astrological condition that inevitably spoils married life. The condition is called *kujadosha*, or Mars affliction, and occurs in about three out of every ten blueprints. It is an indication that a person will be abused, deceived, or victimized in their marriage. In the Western world most people with the affliction eventually find themselves divorced, through no apparent fault of their own. In India the problem is not nearly so devastating because measures are taken to alleviate the problem before any damage is done. Indian society, being more traditional and spiritually oriented, has maintained its acceptance and appreciation of astrology. As such, most parents consult a local astrologer before arranging a marriage for their child. Thus if *Kujadosha* is found to exist in the birthchart a simple but effective solution is offered: marry one with a *kujadosha* blueprint to another who also has the affliction. For it just is not within the nature of people with *kujadosha* to mistreat, in any significant way, their love partner. Therefore, Shastri advised that in the future I should find a wife with *kujadosha*. I stood forewarned.

Eventually our discussion turned to the usual matters of finances, health, future wife, the number and sex of the children I would have, etc. In certain respects Shastri was quite accurate, and in others not so much so. There was not what I would call a great deal of consciousness in the room, and were it not for the fact that this was my first serious exposure to the subject the session could have been forgotten entirely. There was not the usual uplifting and healing, or regenerative process, that regularly takes place in the presence of a spiritual or highly evolved astrologer. But I was, to be certain, receiving valuable information. Also on the positive side I must admit that Shastri made one of the most startling and accurate predictions of all the astrologers I have ever seen. But more of that later.

Regarding health, Shastri correctly noted that the liver and throat were two of the most sensitive areas in my body. Since my father had just recently died of liver cancer, I was curious to know more. According to the language of creation each of the planets has numerous meanings or significations, in other words numerous life functions it is known to represent or rule. Each planet is thus considered to be *associated* with whatever item it rules. There is not necessarily any physical connection between the planet and what it represents. But in the design of the unique language of creation the planet is the symbol, the interpretive tool, used to parallel or mirror the particular life function. In the case of my health, Shastri could easily detect a delicate or fragile liver since the planet representing the liver, Jupiter, was involved in "bad aspects" (adverse spacial relationships with other planets) at the time of my birth.

The question was whether the organ had plans to cause me grief. If so when, and were there any preventative measures I could take. I was informed that since it was Jupiter that was indicating the problem whenever a *dasa* or *bhukti* (planetary period or subperiod) of that planet ran its course such difficulties were indeed likely to arise. Now Shastri explained that the beauty of Hindu astrology was not merely its ability to reveal when certain occurrences would happen but also to advise a client what to do, what remedial measures and antidotes to take in case of dangerous or difficult times. This made good sense. Of what use would the ability to predict the future be if life was completely unalterable? Indeed, how could nature provide a positively fate-oriented means of prognostication without also disclosing precise and concrete remedies to deal with upcoming difficulties?

Hindu astrology offers many different *upayes* or remedial measures designed to relieve or mitigate the difficulties revealed in the birthchart. While the techniques may seem strange, mysterious, and even bizarre to many Westerners, they have been used effectively for thousands of years in the Far East. The simplest and most common method is the use of planetary gemstones. In the same way planets are symbolically associated with certain life functions, they also are known to represent such earthly elements as metals and jewels. In order to affect astrologically evident difficulties one should wear the gem or metal corresponding to the planet revealing the problem. Gems are more powerful than metals, and the larger and better the quality of the stone the more positive its effect.

Why gemstones work, and so profoundly well at that, is perhaps as difficult to discern as why astrology works. But most people today are aware that man is a mass of vibrations constantly affected by other vibrations—chemical, visual, sound-induced, or otherwise. In the same way many arthritic people wear copper for relief, the planetary gemstones have their specific effects. For example, I was advised to wear the gem ruled by Jupiter, yellow sapphire, which would thus improve the condition of my liver. Although wearing the stone would be of immediate benefit, it was specifically crucial during any upcoming Jupiter period when problems are expected. I was also informed that the sapphire would have a good effect not only on my liver but on all the other significations Jupiter represented in my particular birthchart. Thus I could expect a greater sense of optimism, a better relationship with my eldest brother, more opportunity in general, and a longer life.

No one is more aware of the challenge of attempting to convey the power and effectiveness of gemstones than I am. For despite the fact that nearly all the middle class Indians I saw during my travels In India were wearing two or three astrologically prescribed stones on their fingers and necks, it was not for two years that I was sufficiently moved to incur further debts by purchasing my necessary gems. Once I did so I found the results so clearly beneficial I began convincing as many of my astrological clients to obtain their prescibed stones as I could. Positive effects are often immediate. I am especially reminded of a young woman I met who accompanied her friend to a reading. This woman was quite interested in astrology but could not afford a consultation since she had been out of work for a solid year and a half. Out of a sense of service and my love of astrology, I calculated her birthchart after her friend's session. In analyzing her blueprint I noticed that one planet, Mercury, was in a particularly horrific position on the day of her birth. Aside from its usual significations Mercury was, unique to her birthchart, associated with career, self confidence, and the ability to gain recognition. Hence it was not startling that she had difficulties finding a fulfilling vocation, indeed any vocation.

Since the gem associated with Mercury is a green emerald I knew that that was the stone she needed. But before mentioning this fact I noticed on her finger a ring with a large beautiful blue sapphire. It had been a gift from her mother and was quite lovely. Unfortunately however, according to the planetary positions in her particular birthchart, it was the worst stone she could have been wearing! Just as certain stones have beneficial effects others may cause certain harm. The intense affliction to Mercury on the day of her birth was due to its adverse relationship with Saturn. The gem for Saturn is blue sapphire. By wearing the sapphire and strengthening the significations of Saturn she was in fact harming Mercury's condition worse than it already was, which was plenty. I naturally advised her to get an emerald if possible, but in any case to remove the sapphire immediately. Whether she ever obtained the emerald I do not remember, but she did away with the sapphire in front of my eyes. About a week or two later she called to report that she not only felt lighter and easier but also had found a job to her liking! While the story could be coincidental or the result of the placebo effect (what one believes one creates) her favorable experience is not uncommon in the world of astrologers.

In my own experience with gems I have especially noticed positive results from a diamond, also prescribed through birthchart analysis. Although I do wear the yellow sapphire necessary for my liver, luck, and optimism, it will not be for many years that the need for that stone is acute. As for diamond, being associated with Venus, it naturally enhances one's love life. In my own birthchart however, the planet takes on much greater significance as it represents my physical body, confidence, ability to gain recognition, and aptitude for worldly functioning in general. The condition of Venus when I was born, as interpreted through the blueprint via its sign position and interrelationships with other planets, was in an exceptionally adverse and peculiar state. Aside from its revealing shyness and timidity, it is the indicator of my compelling tendency to withdraw from the world, to internalize and focus within. While such propensity is favorable to, and one could say responsible for, my life in mysticism, spiritual disciplines, and let us not forget the inexplicable language of creation, it has not made worldly life easy! Although I generally consider my passion for meditation, introspection, and solitude quite wonderful, the introversion is at times too intense for comfort. This occasionally results in irksome moods of isolation and alienation. Yet because of, or shall I say as indicated by, the condition of Venus this has been my way.

Originally when I decided to obtain a diamond it was not to alleviate these difficulties but rather those of my not-so-simple love life. And although there has since been, to my benefit, a greater sense of detachment in that area, I am most grateful for the resulting balance and equanimity of mind. As it happened, I was constantly reflecting on the effect of the diamond on my love relationships and all but ignoring Venus' other significations. Some three or four months later I came to realize that the annoying moods I had experienced, during most of my adult life, had almost completely disappeared. Such is the power certain vibratory effects can give. As for my great love life well . . .

As Shastri continued with the reading I marveled at the different results Hindu astrology provided compared with the Western system. There were so few statements about my personality. Neither in fact was there even a great deal to say, as certain areas of my life were simply predicted to be favorable, others difficult, and still others mediocre. While Shastri did not know all the specifics of my existence, it was clear that he was identifying much of the format of my life. His view of my possibilities, both on the positive and negative sides, seemed to match what my years of experience and reflection had taught. Only he knew, much more than I, when I was most likely to manifest the best and worst of those possibilities. In short I knew what was possible while he knew what was likely. I knew what could be realized; he knew when!

I recall that foremost on my mind was whether or not my childhood speech problem was apparent in the birthchart. That had been an intense source of suffering and was something I assumed to be destined since there seemed for so long no way to stop it. As the reading progressed I waited to see if Shastri would mention the speech problem. He did not so I did. His reply was that speech, education, and all intellectual or communicative functions were evidently harmed but in a special sort of way. Through birthchart analysis there are certain areas of life which are seen to be utterly ruined while there are others which, though initially devastated, can improve with effort, patience, and persistence. Such was the case at hand and Shastri explained that this particular growing process would never abate. His assessment was certainly accurate, even more so than I knew at the time. For back then my lecturing and teaching, compared to now, had really barely begun. These days when I think that my public astrology lectures are my greatest joy, as well as my greatest strength, his explanation reverberates in my ears. It is also a testimony to the astrological feature indicating this growth process (revealed through *upachaya bhavas* to those familiar with Hindu astrology) that this should be the case for one such as I who contracted a phony cold every time one of my schoolteachers demanded an oral report!

Although I could easily relate to most of what Shastri had to say the conversation took, at one point, what I thought a rather bizarre turn. My judgment was mistaken, however, since four years later the dialogue formed the prologue of my first book, a text on Hindu astrology for Westerners. It is repeated here by my own permission.

Shastri: You are going to write some books.
Braha: What!!!
Shastri: You are going to write some books.
Braha: Are you sure?
Shastri: Yes.
Braha: How many?
Shastri: A few, five or six.
Braha: Are you sure?
Shastri: Yes.

Braha: But are you sure? I mean are you positive?
Shastri: My dear friend, astrology is not an absolute science.
Braha: Ahhhhhh. . . .
Shastri: But you will write books!

Although I had a powerful sense of my destiny as a teacher, and was flattered by his declaration, I also knew I was thirty-one years old and had never attempted any serious writing. I cared little for high school English and was refused admittance to one university because of low grades. I even recall, during college and for some years after that, a series of recurring nightmares in which I am thrust back in time and have to repeat twelfth grade English. So, much as I would like to have believed astrologer Shastri and for all the confidence I had in the language of the stars, this was one matter where I felt Shastri missed the boat. However, his prophecy was a profound one. I consider it so not merely because it has proven to be particularly accurate but because it focused on an aspect of my life almost completely dormant up until then but which would eventually assert itself more intensely than I can describe. By the time of my reading I had already been involved in intellectual activities, both as a teacher and lecturer of meditation, and as an amateur astrologer of the Western system. But writing, in any serious way, I had never considered. It just did not make sense.

Regarding predictions there are two basic ways the Hindu astrologer comes to his or her determinations. Both ways entail judgment born of personal experience. In the same way Western astrologers learn the elements of interpretation through analyzing numerous birth-charts and noting the results in the people's lives, so it is for Hindu astrologers. Of the two ways the Hindu system employs, one is slightly more technical or empirical than the other and, as such, reveals predictions of a more specific nature. This more empirical means is given through Hindu astrological scriptures written thousands of years ago by ancient enlightened sages— masters of astrology. The scriptures contain some 400,000 astrological *yogas* as they are called. Yoga literally means union, and in this context what is meant are unions of various birthchart elements. For example a union is formed if two or three particular planets occupy the same zodiac sign. Or a union may exist if certain planets are in a specifically designed relationship to the Moon or some other planet (these are extremely simplistic examples). When a particular yoga exists in the blueprint certain results are to be expected in the person's life unless there is some strong mitigating factor (thus the need for practical experience).

The method of delineating yogas is a simple one in that once a yoga is found to exist the result can be predicted with relative certainty. What is complicated is that the yogas, as many as one is capable of, must be memorized. The reason they must be memorized is that the astrologer cannot undertake the tedious task of searching the scriptures for days on end to locate the particular yogas inherent in one single chart. The benefit of predictions based on yogas, however, is that the information gained may be extremely specific, much more so than that which is gained through ordinary interpretive methods. For example, consider the prophecy about Swami Prabhupada mentioned at the start of this chapter. The prediction was clearly a result of a special yoga in his blueprint because of its specificity. Although it is relatively simple to identify travel through the Hindu birthchart as well as spirituality, and even the tendency to build temples or "spend for charitable purposes," it is impossible to predict the number of temples Prabhupada would establish. As it happened Prabhupada built not exactly 108 temples but well over 100 before his death. Such is the beauty of astrological yogas.

The other means of prediction occurs through a more logical process of interpretation. As has already been explained, each individual planet is a distinct symbol representing certain issues of life. Likewise the signs of the zodiac have their significations or life functions. Further, spacial relationships between the planets also bear their meanings. And finally twelve consecutive spaces in the blueprint (called *bhavas* or houses) have their effects. This more logical process of delineation simply blends the meanings of the particular elements involved.

For example, to predict that I would write books, Shastri combined the meanings of three separate factors and drew a conclusion. Since I was familiar with Western astrology at the time of my reading and therefore had no basis to judge his interpretation, I was so startled by his prediction that I demanded to know from whence the judgment came. The answer was that in my Hindu birthchart Mercury occupied the sixth space and was aspected by the (almost) full Moon. In other words, the planet designated to represent communicative functions (Mercury) was in an intimate zodiacal relationship with the space symbolizing daily activities and detail work (the sixth space). This alone meant that my daily work would involve any of the communicative arts (writing, lecturing, debating, etc.). The fact that Mercury was in an exceptionally fortunate condition, due to its association with the nearly full Moon on the day of my birth, greatly enhanced the positive effects destined to occur. By virtue of such indications and more importantly because Shastri had witnessed the same astrological aspects in the birthcharts of other authors, he was able to confidently make his prediction. Though nearly all truly competent astrologers readily admit that no indications in the birthchart can be interpreted with *absolute* certainty, based upon personal experience the astrologer comes to trust, quite positively, those indications which consistently and accurately produce the expected result. Thus with his unusual, yet confident, prediction Shastri left the greatest imprint of our meeting on my memory.

The last point worth mentioning of our session was Shastri's description of the present *bhukti*. As already explained the eighteen-year *Rahu dasa* I entered late in 1979 brought on the great spiritual changes, divorce, and my father's death. Within the *dasas*, however, are the *bhuktis*, the nine subperiods coloring or affecting the fundamental energy indicated by the *dasa*. In my case *Rahu dasa, Rahu bhukti* ran from September 1979 until June 1982 at which time the Jupiter subperiod began. This was the *bhukti* I was presently experiencing and this was the matter now focused upon. Shastri explained that Jupiter represented religion, philosophy, and travel, especially travel for religious purposes according to my particular blueprint. Further, the placement of *Rahu* on the day I was born gave indications of spiritual pilgrimages and bathing in India's sacred Ganges River. Therefore now that I was in a period and subperiod of planets both indicating the same direction, Shastri said the entire two and a half years should definitely bring spiritual journeys.

When he then asked if I had visited many sacred spots in his country, I had cause for excitement. It was not simply that I had visited sacred spots in India, it was that from the day the Jupiter subperiod had begun, back in America, I had done nothing *but* visit sacred spots! For several months following my father's death I had been especially depressed. Indeed, I was generally devoid of any ambition whatever. Out of the blue I decided a vacation was in order to relieve the seemingly never-ending melancholia. Since I had friends in California and had never visited the West Coast I decided it was as good a place as any to visit. Though I was right smack in the middle of a process called Reichian therapy (a physically oriented therapeutic technique I was using to help smooth out my grieving) I booked a flight for Los Angeles. This I did in the middle of June, actually within two or three days of the beginning of the Jupiter subperiod. On the night I arrived my friend Rebecca asked what I would enjoy seeing first. I replied that I wanted mostly to get away from city life, to perhaps get out to the country or some secluded place where I could just relax. Rebecca said we could drive to the Anza Borrego desert, to a spot where her guru occasionally took groups of disciples to meditate, chant, and observe certain spiritual ceremonies. The next day we did just that, and I found myself for the first time meditating and spending the night in what for me was a rather interesting setting. Though most of what occurred was the usual sunburn in the day, freezing at night, and coming within two feet of a noisy rattlesnake, there was in the end something of significance in my experience. For somewhere in the peacefulness of the starlit night it suddenly became clear that now was the time to fulfill my ten-year-old yearning to visit India.

Later as I made preparations for my journey I decided that since there was little likelihood of ever traveling to that side of the earth again I should also visit Israel. Though to me Israel had never held a great deal of fascination the idea arose out of a desire to meet my father's brother, a Kabala (Jewish mysticism) rabbi who had been practicing for some twenty or thirty years. However, even though I did have many interesting discussions with my uncle and other Kabalists I spent most of my two or three weeks visiting the sacred sites of the country's three major religions. From there I journeyed on to India and though I went neither in search of a guru nor for other typical spiritual purposes there simply was no way of avoiding the sacred spots. In fact after only one week in the country I had for so long wanted to visit I boarded a bus to Nepal to relieve the assaulting effect

India had on my senses. Though we were told we would arrive in Kathmandu at a designated time, we were more than half a day late since a few Tibetan travelers convinced the driver that what everyone needed was a glorious, which it was, few hours in Lumbini at the sight of Lord Buddha's birthplace. In the following weeks and months there were the continuous visits to the holy temples one after another both in Nepal and India, Vrindaban (Parikarma Marg) and Benares, perhaps most sacred of all.

Some time after my reading I wrote Rebecca to recount what Shastri had delineated of that time of my life. I concluded that the spot in the desert her guru had revealed must have been somewhat special since it began just as my pilgrimage period started. She wrote back to say that her guru had explained to the disciples that the site was one of a few "power spots" on the earth abounding in energy to be used by spiritual people to regenerate and rejuvenate themselves. Whether that was true or not it was obvious to me that these predictive *dasas* and *bhuktis* worked well enough for my money.

Local villager of Vrindaban, at the holy site of Parkiarma Marg.

71

Nepalese temple

Meeting My Mentor

As time passed I continued my travels, heading next to Vrindaban, a village where Lord Sri Krishna lived in one of his various incarnations. There I was to meet an old friend, an Australian I had met years earlier in Europe. Though I had not come to India specifically to learn Hindu astrology, for from what I knew the subject was just too difficult, I had now been bitten by the bug. Before I left America when friends asked whether or not I intended to learn the Hindu system I always answered that I did if it was possible. But I held only the slightest belief that it was. I had been through different books on the subject and had achieved little more than confusion and frustration. Perhaps more than that what I experienced was anger. I knew that this highly predictive system of astrology worked well from all accounts but seemed to be separated from everyone, save Indians and geniuses of the human race, by a huge gulf that defied crossing. However, neither Rakesh nor Shastri were, to my eyes, more intelligent than any of the Western astrologers I knew. So I was now beginning to realistically consider learning Hindu astrology. In Vrindaban I searched without luck to find an astrologer to study with. I did, interestingly enough, come across a volume of astrological scriptures which piqued my interest, but which I could make neither heads nor tails of. Finally I headed to Delhi where there was a Westerner at the local Hare Krishna temple named Yagna Dasa who studied astrology and perhaps could help.

Yagna Dasa was kind and helpful and somewhat versed in astrology but by no means a professional in the field. What I most recall was his advice that I get on the spiritual path of chanting Hare Krishna because the *Rahu dasa* I was now experiencing, he said, would produce a great deal of misery! I countered that from what I understood it would also produce lots of worldly accomplishment and the ability to sway the public. He said it was true that *Rahu* in my birthchart indicated such possibilities but that my effectiveness and associations would be mainly with *mllechas*. *Mllechas* means non-Hindus or nonreligious persons etc., peasants or the masses. From his spiritual perspective he wondered of what use were such mundane activities anyway? He spoke openly since we had already discussed spiritual matters at the start of our talk. He knew I had spent seven or eight years pursuing higher consciousness before coming to my *Rahu* period. It was especially interesting to hear his views since he had recently completed eighteen years of *Rahu's dasa*. Whereas I was quite excited about the possibilities *Rahu* indicated, other than the misery it had brought on, he was extremely glad to be done with it. His concern for me was that *Rahu dasa*, generally indicating such a nonspiritual period, would take me away from spiritual life, bring me to greater material desires, and out into the world where God realization is thought to be far more difficult to attain.

What he understood of *Rahu's* effects I certainly could not argue with. For one thing it was definitely true that in the very beginning of the period I resumed eating animal foods, fish at first and then fowl. This I did after seven years of pure vegetarianism, one of the requisites of traditional spiritual life. For another here I was in India, the spiritual country I had craved for years to visit, seeking astrological knowledge and touring the sacred sites, essentially ignoring the yogis and gurus who would have been the focus of my attention any time before *Rahu dasa*. Indeed as I reflect back to our conversation I realize I could not then truly see just how worldly my desires would eventually become, my books and intention to bring astrology to the public being obvious examples of such.

I recall asking Yagna Das what he thought of Shastri's

prediction that I would write books since it still amazed me. He replied that based upon my blueprint it certainly appeared plausible but that it would be hell for me to get published. And there, he noted, was yet another reason to get onto what he considered the fastest path to God, the chanting of Hare Krishna. At any rate, he was correct on the publishing point. Though I desired from the start to self publish my book on Hindu astrology, I sent the manuscript to three companies to see their reactions and offers. All expressed appreciation for my having considered them but none was willing to take the risk, at least not until after the book appeared on the scene to rave reviews.

Towards the end of my conversation and "mini reading" with Yagna Dasa I asked where I might find a good Hindu astrologer to study with. He replied that that was a difficult question to answer since most of the ones he had encountered were more concerned with taking his American money than providing the valuable service astrology at its best truly is. There was one astrologer in Delhi, however, a very old man named Ojah, who Yagna Dasa had visited and found to be quite capable. Unfortunately though, he could neither remember where the old man resided nor even the entirety of his name. I was therefore out of luck on that account and left Yagna and the Krishna temple frustrated and nearly resigned that after two months in India my learning Hindu astrology was just not in the stars. The most useful information Yagna Dasa provided, though I did not realize it then, was the address of an astrological bookstore called Ranjan Publications, also located in Delhi. Since I had already seen several of the Indian books on Hindu astrology and considered them about as useful as any highly confusing technical manual, I gave little thought to visiting Ranjan.

About three or four days after my visit with Yagna Dasa as I contemplated where my travels should take me next, a powerful astrological transit (current planetary position affecting my natal birthchart) was occurring in my blueprint. Amongst other things the transit was indicative of new contacts and partnerships, especially with spiritual persons or for spiritual purposes. But this I was unaware of at the time since I traveled without my astrology books. In any event the day the planetary aspect became exact (the point of its fullest power) I awoke with an intense urge to "get spiritual." At this point in my life spiritual growth meant many things, the two most important being my meditation and astrological studies. But since I seemed unable to produce a teacher of Hindu astrology, my focus, I decided, would be on austerity via the meditation technique I had practiced for so many years. I thus decided to make my way to Rishikesh, a remote Himalayan village inhabited mainly by gurus and their disciples, to find a secluded spot where I would do nothing but meditate for the next month. As I pondered my decision and considered the boredom likely to occur during nonstop meditating, a thought arose to bring some few astrological scriptures to read whenever my discipline waned. Illogical though it was, since I had already seen the scriptures and found them useless, I resolved to get some books and learn Hindu astrology on my own.

After breakfast that day I hired a taxi to drive me to Ranjan's, the store Yagna Dasa had recommended. Once there I purchased as many of the classic texts on the subject as I could afford. As I did so I noticed a paperback written by none other than "pandit" Gopesh Ojah. I immediately called over the storekeeper to inquire of Ojah's whereabouts. After explaining my reasons I listened to his reply that Ojah was unsuitable to my purposes due to his age, failing health, and heavily distorted English. There was, however, a gifted and learned astrologer in the area, he said, who might just be willing to take me on.

Rangachari Santhanam, an extremely energetic and amiable man, for all of his thirty-five or so years appeared so youthful that I waited for him to announce that he would go round up his father. Instead he immediately sat me down and inquired as to how much time I could afford in order to learn the ancient astrology of the Hindus. I replied that there was one month remaining until my scheduled flight back to the States but that it could certainly be extended another two or three weeks if necessary. Six weeks, he said, would be sufficient to obtain the basics of the system considering the fact that I was already familiar with the Western system. Gaining confidence and proficiency as an Hindu astrologer, he thought, would require about one year depending upon my ability, talent, and experience.

As we spoke and the surprise of his youthfulness wore off it became clear that this was a genuine and accomplished astrologer I was conversing with. I did not yet know that Santhanam was an author and translator of several classic astrological texts. But when I probed his backround and knowledge his self-assuredness and lack of desire to impress or even convince spoke for itself. Quite simply Santhanam was a busy man on the rise with precious little time for anything other than serious business. Consequently our meeting lasted no more than fifteen or twenty minutes at most. We determined a schedule for my private sessions, two hours each night and four hours on Sunday afternoons. We haggled for a minute or two on the price I would pay and settled on a lump sum, which approximated $10 or $15 per session. Though this was a good amount of money in an impoverished country such as India, and for sure the reason Santhanam directed the Ranjan shopkeeper to send me over, I sensed a large dose of the hospitable and pure-hearted nature many Indians have. I therefore felt quite comfortable. Santhanam was, to my perception, a man of integrity, and I immediately considered

R. Santhanam

him to be of higher quality and consciousness than all the astrologers I had previously seen, except for the astrological guru Gopi Nath Shastri mentioned in Chapter one.

After asking some silly questions in my excitement, such as whether predictive astrology *really* worked and when would we analyze *my* birthchart, I set off to return to my living quarters. I marveled at the fact that, just as I had given up on finding a teacher but resolved to learn on my own, a teacher had appeared. Not just a teacher but a respected scholar who was just beginning to enjoy the fame resulting from his highly respected translations. Throughout my journey I had considered returning to Benares to study with either of two astrologers I had met there but I could not bring myself to do it. I was just not sufficiently impressed with either of them as astrologers or as people. How then could I expect to get off to the right start in a field as incredibly vast as Hindu astrology? But with Santhanam something was different and I could see that from the start. Fortunately for me the astrological transit, a once-in-twelve-year occurrence (Jupiter exactly on the seventh house cusp for those who speak astrology), happening that day produced a spiritual partnership which would alter my life forever. I was thrilled and could hardly wait to begin my studies. I knew I was on the verge of something wonderful and that night, like a child on Christmas eve, I thought I would never fall asleep.

In the next six weeks a new world opened—a world in which predestiny took precedence over free will, where so much of the form and structure of people's lives could be perceived even before they lived it. And a world where this could be done without overly sophisticated and complex astrological techniques. As I added Hindu astrology to what I already knew from the Western system what emerged was a profoundly whole astrology, an astrology more the likes of a universal paradigm and clearly more worthy of embracing than what I had previously known. What I had always detected missing and what so many Western astrologers devote God knows how much energy towards—the cut-and-dried predictive element, the objective reality of people's lives —is found quite openly in Hindu astrology. Indeed it is the crux and purpose of the system. Even more astounding, for I had always believed the missing link existed somewhere, was the incredible simplicity of the system. By this I don't mean that Hindu astrology requires less time or effort to master than the Western system or that it has fewer techniques and variables. If anything, Hindu astrology greatly exceeds our system in such matters. However, the *essence* of delineation, the nature of its techniques is more plain, obvious, and circumscribed than Western methods, which so require a kind of meditative or intuitive blending. All this became clear during my study with Santhanam, the core of which were our nightly discussions of some thirty or forty birthcharts of friends and relatives I had brought with me from America in case I should manage to find just such a teacher.

I was anxious to have my mentor analyze my own blueprint immediately if not sooner. To this Santhanam responded that we must first send my birth data to an astrological computer company along with 30 rupees, about $3, to obtain a printout of my blueprint. It was not the actual blueprint that Santhanam was after, however, for that was easy enough for him to calculate in ten or twenty minutes. It was the exact dates of the *dasas* and *bhuktis* as well as a host of other calculations the computer would do, which would take an astrologer ten or twenty hours to do by hand! Mainly what he desired, and what would have been so time consuming, were the results of a computation system called *shad bala* (literally six strengths), which analyzes the powers (positive or negative potentials) of the planets occupying my birthchart. This, he said, was of great importance if we hoped to obtain a truly accurate delineation of my life. As fate would have it though, my printout arrived ten days later with mistaken birth data on it. And even as I returned it to the company making a note of the error the blueprint arrived another ten days later again with fault! So we never did analyze my own blueprint in one complete session but rather in bits and pieces as we went along.

The first technical information Santhanam wanted me to learn was the calculation of the birthchart as well as its sixteen *vargas*. The *Vargas* are "divisional" charts calculated or based on the original birthchart. Each *varga* is an entire chart devoted to one particular facet of life. The information indicated is in addition to, and rather more specific than, what is given in the actual birthchart. For example, there is the *saptamsha* or "one-seventh" divisional chart giving information on one's children. Or there is the *turyamsha* the one-fourth division telling about one's education. In my case the most interesting *varga* was the *dasamsha* or one-tenth division revealing specifics of my career. It showed that my work would be decidedly both intellectual and spiritually oriented, the perfect combination for an astrologer! Since Hindu astrology is a predictive system predicated on the theory of predestiny, my consideration at the time was whether or not this astrology business was my destiny from the instant of my birth. From all I could gather it certainly appeared so. And though as a truth seeker I always attempt to maintain a balance between openness and skepticism this experience to me was as awe inspiring as anything ever in my life.

Thus, as I studied the 6,000-year-old astrology of the ancients night after night in a tiny Indian loft my only doubt about taking astrology on as a profession was my own limitations. Did I have what it takes? Would I ever be as capable as my teacher and did I have the selflessness and quality of consciousness necessary to properly guide people along in their paths of life? Of course only time would tell, but as I witnessed Hindu astrology in action I knew that whatever uncertainty I previously had about the language of the stars was disappearing rapidly. Though there was at least a lifetime of study ahead, between the two complementary systems, it was clearly now time to begin.

Analyzing Friends' Birthcharts
with Santhanam

In time, after Santhanam had taught me the basics of Hindu astrology, each night was spent analyzing one or two particular birthcharts of people I knew. Many were relatives while others were close friends whose lives were familiar to me. It was during these sessions that Hindu astrology so clearly proved itself.

First there was my brother Charles' blueprint. Many of the basic features of his life stood out at once as we analyzed. Clearly this was a man who loved to speculate and an "adventure man" as Santhanam so aptly put it. Both delineations are true and though Charles was a businessman at the time who invested in the stock market on the side, he is now a professional commodities broker. As for being an adventure man, no one I have ever known has ever gotten into more adventures (and mischief) than he, at least during childhood and adolescence as we grew up together. And then there is the tendency towards great financial ups and downs. This showed up in the Western birthchart as a difficulty in holding onto money. Now that such a similar trait appeared in both the Hindu and Western blueprints such experience was easily worth betting on and has, as long as I have known him, been the case.

The two issues most interesting to me were his delayed marriage and his younger sibling—me. Regarding marriage, Charles chose a woman outside of his religion and suffered a good deal of abuse from family and relatives for doing so. I wondered if all of this was reflected in the chart. In this case it was since the Sun occupied the seventh house which, in the Hindu astrological system, nearly always causes marital delays and troubles. In fact it was especially clear to us since Santhanam had the exact same placement in his blueprint. In his instance he married amidst family turmoil because of dowry problems or some such nuisance. Also revealing Charles' marrying against parental desires was an indication in his blueprint known to produce what in India is called a "love marriage." Love marriages are distinguished from other Indian marriages in that the others are arranged by the parents when the children are quite young for all sorts of reasons other than love. Charles, it obviously appeared, was destined to marry for an intense bond of love and passion, not to be dissuaded by others' opinions or criticisms. As for the issue of the younger sibling, I was curious because of the constant fighting with my brother I had to endure for so many years as a child. The astrological explanation for this was that there were two indications in Charles' blueprint that he would receive, as the scriptures put it, "little or no happiness from younger siblings." In other words I was, from his point of view, simply a thorn in his side. So now at the age of thirty-one I guessed I finally discovered at least part of the reason for his compelling need to wail on his little brother! And that to me was fascinating.

It is Hindu astrology's ability to reveal the objective reality of life that so intrigues the Western astrologer. This faculty is especially seen when delineating such matters as children and siblings in the birthchart. For example, in my own Hindu blueprint there are strong indications that I would have no younger siblings. As it happened, immediately following my birth my mother's doctor advised that she should bear no more children. Regarding Charles' blueprint, what was even more interesting to me was the picture of my own life that could be gleaned through his chart. Suffice to say that there were six essential elements providing information about Charles' younger sibling. One factor revealed an artistic or sensitive type, another indicated one who might be powerful or renowned, and the other four were representations of a religious, mystical, or spiritual person. This seemed especially significant to me since I was the only one in a family of five bent in this wondrous direction.

Next there was my good friend Kerry whom I have known since high school. His blueprint is certainly one of the best I have seen from the point of view of Hindu astrology, which is so concerned with a person's comforts and pleasures in life. The first comment Santhanam made was that Kerry was born on the day of the full Moon and that that was one of the greatest benefits a blueprint could possibly contain. This, he said, greatly enhanced the entire chart and meant that life would be filled with luxuries, wealth, and power in general. Most specifically, according to the particulars of his blueprint, the benefic full Moon clearly indicated that Kerry would get all sorts of wonderful homes and conveyances (cars, boats, planes, etc.). This was definitely the case as it seemed that every time I blinked my eyes my thirty-two-year-old friend was moving into a larger, more luxurious home and trading in his Jaguar for the latest Mercedes, Porsche, or Cadillac. More significant to me though, since so many Americans play with cars and houses, was the fact that Kerry also loved boats and had owned a small one as a teenager. Later on, since my sessions with Santhanam, he has owned both motorboats and sailboats. Such is the accuracy of Hindu astrology when birthchart indications are explicit.

Though Santhanam's analysis was right on the mark, what he said about the power and benefit of the full Moon I found quite unusual since in Western astrology the full Moon is considered one of the most difficult of astrological aspects. The reason for this is that on the day of the full Moon the zodiacal positions of the Sun and Moon are exactly opposite each other in the person's blueprint, thereby creating an adverse relationship between the two luminaries. Since the Sun represents one's spirit or will power while the Moon signifies one's emotions and feelings there are generally psychological difficulties or conflicts in the person's thinking or decision making. Quite simply the person's feelings and emotions are not in harmony with their will and desires. Such is the case with Kerry and in many others with the aspect whose blueprints I have analyzed over the years. So I was now being initiated into the many differences between the Eastern and Western systems. It therefore became clear that the systems must absolutely never be mixed or adulterated, but instead should be practiced separately with each method maintaining its own integrity. The results may be appreciated together, but never the techniques themselves.

Another interesting facet of Kerry's life is the "mellifluous voice" Santhanam said that the scriptures declared he would possess due to a certain yoga in his blueprint. Kerry is indeed a singer, a dramatic tenor, and an amazing one at that. However, although his college and professional voice teachers (some of the finest in the US) expected him to *easily* attain great acclaim for his talent, he never pursued the vocation. Instead he chose several other careers. Having heard Kerry's singing over the years and experienced the frustration of watching his ability go unused and unheard, except for his occasional awesome barroom performances, I was curious about the matter.

From what I could assess according to the birthchart the problem came down to a heavily afflicted "tenth house." The tenth house, or tenth space, of the blueprint relates to one's career or life purpose. In this case the particular element connected to that house, the planet involved, was nearly completely devasted by an adverse relationship with the "shadowy planet" Ketu (called the South Node in Western astrology). Unfortunately whenever a planet comes into close contact with Ketu (in other words when the zodiacal position of a planet is close to Ketu's position, within a few degrees) the life functions that the particular planet represents are destroyed in a most unusual, unconscious, or uncontrollable way. Such was the case with Kerry and therefore his singing career was doomed from the start. Although he is intellectually aware of the enormity of his ability and exquisiteness of his voice, there has always been some unconscious or uncontrollable emotional force blocking his capacity to be responsible for the gift.

Interestingly, it is not the case that all of Kerry's career energy is ruined. He is quite successful in his other careers, though there are plenty of changes and ups and downs in that sphere. The reason for this is that the rest of his blueprint is so auspiciously well disposed that he is capable of succeeding generally wherever he places his attention. Most relevant to this ability, astrologically, is the fact that in his birthchart the "desire" houses are extraordinarily powerful. Hindu philosophy divides life into four areas: *dharma*—duty or life purpose, *artha* —wealth, *kama*—desires, and *moksha*—enlightenment or higher consciousness. The astrological blueprint is composed of numerous elements, the most essential being the planetary positions, their interrelationships, and the twelve consecutive spaces or houses containing them.

In the same way that planets symbolize certain life functions so also do the houses. Each house, in fact, represents several different issues so that between the twelve all of life's functions are governed by one of the spaces. Regarding the four functions of human life— *dharma, artha, kama,* and *moksha*—there are three houses designated to embody each category. The *dharma* houses are the first, fifth, and ninth (fire houses for those who speak astrology). The *artha* or money houses are the second, sixth, and tenth (earth houses). The *kama* or desire houses are the third, seventh, and eleventh (air houses). And the *moksha* or spiritual spaces are the fourth, eighth, and twelfth (water houses).

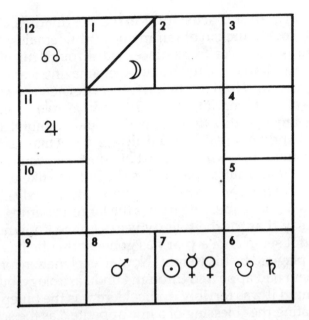

In Kerry's blueprint the *kama* houses are extremely well aspected and more powerful than the others. The meaning of this is twofold. First, it is understood that life itself will center around dealing with constantly arising, intense desires. And secondly such desires will be easily fulfilled due to an innate understanding or mastery of how to make that happen. This inclination of life is distinct from others who having for example, strong *moksha* houses would be more concerned with spiritual evolution than anything else. And it is different from those who have strong *dharma* houses and are thus concerned with their duty or life purpose in the world (making a difference in society). So although Kerry's birthchart indicates a disturbing interference in his life purpose, which has blocked his singing career and fame, yet he may succeed in other vocations unconnected to his own particular duty. And this he has done.

Finally, after discussing Kerry's destined wealth, Midas touch, luck in obtaining beautiful females, and whatever else was to be discerned through his blueprint, Santhanam noted yet another amazing feature of this most unusual birthchart. It concerned the sixth space of the blueprint, which in Hindu astrology represents, among other things, enemies and appetite. This man, Santhanam said, would always defeat his enemies and competitors with the least of effort. He would also have a "voracious appetite," as the Indians like to say. Both were true, and to a degree which I feel nearly inadequate to describe. Regarding the large appetite I can only say that for the twenty years I have known my friend it seems not a year has gone by that he has not been plagued by his weight. Now an explanation for the problem had appeared through Hindu astrology, but to my mind it was terribly ironic. Here was the blueprint indicating the "blessing of a fine appetite," as the scriptures say, and there is my friend constantly bothered by his weight. Unfortunately the values of the astrological sages, I guess, were not the same as mine. For I have noted over and over again, in my practice with clients, that a powerful appetite indicated through the birthchart almost invariably means a person who is overweight.

The other matter, that of defeating enemies and competitors, I found extremely interesting since it is an ability so strong in Kerry's functioning that I had finally assumed it to be the product of some mystical talent he must have developed in a previous lifetime! In fact such a trait is common to many individuals who have attained fame or a very high status in their chosen field. In Kerry's life I have witnessed his continual victories throughout his conquests, romances, and adventures to a point approaching envy. Perhaps not the best, but at least the most humorous, example of this was a contest I had to endure with this great warrior over who would win the presidency of Thespians, our high school drama club. Before the election I counted my close friends in the club versus his, and it seemed quite certain that I would win. Distinguishing the fact was not difficult since because our personalities were so radically different there was relatively little question as to which students would vote for whom. There was, however, a third candidate in the running, but it was obvious that he would place a distant third.

On election night as the votes were tallied, much to my dismay Kerry was declared the winner. Though I accepted the matter graciously I was baffled as to how I had lost. About a week later, at the time we were to be inaugurated, I learned what had occurred. Kerry and I had tied with ten votes apiece, while the third candidate received five. The residing president, not realizing that a new election was in order to allow the third candidate's

Kerry

votes to be cast between us, decided to break the tie himself in favor of Kerry. Had a new election been offered, the tie-breaking votes would have gone my way, each and every one, according to an unofficial count after the issue became public. The turmoil that ensued in the following week was so great that the club was disbanded until the following year at which time such changes took place that neither of us became president. Such was Kerry's luck in overcoming enemies!

Night after night as we continued analyzing birthcharts I became even more enthusiastic about Hindu astrology. It seemed that no matter whose blueprint I presented to Santhanam he would know the fundamentals of that person's life. And this he did consistently through *simple, intelligent analysis*, never through the vastly intricate, time-consuming techniques of the 6,000-year-old system that have so thoroughly scared Western astrologers away from it. We generally spent twenty or thirty minutes on each chart discussing the obvious indications for the person's life and their most likely future. As I gained ability in the system, I came to see that its beauty lay in the clear-cut simplicity of delineation. This is perhaps difficult for the Western astrologer who has seen many complicated books on the subject to appreciate. And even more difficult for the layperson who is completely unfamiliar with the methods of astrology.

Astrological interpretation is the practice of decoding or deciphering the language of creation by considering the meanings of each symbol or representative elements. The process is both visual and conceptual since what the astrologer does is to look at symbols, consider their significations, and finally draw conclusions as to the circumstance being conveyed. The symbols are the planetary positions (expressed numerically using degrees), the map with its twelve symbolic spaces containing the planetary positions, the star clusters (called astrological signs—Aries, Taurus, Gemini, etc.), and all the combinations and permutations of these elements. Although the interpretive work is technical and mathematical, as any method of decoding must be, it is also very much a visceral or intuitive procedure. Astrological interpretation involves an incredible number of factors which must all be considered, weighed, balanced, and judged *together* in order to finally arrive at a conclusive result. It therefore demands that the astrologer acquire a "feel" or "sense" of the blueprint as a whole.

Likewise, both Hindu and Western astrology have their own separate essence and spirit. As I attended session after concentrated session with my mentor and set aside my preconceptions and what I knew of Western astrological wisdom, I began to experience the soul and vital force of Hindu predictive astrology. It was something quite distinct from its Western counterpart. When I analyzed the round-shaped Western blueprint with its "free flowing" demeanor, I had always known that I was viewing a person's "insides," i.e., their behavioral patterns, psychology, interests, and talents. Not that events and circumstances cannot also be perceived, but when they are it is a result of clearly knowing the person's mode of behavior. For this is what Western technique is about. Western astrology delineates the *possibility* of events and circumstances. It delineates possibility that approaches probability through the birthchart, but which because of the nature of the techniques themselves, depends *absolutely* on the person's free will!

Hindu astrology on the other hand—with its square-shaped, boxlike blueprint presenting a rigid and inflexible appearance—is another matter altogether. It is an astrology of fate. It is simple. Not easy or fast, since there are so many variables involved, but simple and direct in its interpretive ways. Unlike Western methodology, which allows for (indeed suggests) the possibility of transforming negative energies and behavioral patterns into positive ones, Hindu astrology is straight, linear, and fundamental. Certain planetary positions are just plain "bad," of no positive value whatever. Certain of the twelve spaces of the blueprint are all-favorable, indicative of great benefit to the life functions they are connected to. Others are malefic, manifesting nothing but disturbance, grief, or misery. Still other houses operate in between the two. Because of the straightforwardness of Hindu technique, the Hindu blueprint represents nothing less than a mirror of the lives of human beings —their manifested, actual lives—not their possible or potential existences. Thus, once Hindu astrology was within my grasp and I was able to make some few accurate predictions, I began to feel privileged, incredibly privileged, almost religiously so. To be able to see people's lives, to objectively see beyond what individuals themselves could see, I considered nothing less than miraculous.

Then came the issue of responsiblity. "Not a joke James," as Santhanam used to say, "It is not a joke." Not a joke indeed. Astrology, as presently practiced, may be nowhere near an exact science, but in my initial brief period of study I came to appreciate, more fully than anything else, that when Hindu astrology worked it worked with unquestionable exactitude. It worked with such precision and simplicity that it was in a way frightening. Not frightening to the Easterner who has been raised in a spiritually oriented culture that teaches the precepts of karma and reincarnation. And not frightening to me, personally, being of a mystical bent. But frightening to consider Hindu astrology in the wrong hands, the hands of the egotistical, the ignorant, or the foolish. The more I learned and the more adept I became, the more concerned I was for my own well being, specifically for my own karma, for the results of the actions I would most likely be taking having learned Hindu astrology.

For as a teacher I had, frankly, a big mouth. What I learned I taught and had recently become compulsive. Withholding knowledge was to my mind a sign of great selfishness. I have tried to be with others as free and gracious as my teachers and gurus were with me. I was proud of that fact and considered it a primary reason that knowledge has always been so easy for me to come by.

Now I had a problem. What was to be done with this profound body of knowledge essentially unknown in the West? Should it be given out to all the astrologers I could gather together in the States? Should I teach only my friends, the ones with abundant common sense, the ones I considered trustworthy? Certainly Western astrologers have seen devastating conditions in people's lives through birthchart analysis without the benefit of Hindu predictive astrology. Certainly I myself had witnessed people's torturous childhoods, crazy parents, marital problems, and divorces through my own practice of the Western system. But such conditions were always "most likely scenarios," they were "possibilities" ultimately dependent on some element outside the astrological paradigm, assumedly free will. Never, before Hindu astrology, had I seen aspects of people's lives appear in the blueprint so definitively and with such clarity and certainty as I now saw. Never had I seen catastrophies such as John Lennon's assassination or Richard Nixon's downfall emerge with such visibility and explicit description as I did through their Hindu charts. Neither had I ever heard an astrologer make such a macabre prediction as the one Santhanam made of one of my acquaintances saying, "He will have a hand in his own death."

So despite the enormous excitement of learning Hindu astrology, I was also torn. The value of predictive astrology was apparent, but so were the risks. Now that I could gain information about a person's psychology and behavior as well as their destiny by using both methods of astrology it was obvious that in combining the two I was in possession of a whole and complete system. With greater accuracy and precision now available to me there was clearly not only an easier but also a more profound means to contribute to people's lives. In my mind Hindu astrology represented the missing link to Western astrology, the answer to its all-too-common lack of predictive efficiency. Astrology as a career and life path, a respectable way to make a difference in the world, finally became real.

How then could I possibly not share the knowledge so fortunately bestowed upon me with other astrologers who had likely experienced many of the same frustrations as myself? Further, the field of astrology itself stood to make great gains as astrologers of both systems became capable of considering and exploring (but not mixing) the interpretive techniques of the other. This was yet another reason to teach Hindu astrology in the West. On the other hand there were plenty of reasons not to do so. Most basic, of course, is the fact that predictive astrology is indigenous to the East, not the West. A fate-oriented astrology naturally belongs in a fate oriented culture. How would it fit into a society where free will is the most acknowledged and acceptable reality?

Although times are rapidly changing and different cultures are, to the benefit of the world, borrowing the best each other has to offer, the transformation is not without its problems. The worst dilemma in bringing Hindu astrology to the West is the probability that certain Western astrologers, being so enamoured of the predictive system, would practice it exclusively. Some would give astrological readings to clients using *only* Hindu astrology, which though it excels in predictive analysis practically ignores the human factor. How detrimental this could be to the innocent client! Imagine, for example, a twenty-year-old hearing his or her astrol-

oger say, "Yes, there is no question about it, you will definitely be divorced in this lifetime. It is your destiny." Or
"there are certainly several pregnancies indicated in
your birthchart, but only two children are scheduled to
live." Without the knowledge of the whys and wherefores so finely expressed through the Western system
there could, with precious little effort, be more damage
done than good.

A culture steeped in the philosophy of free will is an
inappropriate context for a purely fate-oriented astrology. Like it or not astrological information lives within
the understanding of the human being. It lives both
within and for the understanding of the person involved. In the West, where the human race has for so
many centuries been cultivated in the ways of free will,
the whys and wherefores are essential. They are absolutely of the essence. Indeed the whys and wherefores
create free will. For instance, in the example above regarding a person's divorce the Hindu blueprint would
reveal, as the scriptures would say, "loss or death of the
spouse." If the astrological indications were blatant,
there would simply be no two ways about the matter. As
for the possibility of alleviating the problem one could
perform *yagyas* (religious rituals or ceremonies), chant
mantras (prayers of a sort) repeatedly, or choose a more
suitable partner according to the advice of an astrologer.
Such techniques may be reasonable to the Easterner but
impractical or even irrational to the Westerner. On the
other hand, the same person's Western blueprint would
produce information regarding the *nature* of married life
or, of greater relevance, the *reasons* for divorce. The person would thus be forewarned and would have the freedom to alter or modify his or her behavior in order to
have both power over and choice in the matter. If divorce
occurred anyway, it would have been clearly the person's own creation. It could be seen and accepted as
such rather than by some forceful external fate over

which there was no control. Self responsibility would begin to exist.

Furthermore, in the argument against Hindu astrology in the West (or anywhere for that matter) was the question of who is capable of handling it? Who is poised enough to maintain balance and equanimity of mind when perceiving perhaps the most discordant of circumstances in the futures of clients, friends, or loved ones? Who is wise and experienced enough to set matters in their proper perspective, which in extreme cases demands the broadest and most spiritual perspective? The biggest problem in Western astrology, and what has contributed most to its degeneracy and decline over the centuries, is the lack of spirituality of its practitioners. Though this is now being set aright by a new, progressive generation more concerned with personal growth than material possessions, the problem is no small concern. Rectifying the situation is an evolutionary process requiring effort, diligence, intelligence, and most importantly the gradual purification of its practitioners through spiritual practices. Finally, whose consciousness is developed enough to have achieved both the detachment necessary to be able to impassively foresee *anything* as well as the compassion and concern for humanity required to make maximum use of the information discovered?

Here I sat some ten years into my own spiritual journey, seven years of which were spent exclusively devoted to God realization and which produced some wonderfully sublime experiences, and yet I found my own mettle tested well enough. During the six weeks with Santhanam I came to see through Hindu birthchart analysis the divorces of intimate friends looming ominously in the future. I saw that certain of my friends had shorter lives than I wished. And then there were the *dasas* of loved ones, some of whose periods promised far more difficulty and frustration than fulfillment. These were periods that lasted nineteen years in one case and ten years in another and practically guaranteed that these individuals would not obtain what they were after. And then there was my own case. My particular blueprint indicated marvelous spiritual tendencies and an extremely logical, even though slow, mind. But it also revealed a not-so-easy life with limited material comforts and more than a fair share of painful experiences. More significantly, however, since my personal desires were puny anyway, was an issue which Santhanam did not address until I mentioned the indication myself. There appeared in my birthchart a *dasa bhukti* period in the not-too-distant future which could, to no competent Hindu astrologer's surprise, put an end to my life!

To convey to the reader just how intense is the astrological aspect denoting the circumstance (and therefore the likelihood for the predicted event to actually occur, unless mitigated through astrological antidotes) I will relate an interaction with P.M. Padia. Padia was to become my mentor two years later in Bombay. The day we met, just minutes after he had proven his astrological ability by accurately pinpointing the year of my marriage, I posed my question. Of the two-year period under consideration I asked, "Will it kill me?" "Not sure," was his reply. By "not sure" what Padia meant was "not definitely." The reason it was not definite had nothing to do with the element of free will. It was because a separate astrological factor was heavily in my favor. Thus, early death was a distinct possibility but not a certainty. From the very beginning of my days with Hindu astrology I was well aware of the weight and implications involved in this event-oriented system.

Meanwhile as we proceeded in our work, I continued to learn. I had many friends and therefore many charts to analyze. There was my "womanizer" friend whose name shall not be mentioned. The first comment Santhanam made was, "This man has loose morals; he is very sexy (meaning sexual)." I then explained that my friend indeed seemed to be making a career out of his love affairs. The question on my mind was whether he would ever marry. My friend was rather vehement that he would not, but in my judgment I reasoned that he must eventually tire of playing the field, successful though he was at it. Santhanam's reply was that "it is possible but he will never be loyal." Since he is still single and having fun at age thirty-four the loyalty issue is a moot point. I must say, however, that what I learned from his birthchart greatly changed my reaction to his neverending boasting of romantic conquests and virile potency. I naturally assumed that his tales were typical male exaggerations; now I take them quite seriously since his chart powerfully supports his claims.

Regarding sex life I have found Hindu astrology far more revealing of one's actual experience than the Western system. At least this is so in terms of basic birthchart analysis. In Hindu astrology the twelfth space of the blueprint represents "sexual enjoyment." I use the term "enjoyment" as distinct from passion. Passion is signified by the seventh space of the blueprint as well as by Venus and Mars. Therefore, depending on the condition of the various elements in one's chart, a person may be quite sexually passionate and yet very much unable to enjoy the act of sex. On the other hand the opposite is also true. A person may not be particularly passionate yet he or she may be highly stimulated during sex and capable of much gratification. Interestingly, sexual enjoyment is not a designated meaning listed in Hindu astrological scriptures. Sex pleasure is deduced to be a twelfth house affair because the twelfth space literally signifies "pleasures of the bed." The term thus means any and all activities relating to the bed and bedroom. In other words if the twelfth space in a person's birthchart is very well disposed, if it is determined to be fortunately aspected, then the person will enjoy comfortable beds and have a beautiful bedroom. He or she will also get a good deal of sexual pleasure throughout life.

One of the reasons I found this area of information so intriguing was that as I began analyzing the sex lives of my friends a good deal of light was shed on girlfriends I had been with in the past. One blueprint in particular captured my attention. This was the chart of a thirty-year-old woman who had been after me for many years (before my marriage and then after my divorce). Interestingly, or rather frustratingly, whenever we approached physical intimacy her behavior matched that of a frightened teenager. This was especially perplexing to me since, for one thing, she had previously been married for four years. Secondly there was a good deal of love between us. Thirdly, she was quite passionate up to a point. And finally, when I questioned her about the matter she was terribly unaware of the existence of any problem. Though she would not admit to the fact, I eventually could only conclude that she was simply petrified of sex.

Whether that was true or not, what I now saw in her birthchart was indicative of her experience. For her blueprint contained a very weak and badly aspected twelfth house. Sexual problems were, unfortunately, a fact of her life. At very best she would receive little or no sexual enjoyment. It certainly was true in her relationship with me, and so it was with her former husband who, by her own words, had to endure her nightly "headaches!" What I could not help wondering, now that I understood sex from the astrological perspective, was that since this poor woman could not enjoy bed pleasures, whether we would have fared better on the couch or floor.

Next we came to Harold's chart. Harold is a close friend and neighbor I have known since elementary school. While his chart is not extraordinary, it does possess some few elements worth presenting. Incidentally, while each birthchart is unique with a complete life schedule and portrait of the personality only a very few issues for each one are mentioned in this writing. Those chosen are not necessarily the most important or significant aspects of the individual's life. In most cases those chosen are simply the more interesting ones or those that point up the differences between Hindu and Western astrology. In Harold's case one of the most immediately obvious aspects of his life as seen through the Hindu chart is that, as Santhanam put it, "this man will care little of his appearance." As Santhanam, after his statement, asked, "Is it not true?" I had to laugh because I knew just how accurate his delineation was.

I explained that there was no question about the fact and that, unbeknown to Harold, others often remarked about his unkempt appearance saying that he is quite a good looking man if only he would take care of himself and dress properly. Being self-employed, Harold only wears pullover shirts, loose-fitting work shorts, and beach sandals and does so at least 360 days of the year since he is oblivious to the few cold days in Miami. Though I could not say it to Santhanam then, for it had yet to occur, Harold is the only person I have ever known to appear before a judge (for a divorce) in his shorts and thongs. He simply has no concern whatever about his looks. In fact I have grown so accustomed to his dress that when I accompanied him to the courthouse as his witness it was not until we got out of the car that I realized what he was about to do. Since there was no time to return for more appropriate clothing we created a fictitious story so the judge would not feel too terribly insulted.

The astrological factor indicating Harold's apathy for his looks also, to the trained astrologer, indicates a debilitated digestive system. Santhanam's blatant comment was: "This man will have lots of gas." I was unaware that this was so until years later when Harold and I lived in the same apartment building. Often when he visited I would offer him some food or fruit. After some time I came to expect, as often as not, his peculiar answer, "No thanks, it gives me gas." At other times when Harold observed my dinner, he would ask incredulously, "How can you eat that combination? Doesn't it give you gas?" Fortunately his digestive problem has, to some extent, been relieved through the use of astrological gemstones. In his particular case red coral is the stone corresponding to the planet revealing the problem, Mars. Since Harold began wearing coral beads around his neck he has experienced significant relief. He also notes that when he fails to wear the necklace the disturbance returns almost immediately.

Lest I lose a friend I had best now describe some of Harold's more commendable characteristics. Aside from his highly ascetic and spiritual nature some of Harold's most notable attributes are his hard-working nature and extreme efficiency at whatever tasks he undertakes. I have observed Harold in his various careers over the years and have seen the embodiment of a teaching my Indian guru used to give out. It is a message which, though simple and logical, few people are capable of following. The advice—an enlightened philosophy of how to attack daily work, especially the tedious sort—was to "See the job. Do the job. Stay out of the misery." It is something Harold has laudably mastered. Of all the people I have known perhaps no one confronts work and daily tasks, however laborious, more attentively and with less procrastination than he does. Mind you, he clearly does not enjoy toiling any more than the next person. But his approach to the matter is a highly sane one, an art if you will.

The ability is also, from the astrological perspective, something destined from birth since it appears quite openly in his blueprint. This is revealed from an analysis of the third space of his birthchart which, in the

Hindu system, represents a person's "hands and own efforts" (basically anything one touches or handles). Because the house of efforts in Harold's chart is connected with (and therefore "affected" by) Saturn, the planet signifying discipline and responsibility, certain effects must result. For one thing Harold will be extremely reliable at whatever chores or assignments he takes on. For another he will always be engaged in jobs consisting of physical labor. Harold's two alternating careers are landscaping and massage therapy. Lastly Harold, desiring such efficiency, almost never employs laborers but chooses to work alone. The only drawback to Harold's ability is that whenever friends and neighbors need help with heavy work or tedious tasks he is the first to be enlisted!

The other significant issue of Harold's chart we discussed was the fact that he was about to enter a new *dasa*. For the previous nineteen years he had been experiencing Saturn's effects. Those years had, therefore, been of an especially serious, career-oriented, and somewhat burdensome nature. Though that is an extremely general description of his nineteen-year period, it is still an accurate assessment of the kind of energy and focus one would normally feel during such years. And though in an astrological session the *dasa* would be described in much greater detail based upon the person's *particular* blueprint, and the nineteen years would be elucidated year by year, the basic understanding is sufficient for our purposes. The point is that Harold was now about to enter a completely new period, one ruled by Mercury, the planet of intellectual and communicative functions. What was interesting was that Harold, though quite spiritual, cared about as much for intellectual pursuits as he did about his looks. During high school he spent more time at the beach surfing than he did in the classroom. College, I am sure, he never considered let alone attended. Even in spiritual life he was purely the devotional (rather than philosophical) type, ready to serve the guru and accept on faith whatever knowledge was presented. Now according to the language of creation his ways were scheduled to change.

And so of course they did. When I returned to Miami after four months of travel Harold's life was dramatically altered. He had severed a seven-year-old unfulfilling marriage, become restless with his career of the previous ten years and begun a new one, and taken to a new spiritual practice of a far more intellectual nature. Most miraculously, at least to those who knew him, he had enrolled in college and gone back to school. Were it not for my knowledge of his astrological birthchart this action would have been more startling than if he had purchased a wardrobe of suits and ties! Harold had loathed school for as long as I knew him and that was a long time. But Mercury's characteristics were now powerfully exerting themselves and would do so for another seventeen years. The most significant effect however, to my mind, was not so much the external changes taking place, even though that is what Hindu astrology so specially reveals. It was that this man, whose life up to this point had been completely physical and spiritual, was now becoming intellectual. Harold, who had previously not displayed a psychological bone in his body was now probing, dissecting, and analyzing everything in his path. It was fascinating to observe and particularly enjoyable to me since I had yet another friend to indulge in my perpetual philosophical discussions.

Regarding the *dasa* periods it should be understood that the indicated effects depend greatly upon the condition of the planet involved. In other words, although any person entering a Mercury period will become more communicative and mentally or psychologically oriented, the results will not always be positive as they were in Harold's case. As it happens in Harold's blueprint Mercury is well aspected, thus producing the fa-

103

vorable elements of Mercury's representations. Not so for Richard Nixon who entered the same seventeen-year period in November 1970 but whose Mercury is the most afflicted and devastated planet in his chart. The Watergate debacle occurred soon after the *dasa* began (1971) and shows just how simple and accurate Hindu astrology is when birthchart indications are extreme as they were in his case. Since Mercury was the ruling planet and all intellectual and mental functions were now the order of the day, Nixon's downfall came through lying, recorded dialogues, the press, college students, and the intelligentsia, all Mercury principles. In the same way Harold benefitted from Mercury's "energy," Richard Nixon suffered, the difference being the condition of Mercury in their respective birthcharts.

There is an interesting point concerning Nixon's poorly disposed Mercury. The affliction to that planet is said to occur because its position in the zodiac on the day of his birth was conjunct with Mars. Mars, in Hindu astrology, is known to be a "first-class malefic" and as such harms any planet it aspects or conjuncts. In Nixon's case Mercury is conjunct *within one degree* of Mars (there are 360 degrees in the zodiac). As such the affliction is obviously intense. However it is also true that whenever these two planets join together in the birthchart the person will be exceptionally practical and political. He or she will also excel in technical fields such as law, architecture, drafting, and engineering. And it denotes that the person will be an excellent speaker or debater. Such features are, of course, strong characteristics of Richard Nixon.

The same Mercury-Mars aspect also represents that, as the ancient Hindu sages have so bluntly stated in the scriptures, "the person will be a thief or a liar." What is important is not that Richard Nixon has this astrological aspect and was caught lying. It is that the Mercury-Mars aspect that indicates lying and/or a career in politics occurs in some way or other (there are four ways the aspect can occur in Hindu astrology) in the charts of incredibly many politicians! It is especially common in the charts of presidents. The aspect, incidentally, does not indicate that the person is immoral necessarily or that he or she lies for detrimental or even selfish reasons; that depends on other factors in the blueprint. But the aspect makes the person highly practical and able to perceive the actions necessary to achieve desired goals. Therefore do most politicians operate out of an "end justifies the means" philosophy, perhaps an obvious requisite for political success.

Even Jimmy Carter—whose Hindu birthchart indicates an extraordinary dose of honesty, humility, and integrity—contains a Mercury-Mars aspect (this occurs in his Hindu chart but not in his Western chart). Of the last several presidents the aspect appears the strongest in the charts of Kennedy, Nixon, and Johnson. However, Johnson's chart, because it reveals a blatant lack of morals is the most interesting. As it happens the Mercury-Mars aspect, said to make one a thief or liar, occupies the second space of the birthchart which in the Hindu system represents truthfulness. The results are that Johnson's lying was so extreme, according to Robert Caro's literary masterpiece *The Path To Power*, that Johnson was described by a college classmate as "a man who just could not tell the truth." More succinctly, the same book reveals, he was nicknamed "Bull Johnson" at school which, outside of his presence, turned to Bullshit Johnson.

Eventually, during our nightly sessions, I presented Santhanam with the birthchart of my ex-wife Anna. After commenting that hers was one of the best blueprints I had brought him so far, he immediately asked, "Is she not involved in dramatical life?" This to me was especially startling because one of the most perplexing problems I had encountered in Western astrology was in discerning what blueprint indications were responsible for revealing a career in the arts. Having been an actor from the age of fifteen to twenty-one, I naturally had analyzed birthcharts of numerous friends in the theatre. And though I followed traditional Western astrological teachings—which assert that the fifth house of the birthchart reveals self-expression, drama, and theatrics—the blueprints of these actors almost never contained a particularly strong or significant fifth space. I had yet to resolve the matter and never knew why, astrologically, these friends of mine were actors. Now Santhanam, in less than two minutes, predicted that the chart in front of him belonged to a dramatist. It was quite a simple matter for him since in Hindu astrology the fine arts are revealed from the third space of the blueprint and Anna had about the strongest third house an astrologer could imagine. I was excited. Such simple and practical tidbits of knowledge to an astrologer longing for predictive ability made my entire trip to India worthwhile, dysentery and all.

The next element of the chart we discussed was finances. Though Anna had not yet earned much wealth Santhanam was confident she eventually would, especially after her twenties. What was most insightful though was Santhanam's comment that her husband would make plenty of money. Since I was once her husband it was not hard to assess the accuracy of his prediction. The long and short of the matter was that the analysis was right on the mark. I had in fact been successful during the five years of our marriage and was terribly obsessed with wealth. At least I was as obsessed as my ascetic nature would allow. It was now apparent that a good deal of the reason for this was because of Anna's destiny! Of course it could have simply been the case that wealth was always a major desire of mine. But nothing was further from the truth.

Money had never, before marriage, been much on my

106

mind. I had certainly not become an actor, of all things, in my earlier years to gain riches. Neither had I traveled back and forth to Europe seven times to be with my guru and meditate for months on end in order to enhance my finances. Significant wealth was not even to be found in my birthchart. Manik Chand Jain, a renowned Hindu astrologer, had previously commented to me that "the ruler of your second house is in your sixth so you do not want money." I could not argue with that since a year or two earlier, only a month after my divorce became final, I handed my tee-shirt business, lucrative though it was, over to Anna. I did not do this as part of any divorce settlement but just to be done with a part of my life I now had no interest in. In other words money was of little concern to me both before and after marriage to Anna. It was just not my karma!

What is even more interesting is that although it was Anna's fate to have a wealthy or money-minded husband, this was a completely unconscious matter for her. For she, being of an artistic and altruistic temperament, never cared about wealth, never much sought it, and never even asked me about it. If anything she made it harder, I felt, for me to earn! For aside from the fact that so much of her energy went into theatrical projects all of my endeavors had to be undertaken with care and consideration for her interests and life in the theatre. Most revealing of the matter, I suppose, is the fact that before we were married I warned Anna that if wealth and comforts were at all important to her that I was not the one to marry. My intentions were clearly spiritual and ascetic. A lot that mattered since her destiny proclaimed otherwise, and I found myself for the next five years "living in the material world!"

How one person's destiny affects another's is, to borrow from Santhanam's vernacular, "not a joke." I have witnessed the phenomenon in my own and my clients' lives over and over again. In fact it is not uncommon that a Hindu astrologer will advise clients that their lives will improve when a certain close relative is gone (one could also, of course, advise that a person's life might deteriorate with a relative's absence, but that is rarely done since astrology is used to uplift not to depress). In my life I have grown accustomed to the matter and learned who to associate with and who to avoid. Whenever I doubt my achievements and future career success, I need only hang out a bit with my brother Charles who is destined to have a powerful or famous younger sibling. The only trouble is that it is sometimes, due to my shyness, hard to take. For he always proudly introduces me to his friends as "Jimmy, the one who wrote the Hindu astrology book" or "Jimmy, the astrologer who goes on the radio." I even recall being harrassed by him during the writing of my first book because he was constantly protesting, "Why don't you write a book for the public?" Not that he cared one iota that the public learn anything of astrology, mind you. But how could he have a famous brother if my writing was geared to an infinitesimally small audience of quirky professional astrologers? How was his karma ever going to actualize!

I have also, over the years, been extremely aware of the effects various girlfriends caused to my life, each having her own destiny with love partners. Though I have examined both the Hindu and Western charts of these women, it is the Hindu chart I am usually interested in since it is most revealing of actual life rather than the psychology of our relationship. An obvious example of how well Hindu astrology works is that ever since the acclaim of my first book among astrologers worldwide nearly all the women I have dated (dated seriously enough to ask them for their birth data) have had a very powerful seventh house in their birthchart. The seventh space is, of course, the area of the chart revealing one's love relationships. As such the women now being attracted into my life have the destiny to have a special (in the worldly sense) husband. This was never the case before any large-scale success in my life.

There has, however, been one woman I was serious about marrying, until the relationship proved too burdensome, whose destiny was not particularly to have a famous or special husband. Her fate was similar to my brother Charles' in that she was headed for a "love marriage" as the Indians call it. This was fine with me as our love was most intense and wonderful. However in our wonderful affection, which in my opinion was never going to greatly subside, I could easily see that my work in the world was going to assume less priority, *by my own doing*, being with this woman than with the others. It was, I must say, rather disconcerting. This was the first time in the past two years I had been with a woman not waiting for a powerful husband, and it was definitely uncomfortable. It was the first time I ever considered that something could seriously sidetrack my dream of clarifying astrology for the masses.

Free Will Versus Predestiny

In light of people being significantly influenced by others around them, this is perhaps as good a time as any to finally address the issue of free will. It should first be understood, though, that the view presented is only for the reader's reflection and consideration. Unfortunately, like Hindu astrology the matter is simple but not easy. However it can be grasped if one has great curiosity, patience, and humility. I might add that because many people are unwilling to rigorously confront the question it is the only opinion relating to astrology about which I am stingy in my lectures. Quite simply, people are often too threatened by the subject to truly hear the concepts, traditional though they are. Furthermore the issue is, from the point of view of an astrologer who practices Hindu and Western astrology and thus daily sees the workings of *both* fate and free will, clearly meant for prolonged thought, not for spur-of-the-moment speculation. The question of free will is far and away the most important matter to be handled by an astrologer for it is absolutely at the heart of all astrological counseling.

Proper understanding of free will nearly always determines whether an astrologer will benefit or harm his or her clients. People who are in distress and thus visit an astrologer to "see what the stars say" do so in order to address a discrepancy in their experience of their own power, their own free will. As such the astrologer deals with essentially two kinds of trouble. Either the client is not taking enough responsibility and doing what is necessary to solve the problem or they are neurotically anguishing over an interest that is simply not in their power to control. Aiding the person through an objective analysis of the situation is not terribly difficult. But it does require open-mindedness and a deep, rigorous understanding of free will versus predestiny.

The foremost reason for my journey to the East was to "cool out" from the loss of my father. Since I was, at the time, unaware that Hindu astrology could ever be accessible to a Westerner, learning the subject was not my second priority. Coming to grips with the issue of free will was. It had been on my mind ever since I began to study Western astrology. It was there daily, upon waking and upon retiring. I assumed that in my travels to India and Israel there would be enough priests, saints, and gurus to confer with after which I might finally draw my own conclusions. There were and I did. While I had no mind-altering or highly mystical experiences regarding the matter, everyone, regardless of religious or spiritual backround, said the same things. Though superficial teachers did not draw identical conclusions to those of the profound thinkers, all acknowledged the same basic tenets. And well they should for the principles are as traditional and conventional as knowledge ever gets.

Quite simply, nearly every religion, every doctrine attempting to "bind man back to God" (for that is the meaning of religion: "re" meaning again, "ligio" from "logos" meaning word or source; literally "again source") appeals to man to behave in certain ways. In doing so, in requesting man to perform certain actions while avoiding others, religion implies the existence of free will in no uncertain terms. And since free will fully matches our experience, the philosophy needs no clarification. The other maxim given out in nearly every belief system is that God or "source" is omniscient, knowing all even to the extent of every detail in existence, be it past, present, or future. Now this premise, which implies predestiny (or as the mystics teach that in the same way a seed contains the entire finished product of a tree all of creation was completed at the instant it was created) is, at least seemingly, diametrically opposed to free will. What is present then is a giant paradox (a statement that seems contradictory or opposed to common sense and yet may be true): a paradox most people easily ignore because the first premise, free will, lives in their experience while the second, predestiny, lives in their belief system, which therefore need not have any basis in reality. Not so simple, however, for an astrologer, especially an Hindu one who witnesses predestiny regularly in the course of daily work.

What religions and philosophies say regarding free will does not, of course, make that information true. But since paradigms and thought systems are not created by fools, even if they are often followed and corrupted by fools, it does make them worth considering. Here I might add that the original meaning of the word consider was to "confer with the stars" ("con" meaning with and "sider" from "sidus" meaning star; literally "with stars"). If one confers with the stars (and not through the horoscope section of the daily news or the local gypsy) one does indeed find, quite openly, the element of fate. So do consider, that is confer with the stars, if you would understand free will versus predestiny.

Now, according to what has been presented, the astute reader will conclude that free will versus predestiny is not the issue; free will *and* predestiny is. Free will exists, absolutely (without reservation and free from imperfection). Predestiny exists, absolutely and unconditionally. Everything was already determined the instant creation began. The combination of the two realities does *not* mean that certain events are predetermined while others are, somehow, not. The truth is closer to: we choose with our free will and that choice, once made is predestined *even though our free will is indeed real!* If this does not seem to make sense, it is not necessarily meant to. That is the nature of the issue. Paradox is not easy for the human mind to grapple with. It is nearly as difficult for those who have practiced mysticism and meditation for twenty, thirty, forty years or even an entire lifetime. In the Far East there exist two fierce stone lions at the front of every temple, as if guarding the entrance. Tourists marvel at their elegance. The wise know what the lions represent. They stand for the two greatest obstacles on the path to God. One is doubt, or lack of faith; a problem, certainly, but one which many manage to overcome. The other is paradox. It is rarely conquered.

Lions guard the entrance of a Nepalese temple.

Astrologers wrestle with paradox daily. For interpreters of the heavenly language experience the same free choice as everyone else and at the same time go about predicting the design, purpose, and life schedule of people's lives. Often, as I have tried to show through the accounts in this book, the "magic" works and predictions occur like clockwork. At times, for generally no rhyme or reason, they fall flat. Regarding predictive failure I feel obliged to address those who quite naturally believe that if astrology works so much of the time then it must in fact work all of the time, the fault then lying in the astrologer's lack of expertise and/or the complexity of the subject. In one sense I would agree. Since predestiny is absolute, all is predictable. And where, of course, better to find the prognostication than through the heavenly language which has survived, incredibly, the test of time, charlatans, gypsies, and newspaper columns. Yes, ultimately the stars, if they are generally and routinely correct in their revelations, must be always exact. Logically it would seem so. And as I began my work with the Hindu system, which so often proved wonderfully simple and precise, the assumption made perfect sense.

In practice, however, I think all is not predictable. For example, while John Lennon's violent death and Richard Nixon's political downfall appear with such blatant obviousness in their Hindu charts other major occurrences such as the sudden deaths of James Dean and Ricky Nelson are nowhere to be found (at least not in their Hindu charts). It seems, at least from experience, that there will always, regardless of the astrologer's ability, be predictions that flop and occurrences that happen and cannot be found in the blueprint. The reason for this lies not in the simple fact that no one has ever experienced total accuracy from astrology but in the paradoxical existence of free will and predestiny. For from the free will reality all, obviously, cannot be predicted. And it never will. From that reality astrology can neither be nor even evolve to absolute perfection.

Free will is the counterpart reality to predestiny. And though it is not one iota greater or more real than predestiny, it must be given equal weight and consideration or we will never even approach, let alone understand, the truth of the matter. At this point I feel especially inadequate, more so than in expressing the authenticity of the heavenly language to nonbelievers, to argue the imperfect, or shall I say nonabsolute, nature of astrology. For when I assert that there are plenty of cases of blueprints not mirroring, in completeness, individuals' lives one can always assume the fault is in the astrologer's analysis and judgment. Worse, one can assert that our understanding of astrological technique is lacking. I have, to be sure, no way to prove that such is not the case. In fact I have even no great argument against such intelligent logic. In the reality of predestiny such assertions are absolutely correct. What I do offer are three premises. The first is that in the actuality of absolute free will astrology must, on some level, fail. Secondly, no one has ever been completely accurate in his or her work with the heavenly language. And thirdly I would offer my own brief experience which in influence and contact with peers and mentors is quite ample. At least it is ample enough for rational speculation.

When astrological analysis works, really works, it does so simply, easily, and openly. It works with integrity and without great complication and tedious technicality. Therefore, on those occasions when predictions and delineations fail, after all the blueprint factors have been noted and properly analyzed, and the basic fundamentals have been found to be in place, astrology has indeed failed. At least it has failed within "practical reality." There is, of course, another reality and viewpoint, which we may call "ultimate reality," which presupposes that astrology is perfect and in time will be practiced as such. And it is true also. But this reality has less impact since we live in relative existence where the practical always takes precedence over absolutes and ultimates. To attempt some sort of summary to the issue of predictive failure let us say that astrology will never work completely unless there is a way for it to work completely *and* not at all.

The issue of free will and predestiny is difficult and paradoxical.* For many, unwilling to rigorously confront an issue, paradox invokes anger. At any rate, as a final personal note: while I am fully aware that within one reality predictive perfection is impossible yet I intend to use my free will to regularly return to India to study with as many experienced astrologers as possible. This I will do in the quest for predictive perfection, which absolutely exists in the reality of predestiny. This way of living is the same one of which every astrologer is hopefully aware: that all is possible and at the same time predetermined but the only sane way to live is in the reality of free will, with an understanding and acknowledgment of predestiny. A humorous quote by Isaac Bashevis Singer expresses the matter: "We must believe in free will, we have no choice!"

---

*For a practical explanation of how free will and predestiny function simultaneously please see the section titled "How And Why The Star Language Works" on page 292.

More Birthchart Analysis

Back to the chart at hand, Santhanam mentioned that Anna's birthchart revealed extremely fortunate career success. Although his point was easy to agree with since the blueprint indications were so strong, the astrological analysis seemed to me to stray somewhat from the truth. Anna had, indeed, graduated from one of the finest drama schools in the country. But career success in the outside world had been just as difficult for her as it had for other actors and actresses. When Santhanam made the statement that her chart was one of the best I had brought him, I remember wondering if there was something about her life that I was missing. There was. In the years after we separated Anna rather quickly established herself as a prominent director in her city. Of all my college classmates she became one of the rare few to make a living in the theatre. As we closely examined her chart it became clear that she had just entered a very favorable period, which would last for two or three years. The period promised financial reward and powerful success in general. Since Anna's blueprint was one of the few that contained such strong professional success and even the possibility of fame I was excited to tell her the good news. What was especially pleasing was that there was good fortune indicated at present rather than five or ten years in the future, which is often the case.

When I left India, I stopped in Anna's hometown on my way to Miami. We met for lunch and I immediately told her, "Your birthchart looks like you're going to have some fame soon." She replied, "I think it's already happening. I have won three theatrical awards in the past two months." Strike another notch for Hindu astrology.

"Doesn't anyone in America have peaceful married life?" Santhanam asked after scrutinizing the next blueprint placed before him. Having by now seen a different birthchart each night in our studies Santhanam was, I surmised, beginning to notice a pattern. I was loathe to answer the question but nevertheless replied that few people, of my acquaintances anyway, seemed to have mastered the art. "This man is corrupt, he has no morals at all," he continued. "Married life for him is a total disaster." To myself I jokingly wondered which marriage Santhanam meant. Was it the first one that had burned out after less than two years? Was it the second one which had ended also in just as short a time? Or was he saying that if my thirty-three-year-old friend should tie the knot a third time that the union would again be doomed?

Santhanam had, of course, been correct in his analysis and he knew it. Anyone having even a rudimentary knowledge of Hindu astrology could see that married life through this birthchart carried with it very little, if indeed any, luck whatever in terms of relationships. Domestic life for this man was, as Santhanam proclaimed, a disaster, in the original meaning of the word ("dis" meaning against, "aster" from "astrum" meaning star. Literally "stars against"). Furthermore, the man was both corrupt and immoral. He constantly seduced women with no regard for anything but his own physical pleasure. Worse yet he seemed to gain much greater enjoyment from sleeping with married women. There was a time, following his second divorce, that he was having affairs with three different married women with whom he worked.

As if it were not enough that this man's stars were against his relationships, they were also against his life. The eighth space in his blueprint, the space revealing length of life and means of death, was so badly marred that Santhanam's statement regarding that fact sent shivers up my spine. "This man," he blurted out, "will do suicide. He will have a hand in his own death." I was shocked. "But he is actually spiritually oriented," I protested. "He has been meditating for many years." In fact this ex-colleague of mine had taught meditation for a long while and was very devoted to gaining enlightenment. But his life was, in my mind, one huge contradiction. For he was also about as selfish and therefore miserable as I imagine one could be. So the longer I considered Santhanam's statement the more sense it made. It seemed especially logical, I reasoned, if the man continued to pursue higher consciousness with such vigor while at the same time remaining so cruel-hearted. For if there was no significant change in his behavior and motives, he would eventually have to confront his own nature and then would certainly wind up in a bad way.

We did not discuss, or if we did it was quickly forgotten, the timeframe of when this man's life might end. Foremost on my mind, as we spoke about this most significant subject, was just where on earth was this free will we were all supposed to have. Granted Santhanam and I had been dissecting people's lives by the night and I was thoroughly initiated into the reality of predestiny, but this issue somehow left my mind reeling. Suicide, according to gurus and mystics, is by far the worst action a person can undertake. It just seemed very strange that such an activity could really appear in a blueprint as if destined from birth. I was perturbed at Santhanam for his analysis, and one part of my brain wanted to drop the matter of death completely. There was of course no way to know if his conclusion was accurate except to wait who knows how many years. But even that was not the point. Whether this prediction was correct or not was unimportant. The fact was that suicide appearing in a birthchart was no odd concept to my mentor. It was to me and therefore sat with me philosophically, more tied in with the free will question than anything else.

Through the language of the stars I have come to see

clearly that many of man's experiences, which seem absolutely "chosen," are quite predictable. One of the most interesting and relevant to this theme concerns the act of abortion. As it happens children and childbirth are seen from the fifth house of the blueprint. When the space is well disposed in a person's chart, he or she will have children and they will be successful or a source of joy. The amount of offspring is determined by the number (and quality) of planetary aspects made to the house and any planetary positions coinciding with the space itself. However, if the malefic planets, the planets considered negative influences, aspect the house then problems will exist. The difficulties can, of course, occur in any number of ways, but there are two aspects which are rather simplistic in their effects. When the planetary positions of either Mars or Saturn aspect the fifth space (special exceptions notwithstanding) the person will, as the scriptures say, "suffer on account of children." What this means in practice is that the person having such an aspect will have a miscarriage or a child that will die very early in its life (generally within a year or so). However, that is the effect occurring to individuals living in underdeveloped, third world countries.

Interestingly, in the West where modern medicine has so greatly diminished child fatalities what occurs to individuals with the malefic aspects are abortions. The same blueprint that to an Indian indicates two or three children dying in infancy means two or three abortions to a Westerner. In charts of Westerners the fifth space must be very greatly marred to indicate a miscarriage or child death. But in any event after only a few years of astrological practice it has become obvious that abortions are no more or less chosen than anything else. They are indicated in birthcharts quite openly, more so I would say than many other delineations that are often very tricky. This is not to say that one is not responsible for such actions as abortions or suicide. This is not to say that there are not great consequences incurred. Most likely there are. But neither are such acts as simple as they appear.

As we discussed the chart in front of us, I was curious to gain some insight as to how one who was so spiritually oriented as this man could at the same time be so sexually promiscuous. Celibacy seems to exist as a requisite to enlightenment in so many traditional paths to God. The reason for this is not moral but practical since the sexual energy, being so intense, is an important aid in opening up the subtle channels of consciousness in the body. What I learned through the language of the stars gave me to think that our Creator did not lack for a sense of humour. Celibacy, which almost all agree demands incredible strength and resolve, appears an even greater struggle for spiritual seekers than it is for the worldly. The way it works is that the same space in the Hindu blueprint "ruling" *moksha* (enlightenment or final liberation) also governs sexual pleasure. Therefore when the twelfth space of the chart is powerful, thus indicating that the person will take to spiritual life, it also means he or she has the great good fortune to experience plenty of heightened sexual pleasure.

The twelfth space is not the only birthchart indicator of these attributes. The dispositions of the planetary positions of Venus and Mars are important to sex life, while spirituality is greatly affected by Jupiter, Saturn, and Ketu (known as South Node to Westerners). And of course there are certain yogas or planetary combinations that declare a person is meant to live the life of a monk. But in most cases the spiritual-minded seekers of enlightenment, being guided by their teachings to strive for celibacy, are hounded and plagued by their "good fortune" to receive plenty of sexual enjoyment. Needless to say the twelfth house of my ex-colleague's birthchart was massively strong. And needless to say the issue of the struggle comes up almost routinely in the sessions with spiritual disciples and new-age-movement followers who have contracted my services. There is, of course, no magical solution to the problem, but it is at least consoling to understand the dilemma from a perspective not at all conducive to guilt.

As for the issue of death being revealed through the birthchart, it is a delicate matter at best. Predicting the time or nature of death from ominous blueprint indications is certainly not to be done with absolute certainty. Yet neither is it to be taken lightly or ignored when one can be appropriately warned of a dangerous period. Though I have had little experience in predicting death, the issue has not escaped my attention. Discerning whether the length of one's life is short or long through the Hindu blueprint is no more or less complicated than any other signification of the star language. The eighth space of the birthchart, representing the overall life force, when strong and well aspected indicates great longevity while the opposite reveals early death. What is somewhat tricky, however, is that in certain charts the "natal" or basic blueprint indications show extremely strong life energy and yet the person may indeed die early because of a particularly life-threatening *dasa bhukti* period.

Such was the case with Marilyn Monroe whose eighth house was extremely powerful but whose death occurred as if on schedule in a terribly foreboding period. Monroe died in a *dasa* or major period of Jupiter and a minor period of Mars. That alone is indicative of very little without a knowledge of the position, aspects, and rulerships of the planets. The significant point is that the zodiacal positions of Jupiter and Mars both occupy the eighth space of her chart, the house of life—and death. And Mars, being a "harmful planet" by nature, could not influence Jupiter's energy in any way but negatively. Therefore the period was undeniably dangerous. Incidentally, in discussing Monroe's chart one point is especially worth mentioning. The eighth space, though it does not represent sexual activity in the Hindu system as it does in Western astrology, does reveal sexual *attractiveness*. Hence the sex symbols of our day— such as Monroe, John Travolta, and Paul Newman (John Kennedy, too)—all have phenomenally strong eighth houses. It is also worth noting that nearly every world champion boxer has an immensely powerful eighth house. This is because great fighters must have enormous life energy to withstand the beatings they incur. Floyd Patterson, Joe Frazier, and George Foreman all have extremely positive eighth houses in their Hindu charts. The result is that they could not have the life force knocked out of them, even briefly.

Regarding longevity, almost every person whose Hindu blueprint shows an extremely long or short life instinctively knows the fact. Since the eighth space also represents intuition, it is perhaps natural for those with a powerful eighth to be so aware. But somehow even those with weak eighth houses, and therefore minimal intuition, know of their curtailed lives. Though it is extremely rare that I have informed anyone of the likelihood of a very short life (for obvious reasons) I have on occasion done so. I have given out such delicate information in the occasional presence of highly spiritual persons who, being unafraid of transition, might benefit from the knowledge. There is also less chance of such responsible persons causing any "self-fulfilling prophecies." The others it has seemed wise to advise have been clients with intense purpose and far-reaching goals in life. For such persons the knowledge that their future existence, after a specific date, is uncertain could be beneficial in terms of designing their strategy.

Though, as mentioned, it has rarely been appropriate to relate to someone the likelihood of an early death, the few times I have done so it has never surprised the client. Since the behavioral patterns and experiences expressed through astrology are essentially hereditary many, if not most, persons with early deaths have witnessed the same situation with their ancestors. In fact the most graceful way I have found to inform a person of such sensitive information as this is by asking how their parents and grandparents have fared with longevity. They then understand through logic their most likely outcome.

Oftentimes in dangerous *dasa bhukti* periods which portend death the person does not die but simply experiences an especially difficult time of life. There are usually intense accidents and other serious misfortunes. It has happened more than once during the past few years that persons undergoing such dreadful planetary periods have arrived at my door with bandaged heads and stories of calamities, fires, etc. Also common in these instances is for the individual to relate that he or she has been threatened or assaulted. Such a case recently occurred to a relative of mine. One day while I was analyzing this man's birthchart I noticed that he was at the end of a *dasa bhukti* which indicated an extremely strong chance of violent death. Because the period was almost over and because he is not the sort to act on astrological advice, I decided against burdening him with the information. There was, in my opinion, nothing to be gained by doing so. I thus crossed my fingers and prayed that whatever had kept him safe so far would continue for another two months. At last when the period ended and I told him that he had just finished an intensely dangerous year and a half, he replied that there was indeed a man trying to kill him. He refused to elaborate or say why the man was after him but was glad to hear that the period was finally over.

John Lennon, during 1980, was not so lucky as he was assassinated some seven or eight months into a terribly inauspicious two-and-a-half-year period. Like Marilyn Monroe, the *dasa bhukti* planets were both situated in the house of death. In this case it was Jupiter's main period and Saturn's subperiod. Far worse than the planets simply being situated in the eighth space was the fact that the positions of the two planets were conjunct within one degree of each other (out of a possible 360!). Whenever two planets are so closely joined together in a Hindu blueprint, there is said to exist a "planetary war." The outcome of a planetary war is determined by the planet occupying the earlier longitudinal degree. That planet is known to win and give good effects while the losing planet is then designated to produce (actually indicate) nothing but grief, misery, and destruction. As it happened Jupiter, which was the *dasa* planet or essential influence, lost the war. Furthermore, because of "house rulership" (in other words, the space Jupiter was *inherently* connected to, in this case the seventh) Jupiter became what is called a *maraka* or death-inflicting planet.

Between the combination of all these intense factors was the great danger. Lennon incidentally, being mystically oriented, was reportedly in close contact with a Western astrologer when he died. Unfortunately the peril went unseen which is no great shock knowing the nature of Western astrology. Sometimes events and circumstances can be seen through our Western system but that is not its forté. At any rate the danger indicated in his Hindu blueprint was so obvious that even a novice would have been immediately alarmed. Had Lennon visited an Hindu astrologer he would have been warned about the period and advised to take precautions. The first recommendation would have been to obtain a large, high-quality yellow or gold sapphire and wear it on the body throughout the entire sixteen years of Jupiter's *dasa*. That would, however, be somewhat insufficient to counteract the extreme negative effects of the Jupiter Saturn cycle even though it would have been partially helpful. The most important antidote to ameliorate the situation, aside from simply being very careful, would have been to chant a Jupiter mantra or have a *yagya* (Indian religious ceremony) performed. If the wearing of gemstones to effect certain results seems odd to the reader, then mantras and *yagyas* may appear even more so. But they have been successfully employed by Indians for thousands of years and therefore will be mentioned, though briefly.

Mantras are Sanskrit sounds or phrases, the effects of which (when chanted) are beneficial. The phrases are very much like what the West considers prayer except that they work on a different level than devotion. This is because Sanskrit is the language of the *Vedas*, the Indian body of knowledge that predates religion and is said to have been cognized by enlightened beings. It is revered as a "pure" language in which a word and the object it represents are essentially the same. In other words, the sound or vibration of the name is the same as the vibration of the object. Hence chanting or mentally repeating a specific vibration invokes the form that the word suggests. Sanskrit, being aptly titled a "name and form" language, is therefore especially unique.

In Lennon's case chanting the Jupiter mantra would have been the appropriate action to alter the danger indicated through his Jupiter Saturn *dasa bhukti*. The prescription for that particular mantra is 19,000 repetitions but not necessarily in one sitting. Generally one chants ten or twenty minutes per day for some months until the allotted number has been completed. Astrological mantras are somewhat lengthier than the simple one- or two-syllable phrases (such as OM) that most Westerners know. The Jupiter mantra in transliterated form is as follows: *Deva-nancha rishi-nancha gurum-kanchana shan-eebam boodee bootam treelo-keysham tam na-mamee brihaspateem.*

There is little to say about the power and efficacy of chanting mantras since until one has experienced the process there is no basis for judgment. Further, there is no way to prove that astrological mantras work. For how is one to prove that chanting a mantra has mitigated a dangerous event? But Indians consider them to have been successfully employed for thousands of years. The way mantras work is by their vibratory effect on the human nervous system. The reason they are more powerful than gemstones and metals is perhaps because sound and thought vibrations are more subtle than those of the grossly physical. I have not yet had any great need to chant an astrological mantra but I did, for a short time, chant the Mercury one. The effect was a powerful calming influence. This was natural since Mercury rules the nervous system. Also, clients I have prescribed mantras for occasionally call up, out of gratitude, to report the significant benefits they are gaining.

The most interesting stories I know to relate are two which were told to me by another Hindu astrologer. The first regards a man who was approaching an extremely dangerous period, one which was interpreted to mean death. The astrologer prescribed an appropriate mantra. He also advised that the man obtain a goat, which he should shower with love and affection. The idea was that when the bad period arrived the goat would somehow take on the negative effects rather than the man himself. Having followed the advice the man passed through the dangerous *dasa bhukti* unharmed while the goat, at the very beginning of the period, died suddenly. The other account concerns a famous Indian Yogi, the father of Guru Maharaj Ji (the famous child guru now residing in America). It seems that the local astrologers had foreseen the death of the elderly guru and warned him of the danger. The guru was unconcerned however and took no precautions. His wife, stricken with fear and unable to persuade her husband to take care, finally hired priests to perform *yagyas* to try to alter the situation. *Yagyas* are ritualistic ceremonies also performed in the Sanskrit language, which may be done by priests or pundits for the benefit of another person. When the priests entered the house chanting mantras and waving incense around the room, however, the guru quickly threw them out. He died, shortly thereafter, as predicted.

Throughout my stay with Santhanam we often analyzed my own birthchart, mostly focusing on one or two details in isolation rather than the chart as a whole. The sense I left India with was that my life contained the potential for some strong worldly accomplishment but was far more well disposed in the area of spiritual values. I also knew that astrology, now that I had access to both systems, was for me. Since these were such early days in my study of the Hindu system, much subtlety was lacking. I had merely the tiniest bit of practical experience with Hindu birthcharts and was unaware of much astrological technique. Certain matters Santhanam may have avoided since I was a beginner. Other knowledge I perhaps considered of a lesser priority and therefore forgot rather quickly. In a system as vast as Hindu astrology prioritizing is essential, lest one end up in a maze of confusion. It should also be said that my mentor was a scholar, more than a practitioner, and a relative youngster at that. So although a solid basis for future practice was established I later came to find that the understanding of my life and its schedule was at this point incomplete and therefore somewhat inaccurate.

Basically, I was so fascinated by the accuracy of the *dasa bhukti* system of prediction that I overlooked other, more subtle factors. Most importantly, I was nearly ecstatic just to have finally decided on a profession I could devote my life to. I did not dwell on the glaring reality that astrology was an impractical way to earn a living or even that it was almost entirely misunderstood by society. The fact was that between the ages of twenty-nine and thirty-one I had been professionally passionless for the first time since my teens. I was now getting back on track after two and a half years of what is known as "Saturn return" and that felt just fine!

Saturn return is a highly significant astrological condition in Western astrology. The influence is a cycle that occurs to all individuals beginning at the approximate age of twenty-nine and ending around thirty-one-and-a-half (it also occurs again at fifty-eight). The reason it is called Saturn return is because after twenty-nine years Saturn has completed its transit around the zodiac and thus returns to its original position in a person's birthchart. The astrological meaning of this is that the person undergoing the transit has lived a substantial degree of experience in each particular area of life. Therefore a succession of lessons have been learned and hence adulthood begins. The usual occurrence during these years is for the person to experience great pressure to let go of any life features not conducive to fulfillment or in accord with the overall life purpose. It is as if twenty-nine years of experimentation are over and now commitment is the order of the day. Saturn return is frequently quite painful since many people at this age find themselves in crisis as they are confronted with inappropriate careers, unhappy relationships, and other inadequate life situations.

My own Saturn return was, obviously, a perfect example of a difficult expression of the transit. At the age of twenty-nine I dissolved an incongruous marriage, quit an unfitting career, and began a search for a course of action more in sync with my spirituality, purpose, and intention. By the time my goodbyes were said to Santhanam my Saturn return was, thank God and Santhanam, nearing a successful end. When I arrived home in Miami and told my family of my plans for a career in astrology my mother reminded me of something I had long forgotten. She said that during my first or second year of school when I heard about the study of planets and stars I had declared that I then knew what I wanted to do with my life!

CHAPTER **III**

PRACTICING HINDU AND WESTERN ASTROLOGY

Having returned from India and my studies with Santhanam, astrology was about all I could think of. If the subject was fascinating to me it was even more so to everyone I came in contact with. So although my plan of action was to keep to myself and analyze and research as many charts as possible, the people I was meeting had other ideas. Everyone, it seemed, wanted to know what his or her astrological birthchart "said." On the plane home from India I had to truly put up a fight in order to escape astrologizing for one of the flight attendants. Though I gave her the name of an astrologer in the town she lived in she insisted "I want *you* to do it." I explained as best I could that I was not yet ready to do that. It must have seemed terribly strange to her because in my excitement over the wonderful learning experience I had just completed I was nearly bouncing off the walls to tell people the merits of Hindu astrology. She finally relented and I was off the hook. But the relief did not last long. Shortly thereafter a landlord I met while apartment hunting also insisted that I interpret his chart. Though I again protested that I felt unready to practice for the public he refused to take no for an an-

131

swer. If I would not take his money for the work, he said, then he would repay me through his professional activity of haircutting. Having made the agreement we exchanged services and I was off to a running start. The man, to whom I am very grateful, was thrilled with the reading and spread the word to all his friends. When my phone started ringing, I realized I was in business whether I considered myself ready or not.

My first professional session. I painfully asked $45 and was petrified of charging money for what I considered birthright information. Though I certainly had enough knowledge between the two astrological systems there was no university degree proclaiming me a professional interpreter of the language of the stars. More than anything I was concerned that people would be paying money for information about which a certain amount would be accurate and a certain amount would not. My astrologizing was not flawless, especially early on. The strategy therefore was to work as diligently as possible on each blueprint in order to gain as much precision as I could. I am ashamed to say how long I labored over the two charts of my first paying customer.

Finally, after some days I felt as ready as I ever would be. However because of my fear of inadequacy and the resultant desire for accuracy I was insensitive to the astrological counseling process. Rather than first gaining the client's trust and confidence by gradually providing her with correct but relatively innocuous information and then approaching intense issues, I went straight to the point. "Well, your life seems to center around love relationships which are quite difficult because of what happened with your father. It appears from the chart that there were real problems there." "No," she said, "everything was fine with my father." "Well, was his life rough?" I asked. "Did he die very young or leave you and your mother or something?" "No, everything was good. We had a good relationship," she replied. "Wait a minute," I interjected. "Was there not something strange or weird going on? *Were you not missing a father emotionally?*" (From analysis of the Hindu chart I knew there was a problem with the father. From Western astrology I could see she psychologically had no father). "No, everything was fine," she repeated. "Well are you sure you've given me the correct birth time," I asked. "Yes, definitely," she said. "The birth time is accurate."

Panic. How can astrology work so well for me and my friends and so poorly now that someone wants to pay me I wondered. What was odd was that this particular birthchart would not greatly change unless the birth time was extremely off, meaning thirty or forty minutes. Some charts change drastically with a four- or five-minute discrepancy, but this was not one of them. To alter her Hindu chart, which clearly indicated great suffering at the hands of the father, the time would have to have been way off. And she swore it was not! Since I had no astrological experience with the general public or as a professional, I was quite at a loss as to what was happening. So I simply told her that the chart did not seem to work and I had no idea why. She was not nearly as bothered as I was and asked me to please continue. There seemed little point in that. I had examined both her charts for plenty of hours and all the data pointed to the same reality. If the information I had just presented was inaccurate then there was no reason to feel confident in anything else that was delineated.

But strangely she bade me go on so I did. I continued with the reading for another twenty or thirty minutes speaking on different topics of her life. It then finally came time to address her home life as a child in terms of her mother. Since this was another disaster area about which the blueprint was truly implicit I was loathe to put my opinion forth in fear of being wrong again. But I was not going to lie. I meekly stated "I may be off again, but from the chart it seems that your mother also had a very hard life. Your relationship with her appears as difficult as it does with your father." From her reply it became obvious that interpreting the stars for myself was one thing; Practicing it for others was quite another. "Well," she said, "my mother never had any time for me. You see she was always taking care of my father. He was a terrible alcoholic."

Then and there I contemplated drawing a picture of myself strangling a woman and then saying, "Now look closely. What's wrong with this picture?" But the truth was it was an excellent lesson. There was much to be learned from it. And I was fortunate to have been confronted so early on. For one thing I learned that I would have to decide from the very start which to trust, astrology and my own experience or the client's word. Also, I now realized that from my tongue to another's ears there could exist a mind-boggling gap. Finally, I came to find that although astrologizing is not therapy or counseling per se, it is similar in nature. Thus, to successfully practice the "art" of astrology is to deeply understand the human experience, to possess the greatest communication skills, and to appreciate the nature of life itself.

Though I was no greenhorn to these matters, in the quest to prove myself I managed to somehow let them slide. I, insensitively, did not realize that people are often quite nervous in the beginning of an astrological session and are consequently not about to discuss their most delicate concerns with a total stranger. Not at least until a significant degree of harmony and trust is established. The woman I astrologized for was not crazy when she originally spoke of her father. She was scared. Furthermore she had been through years and years of psychoanalysis dealing with exactly the issues I had raised! What she was thinking and really meant to say was that at this point in her life she had *resolved* the issue for herself, and there was now no problem between her and her father. So be it.

For the next year and a half I enjoyed a field day, astrologically speaking. I was no longer tormented by the inconsistency I had experienced in using only one astrological system. Furthermore, for every particular life function worth analyzing there were now two completely different methodologies providing insight. Because of the complexity of astrological analysis, the ability to determine any feature with certainty boils down to a matter of percentages, especially in the Hindu system. For example an astrologer may conclude that someone has, free will notwithstanding, an eighty or eighty-five percent chance of becoming wealthy in his or her lifetime. Someone else may have a ninety percent chance of getting married in a certain year. Another person may have only a ten or twenty percent chance of ever creating a fulfilling career, etc. There is a common saying among astrologers: "See an indication in a birthchart once and it is a possibility. See the indication twice and it is a likelihood. See it three times and it is a certainty."

With the two systems available to me the potential for accuracy greatly increased. Not only was there more data, but there was also a means of perspective with which to consider astrological information. Now I could see for instance that a person's Western birthchart might indicate fame while their Hindu chart could contradictorily reveal very limited success. Since the Western chart focuses more on the psychology, behavior, and motivation of the person, he or she would quite naturally be consumed with that form of desire. However the probability of fame actually occurring would be minimal and almost completely dependent on free will, meaning the dedication and commitment towards such a goal. Another fortunate result of possessing both systems was that I had the ability to see a person's talents and fascinations through the chart but also to know which ones were likely to ever be taken beyond hobbies or enjoyments.

For some reason, though I analyzed charts week after week and month after month, I never ceased to be amazed that people's lives could actually be reviewed from some thirty or forty symbols placed on a few pieces of paper. What was also interesting was that the clients who came for readings took this fact in stride. They evidently "believed" in the language of the stars without having had any hands-on experience themselves and were content to have the interpretation of their life and its schedule delineated by a stranger. I found this very curious. In my own life, being the seeker that I am, it has always seemed a necessity to maintain a hefty dose of skepticism if there was any intention of ever finding truth. Not that one should necessarily be skeptical of astrology, mind you. That is not the point. One must certainly, in the beginning, seek out an experienced astrologer in order to realize whatever benefits are to be gained from the subject.

Indeed, just as the people I astrologized for came to me, I had years earlier visited my first astrologer without any knowledge whatever of the mystical language of the stars save a minimum of information about my Libra Sun sign. Even then I was naturally skeptical of the astrologer called upon to do the honors of interpretation. And my skepticism had nothing to do with the astrologer's ability. My skepticism, or concern in the matter, derived from the question of whether the highest good could ever be obtained by having *anyone* other than myself interpret the blueprint for my existence. It seemed to me that if at the moment of my creation nature had laid out a plan and design for my life that it should at least be *me* who was doing the interpreting! There are, to be sure, very powerful arguments against that line of thinking but to this day the issue is, in my mind, quite of the essence. This concern is, incidentally, the reason that in my own astrological work I always convey to the client, as simply as possible, the astrological indications (the interpretive details, that is) responsible for my analysis and predictions of their life. Such a way of working is distinct from merely giving out my prognosis and opinions without explanation or reason.

Astrological interpretation is, unbeknown to most people, an extremely rational and analytical procedure. Though an accurate rendering of one's blueprint depends completely on the astrologer's understanding of and experience with the heavenly language the judgments made are merely the result of logical inferences. It is all a matter of deductive reasoning or piecing together informational elements in a sequential way to arrive at specific meanings. Once the elements of the language are understood the person possessing the more logical, more unrestricted, and unbounded mind is capable of drawing the most accurate and profound conclusions. That person is sometimes the client rather than the astrologer. Furthermore, if the client is given the essentials of how interpretations are deduced, he or she may, long after the astrological session is over, play with the information (consciously or unconsciously) and make certain important realizations. So from the beginning of my professional days I attempted to treat those who came to me with the same respect I would have desired had I been in their places.

One of the first tasks I wished to accomplish once I was back in America was to determine my father's accurate birthchart, if that was possible. Boss, as he was affectionately called, never knew his exact date of birth. Birthdays in Allepo, Syria, during the early part of the century were evidently of no great concern. What the Boss did remember was that he was told the birth occurred on the very last day of the Jewish holiday *Succos*. The year, as best he knew, was either 1906, 1907, or 1908 (he believed it was 1907 but could not be sure). The day he celebrated as his birthday was October 1 but there was no way to be certain that was the correct day. Some days after Boss' death I asked the Rabbi performing the funeral rites if it was possible to ascertain the exact dates of *Succos* for the three years in question. He said it was a simple matter and quickly produced the desired information. I had no idea whatever of my father's birth time but that was not the main concern now. At this point I was most interested to establish the date of birth which, in using Western astrology, would reveal a good deal of information about his psychology, behavior, and motivations.

Before my journey to India I had, without success, examined the three charts and come to no conclusions. There were many factors in each of the blueprints that could have fit my father's way of being. There were also elements that seemed questionable as far as I could tell. At any rate from none of the charts did I gain any sense of certainty of connection to the Boss. I hoped that perhaps through the Hindu system more knowledge would present itself and thus help me to draw some conclusion. As it happened it was through the use of both the Hindu and Western systems that success was finally achieved.

One day during morning meditation, after having looked over the three charts for a few minutes, I was struck with an interesting insight. One of the charts, the one for September 30, 1907, contained an astrological factor which appeared in one way or another in the charts of all three of the Boss' children! Since behavioral patterns and even events and life schedules are hereditary, as I had witnessed time and time again over the years, I knew I was onto something. The particular feature, an *extremely* prominent Mars position (revealing great ambition and courage) did not occur in the 1906 or 1908 charts. Furthermore, luckily for me in this discernment process, the Mars aspect was nowhere to be found in the blueprint of my mother. It therefore made perfect sense that since I and my two older brothers all had intense Mars aspects (two with the conjunction and one with the opposition, for those who speak astrology) and so did the 1907 chart for the last day of *Succos* that I had at last determined his date of birth. I was excited.

The next step, now that I knew the zodiacal placements of the heavenly bodies for that day, was to place the planetary configurations into a Hindu format which would reveal the actual life (as opposed to the psychological profile) he had just lived. Since the arrangement of the planets, in their relationships to each other, does not significantly change in a twenty-four hour period (other than the Moon) the distinction to be determined was from which zodiac sign to begin the twelve spaces of the blueprint. Once that point was located it would be a simple process of setting down the planetary positions in their order of sequence. There being only twelve spaces in a blueprint, the process is easy if one knows for certain the detailed circumstances of a person's life (although there are astrologers willing to "rectify" birthcharts for clients completely unaware of their birth time I am not one of them. The reason I felt confident in doing so for my father was because of my absolute certainty of the specifics of his existence. However, in such cases where a person knows his or her birth time within an hour or two it is relatively simple to determine an approximate birth time implicit enough to facilitate an accurate blueprint interpretation. Such process is easily attained through the Hindu system because of its event-oriented nature. Instances will later be described).

The way to begin to find my father's Hindu chart was to simply work backwards, in other words to fit the planets and the zodiac signs they occupied into the numerical spaces indicative of the life he lived. I therefore pondered some of the most definite features of his life and contemplated where I wished to start. This was a matter of convenience, and fun I might add, since I knew so much about my father. I, sportingly, decided on the signification of gambling and speculation. This I did because it was the Boss' favorite means of play, essentially the only recreation that took him away from his retail gift shop where he was a workaholic. The subject came to mind, I suppose, because my oldest brother had jokingly suggested engraving "He loved the dogs" (dog racing, that is) on Boss' tombstone. This was not at all a disparaging remark but rather a tribute to the Boss' wonderful sense of humor.

At any rate, the strongest factor revealing the tendency to speculate is Jupiter's planetary position occupying the fifth space. I thus placed Jupiter in the fifth and fit all the other planets in their respective houses. I did this rather automatically by virtue of the other planets' relationships to Jupiter within the zodiac. That completed, the chart was now whole. Saturn occupied the first house. The Moon and Rahu were in the fourth. Venus and the Sun were in the seventh. Mercury occupied the eighth while Ketu was in the tenth and the powerful Mars sat in the eleventh. Interesting . . . very interesting. There was the same Sun in the seventh (indicating marital delays) such as my brother Charles possessed. In Boss' case the marriage was not delayed by family interference but simply by time. My father did not marry until he was thirty-nine years old, an extremely odd fact for someone of his generation and culture. The Sun, which represents power and authority, in the space of the spouse accurately described my mother with her forceful and dominating character. Venus, the planet of love and beauty, also in Boss' partnership house revealed my mother's good looks and youthful appearance.

Venus, however, because it was in its *neecha* or "fallen" position (each planet has one zodiac sign where it functions best and one where it functions worst) revealed a great deal more. Whenever a planet occupies its fallen, or worst, position tremendous grief and hardship occurs to the significations of the house containing the planet. In marrying my mother the Boss unknowingly chose a woman headed for a severely difficult life. In deference to my mother the reader shall be spared unpleasant details. In any case, the Boss, in his involvement and responsibilities in the matter, definitely endured more than his fair share of suffering. All this was accounted for in the placement of Venus in its *neecha* sign in the seventh (as well as two other more subtle, but equally powerful, disruptive birthchart factors).

So there it was. Tedious married life and an afflicted spouse in three or four simple astrological strokes. If there had been for a moment any doubts that this was my father's blueprint they were now absolutely gone. I had found the Boss' chart on the first try.

As I continued analyzing, one of my long-standing questions was answered. How, I wondered year after year, did the Boss remain married under such difficult circumstances. The answer sat on the piece of paper in front of my eyes. It was the Sun in the seventh space. The Sun in Hindu astrology is known as the *atma-karaka*, the indicator of the soul. Because it represents a person's soul, whichever blueprint space contains the *atmakaraka* takes on vast importance. It is as if the spirit and soul of the person are connected or "tied" to the significations implied by the house. In the case of the Sun in the seventh the person belonging to the blueprint can never, once married, run away (astrologers are cautioned not to apply this explanation to Western birthcharts. Because of the different zodiacs and house systems of the East and West, planets in houses in Western charts do not necessarily occupy the same spaces in Hindu *chakras*). Because the soul is so innately attached to relationships the person may not leave the spouse under *any* circumstances. He or she may wind up divorced but only if it is the decision of the spouse. It is simply a karmic condition and a difficult one at that. Throughout my astrological practice over the years I have attempted to work with several people with the Sun in the seventh, some living under the most agonizing marital situations. Never have any of them given up and walked out. Occasionally their relationship debts are paid off and in the more fortunate cases the partner sets them free.

In placing Jupiter in the fifth space of Boss' chart many other important features, other than a love of speculating, were expressed. Jupiter in the fifth generally indicates a great sense of humor and optimism, masculine children (the amount depends on several factors), and a religious, or at the least, highly moral character with a deep faith in God. In the Boss' case all of these significations were strengthened to an especially significant degree because Jupiter was in its *uchcha* (pronounced oocha) or "exalted" position on the day of his birth. In other words Jupiter was in the best zodiac sign for its functioning, the placement where it gives its finest results. Therefore all the above mentioned issues were incredibly strong. As for my father's optimism it seemed to know no bounds. As a child living through an intensely difficult domestic scene, one which my father had infinite trust would improve, I constantly tried to decipher whether he was the world's most gullible human being or the second coming of the Biblical character Job. The Boss' faith in God was simply unshakable. No matter how bad circumstances got the Boss never gave in to doubt. I incidentally, being a "realist" with a blatantly different viewpoint of the situation, experienced a good deal of guilt living in the face of this man whose trust was "as constant as the Northern star."

Religion and a highly moral character were facts of my father's life. From his thirteenth year until the day he died the Boss performed the daily Hebrew praying ritual every morning upon wakening. He also practiced twenty minutes of meditation each day from the age of sixty-six to seventy-four when he passed on. As for his moral fibre it was absolutely irreproachable. I experienced this regularly during my adolescence when I worked for the Boss in his gift shop. It seems not a week went by that my father did not send me chasing after some unwitting customer who had accidentally misplaced a package or wallet somewhere in our store. Having done the deed I would return to the shop to hear my mother explaining to the Boss the ways of the world, "Al, you don't have to be *that* honest!" "Yes Lilly, you right," Boss would say in his broken English as the words went in one ear and immediately out the other.

As soon as I started using the diametrically opposed astrological systems side by side the profound value of doing so became apparent. Although I knew the moment I came upon Hindu astrology that I had found a great, if not *the*, missing link to the Western system, I was very gratified to have that fact born out through practical experience. In the case of determining my father's birthchart it was clearly because both methods were within my grasp that I was able to succeed with ease and certainty. What was gained from the Western system was the ability to make an educated guess as to my father's birthdate. Through the use of the Hindu chart I was able to determine the accuracy of that date and then establish the approximate time of birth.

In the case of my first professional session—with the woman who suffered on account of her father—the information revealed from both systems made two realities of her life apparent. The Hindu chart demonstrated that there was a significant *actual* deficiency about her father. The Western blueprint showed that she had experienced great suffering in her relationship with him. As the reader may appreciate, possessing the knowledge of a client's objective and subjective experience of life is extremely useful to the counseling astrologer. That is an understatement. Possessing knowledge of both realities is crucial. It is crucial, that is, if astrology is to be utilized as the profound aid to human evolution that it is. As great as Hindu astrology is, what use can the predictive accuracy it provides be without understanding the person's psychology and inner experience of such circumstances? Subjective experience is at least as important, if not more so, than one's actual physical reality. At least this is so if our purpose is to evolve to higher states. For what is then most essential is the individual's interpretation of and reaction to his or her life.

Psychologically speaking, in the human experience there is no absolutely ordained reaction to any particular event or circumstance. Different personalities generate different observations and reactions to the exact same reality. If I have learned anything during my years in astrology it is that people's perceptions and responses to their lives are inevitably, almost absurdly, unique. And these "personal" opinions, feelings, and constructs are just as programmed as the events and situations able to be predicted from the Hindu system. Incidentally, the fact that one's inner experience does not necessarily match one's objective or outer reality I learned from both systems of astrology. I learned it from Santhanam when he taught me how to determine whether a person would be happy in life (happiness here is to be distinguished from contentment which is a function of spirituality and therefore, I believe, greatly subject to free will).

Happiness, or the "sweetness" of life if you will, is analyzed in the Hindu blueprint from the condition of the fourth space and the planetary position of Venus. Indeed there were charts my mentor Santhanam and I discussed that clearly produced great worldly benefits but very little happiness. John Lennon was a typical example. Contentment, according to his chart he could gain, being the spiritual man that he was. But happiness would always be elusive. There were also charts revealing the opposite; minimal wealth or "name and fame," as they say in India, yet great cheerfulness. The reason, by the way, that this issue of happiness is so important in India is because so few people there ever manage to obtain significant wealth or comforts. Therefore it is important to note whether an individual could be happy with his or her lot in life.

From Western astrology I learned almost immediately that there is no particular connection between a person's outer reality and their inner experience. This revelation came as I analyzed the birthcharts of my two older brothers in my beginning days of study. Certainly they and I shared the same household and day after day saw the same domestic events. Yet only Herb, my oldest brother, and myself considered that we had drastically difficult childhoods. Charles, who in his Western blueprint, has two very "benefic" influences (the Moon and Jupiter) in the fourth space of his birthchart, was quite another matter. As the fourth space indicates the home and mother, Charles was destined to experience an extremely happy upbringing. And so he did. How this occurred, of course, was an enormous curiosity to Herb and myself. In fact we never discussed our childhood experiences until one day as adults we sat down and shared perspectives. As we indulged in our complaints of how rough early life had been Herb amusingly blurted out, "What ever happened to Charlie? God, he was in Disney World!" Incidentally, it is fascinating to note that the beneficial astrological influences of Moon and Jupiter which occupy Charles' fourth house in his Western chart thus smoothing over his early life experience do not occupy the same blueprint space in his Hindu chart. Those planetary positions occupy the fifth space and describe his extreme optimism, speculative tendencies (just like the Boss), and his career as a stockbroker. The fourth house, in his Hindu chart, is of course severely afflicted since the objective reality of his early home life was no better than Herb's and mine. But, unlike us, because his Western blueprint decreed it so, he somehow managed to have a grand time of it.

So the more experience I gained, the more I realized the benefit and privilege of using these astrological systems together. I was grateful and happy. And yet oddly, though my greatest fascination was the Hindu predictive system, I soon realized that Western astrology, if it came down to an either/or comparison, could almost be said to be more useful to my purposes. For what I desired for my life was a spiritual career, a career that could create harmony and move people forward in their lives and thereby make a difference. I had previously rejected astrology as a serious course of action when the Western system was all I knew. This was not simply because the predictive element was unreliable. For even in the Hindu system there are plenty of discrepancies yet to be resolved. Hindu astrology must also be used with discretion and taken with a grain of salt. But the more I practiced Western astrology exclusively the more incomplete the work appeared to be. For this reason Western astrology to my eyes lacked integrity.

Much of the reason for such an assessment was because of a particular aspect in my Western blueprint indicative of my approach to life. That aspect is called the "Sun conjunct Neptune," which means that in my birthchart the zodiacal positions of the Sun and Neptune are close to each other. In my case they are extremely close and therefore the aspect is especially intense. When Pam Raff had analyzed my birthchart back in 1979 I distinctly remember her commenting on the aspect: "You have this absolutely beautiful conjunction in the sixth house." She then went on to explain that the aspect meant I was extremely spiritual or mystical, highly idealistic, and always looking for perfection. That was true, no doubt, but what she did not say was that according to C.E.O. Carter, one of the most influential British astrologers of the Twentieth Century, this particular conjunction is the most common aspect to be found in the blueprints of astrologers, "especially of those who are particularly interested in the predictive art" (*Astrological Aspects*, Fowler & Co. 1977). So by this reasoning it was only natural that I had been frustrated with Western astrology.

Now that I had solved my problem by learning the Hindu system I had, in a sense, come full circle. Having fulfilled my personal cravings for the predictive element, I could now with some perspective see the greatness of Western astrology. Aside from the fact that the knowledge it reveals fits in perfectly with the free will philosophy, Western astrology is wonderfully spiritual. The information Western birthcharts provide allows us to determine our greatest resources and potentials, and to zero in on our foibles and character flaws that we can overcome or at least embrace them with acceptance and compassion. The Western blueprint serves as a guide to the course of actions most conducive to our evolutionary growth. These are the fruits of the Western world's rendition of nature's communiqué. Clearly, the Western system is the very essence of a spiritual tool. And in my search for a meaningful career, that was all I had ever really desired!

Indeed, what bothered me most during the previous two and a half years was that my attention was so captured by what I, then, considered mundane business. I had spent seven or eight years pursuing higher consciousness and teaching several hundreds of people meditation, which to my mind meant bringing them back to God. It was no oddity that I found my fascination (really compulsion) with astrology disconcerting. Why, after such "high" activity should I be entranced with astrology I constantly wondered? What was so valuable about being able to predict people's relative existence after having worked with their journey back to "the absolute?" But even though my instincts would not allow me to embrace Western astrology as a career there were extremely compelling reasons for my interest. Just from my work with the one astrological system I had gained so very much; so much, incidentally, which would never be gotten from the purely predictive, black and white, "practical" system of the ancient Hindus.

In terms of understanding my own life, Western astrological delineations answered questions I had nearly given up asking. Why, for instance, was my social behavior always so conservative, restrained, even uptight? Why, having finally made it through my childhood and teens relatively intact, was I so stiff whenever it was time to have fun? How was it that I could be a proficient actor in a great and competitive drama school and yet be mortified at the prospect of dancing at a party? Why had love affairs been so incredibly few and far between? And what was the meaning of the fact that, at the age of eighteen, the first woman I ever slept with became pregnant; became pregnant even though precautions (obviously not enough) were taken. Was this pure coincidence? Was it my bad luck? Her bad luck? Was this simply the way of the world? Or was there a message, a lesson to be deduced, specifically for James T. Braha?

Through Western astrology I learned that there was actually a good deal of reason to all of the above madness. This is not to say, for example, that the pregnancy event was necessarily "predestined." Western astrology just does not work that way. Such a conclusion would have to come from the Hindu system. But based upon my Western blueprint the occurrence was clearly "an accident waiting to happen" because Saturn, the planet representing discipline, loss, delays, restriction, and limitation occupies the fifth space of my Western birthchart. The fifth space represents (among other things) pleasures, amusements, fun, children, and love affairs. Since Saturn represents what it does the space it occupies reveals those areas of life where a person is likely to experience hardships. Such areas are also the spheres within which the soul must learn responsible behavior. Further, because Saturn is the key indicator of karma (action/reaction, an eye for an eye, what you sow so shall you reap) its house placement indicates areas of life which may simply be difficult as a result of negative actions a person has taken in previous lives (I have no particular interest in preaching the philosophy of reincarnation. Whether or not it exists I cannot prove. But describe the astrological placement and condition of Saturn in a person's birthchart and what will be found is a life function about which the person feels they are repaying "debts" which there is no memory of having ever incurred.). The extent of hardship depends of course on the condition of Saturn, whether its position is well or poorly disposed, meaning in good or bad aspectual relationships with the other planets.

Unfortunately for me Saturn is one of the most "afflicted" planets in my Western chart (it is the absolute best planet in my Hindu chart so the reader should take note not to become confused when Saturn's great virtues are extolled later on in this book. This, by the way, is yet another demonstration of why Hindu and Western techniques must never be mixed.). My knowledge of having Saturn in the fifth house, which I learned at the age of twenty-eight, did not in any way alter my social behavior, love affair inhibitions, or aversion to dance floors; but it definitely provided insight, understanding, and answers to persistent questions. No, I realized, there was nothing faulty about my early-life impressions and perceptions. There were indeed certain areas of life in which I was somehow, in some way, innately disadvantaged. Although such reasoning could, with little effort, lead one to adopt a victim's attitude, it could *just as easily* serve some valuable purpose. With that knowledge I could finally know, with a degree of surety, that part of the reason for my earthly existence is to learn discipline and responsibility in love affairs and other pleasures or indulgences. The knowledge that powerful psychological restraints to these albeit normal life functions were inbred in my psyche from my first breath could allow me a significant measure of self acceptance in an area I had always considered myself "crippled." Though to any observer I could be considered, quite deplorably, to be holding back from certain joys one is obviously meant to experience, the knowledge that I am as an evolving organism, spirit, or soul receiving the necessary and proper life experiences for my growth is both heartening and healing.

To learn that anyone with Saturn in the fifth house had better be responsible in love affairs "or else" has been an extremely important lesson. This has been useful to me more than as a reminder to always take birth control precautions. The astrological knowledge has saved me considerable worry. For as it happens Saturn in my chart is so afflicted that in nearly every one of my love affairs the woman involved has reported (strike me dead if I lie) like clockwork that she is "*sure*" she is pregnant. Because of the knowledge at hand (and because practical experience has borne out such reality) I have spared myself a great deal of unnecessary angst. I know both the purpose and the reality of the situation. The circumstance—a natural, though powerfully confronting, repercussion of my action—is nature's way of giving me an opportunity to reflect on my love affair pleasures, an area evidently misused in the past. Interestingly, even on the occasions when I have tried to defuse this monotonous occurrence by warning my lover, after our first intimate encounter, that her body will, no doubt, be scaring the daylights out of us in the next month because of my "wondrous" karma it has not stopped nature's attempt to plague my life. My lover still manages to wind up at my house one day with the most urgent look on her face. "Astrology my a--," she will say. "I know I'm pregnant. I can feel it!"

It is, by the way, worth noting that love affairs are a completely different signification in the astrological blueprint from married life. Marriage for me, right up until the fateful events detailed in Chapter One, was a source of joy. This is in keeping with my Hindu chart which, aside from blatantly indicating divorce (because of *Kujadosha*) declares quite openly happy married life to a beautiful, special, or artistic woman. (Mars, the ruler of my seventh space is conjunct within two degrees of Venus for those who speak Hindu astrology). So whereas in the matter of love affairs I could "quite some hair-raising tales unfold," married life was, fortunately, nothing of the sort. It was, in fact, very enjoyable. Further, during our five contractual years together— wherein Anna and I used the most unorthodox, counter-culture, nontraditional, quasi-mystical means of birth control—never once did my wife get that most urgent and terrible look on her face. Lastly, regarding the benefits of understanding my Saturn in the fifth space was the fact that I finally knew, partially anyway, what Pam Raff meant during my first astrological reading when she made a statement I have, to this day, had no success in exorcising from my brain. What she said was something to the effect of, "You know, James, your relationship karma, according to this chart, is so peculiar that I think in your last life you must have had a harem!"

On the more positive side, there is a benefic element of my existence expressed in the Western blueprint but not expressed in my Hindu chart. At least it is not found by me nor any Hindu astrologer who has interpreted my chart. The matter is not indicated by one simple astrological influence such as an "afflicted Saturn in the fifth house." The issue is actually a theme of my life and therefore appears through several birthchart factors. It is an acute ability to develop, regenerate, and self-improve in whatever area of life my attention is placed. For my part I would say that my life thus far has been, fundamentally, something of a case history in the arena of self-improvement. Yet what I'm describing is not so much an ability as it is a part of my psychological makeup; who I am, so to speak. As such it is perfectly logical that the delineation would appear in my Western chart and not the Hindu one.

The indications for all this are found mainly within two astrological features. One is the sixth space of the blueprint, which represents, among other things, self-improvement and healing potential. The other is the placement and condition of Pluto. Pluto is the planet of resourcefulness, regeneration, and transformation. As it happens both Pluto and the sixth space are the two strongest and most influential elements in my Western blueprint. The reason the sixth house is of such significance is that three planetary positions (Sun, Mercury, and Neptune) occupy that space. But more importantly the *condition* of the planets and the house they occupy are well disposed. In other words the three planets in the sixth space are well aspected by virtue of their favorable zodiacal relationships to other planets elsewhere in the chart. Even this, however, is not quite the decisive factor making the sixth space so important in my life. The significant point is that the sixth space and the planets within are about the only factors in my Western chart not afflicted. In astrology, birthchart spaces and planetary positions that are afflicted represent life functions or spheres of life that are tedious, difficult, or subject to various kinds of upheaval. Elements that are well disposed signify, of course, areas of life that function smoothly, easily, and comfortably.

So in my case since nearly the entire Western chart is afflicted except for the sixth space I have essentially lived my life in the areas governed by that house. That for me has meant a preoccupation with detail work, healing diets, perfectionest tendencies, and serving others. In terms of my overall functioning it has meant that my energies have been directed toward improvement and self-healing (not just in health matters but wherever deficiencies have existed). It even appears, to me anyway, that a peculiar pattern relating to this matter has followed me around since birth. The pattern is one wherein my initial endeavors fail and are then turned around by my ability to ameliorate the situation. This has occurred in my starting out as a child with a speech problem and turning out an effective and articulate lecturer. It has occurred in my near failure of twelfth grade English, falling flat on my face in my first attempt at writing my Hindu astrology book, and finally completing what reviewers have declared "a superbly written astrology book," "the clearest exposition of Hindu astrology I have ever seen," and "the classic reference on Hindu astrology." On meditation courses I attended years ago, where we would meditate several hours a day for months at a time, it was typical at the end of the course for peers to comment admiringly "You seem to have grown from this course more than anyone else."

This ability to change a situation for the better was evident in my acting days. The school I attended, Carnegie Tech, used to accept forty students out of hundreds of auditioning applicants. Out of the forty only ten or fifteen would make it to graduation four years later. In my case, I was initially refused admittance to the college. Although my audition was acceptable, I was later told, I appeared extremely inhibited in the interview (I was, in fact, scared silly). In any case upon my pleading the acceptance committee reconsidered and I was admitted. From there I was in for some incredibly rough sailing, and that is an understatement. My theatrical ability did not, according to the professors, make the grade. I was thus placed on a warning or probation status for a solid two years. But with my usual growing and developing tendencies I managed to graduate. This was no small feat. It was especially significant since I am not truly suited to the acting profession. My theatrical experience lasted ten years during which I was in a Moon *dasa* in the Hindu system. The Moon in that chart rules (is innately connected to) the third space, the space signifying fine arts. So naturally during those years I acted. Immediately after the Moon period ended my spiritual days began, and I became increasingly puzzled as to my willingness to endure the hellish stage fright I always experienced as an actor. My success in graduating, incidentally, was no less a feat for the fact that in 1973, for a host of reasons, only six of us succeeded in receiving Bachelors degrees. Out of the six of us I was the only one to have had such a troubled start.

It is not as if, at the age of 28 or so when I learned Western astrology, I did not already know my own way of functioning. Of course I did. Yet there is quite an effect in having one's experience verified from an objective source. This effect is stronger still because the heavenly language is not just an objective source, but a language conveying destiny. Thus I came to see that the talents in question were meant to be, that they were inbred or part of my genetic code. Knowing that my intense transformative and self-improvement abilities could be summoned at will and utilized in any area of my life has been extremely beneficial. At the very least it has provided confidence and courage at the outset of new ventures. It has also been a cushion of comfort that should any particular aspect of life ever get really rough my resourcefulness to heal would not be lacking. Most of all this knowledge has quickened the realization that I can, to a considerable extent, play in any area of life I wish. For no matter how inept my beginnings (and they have at times been *incredibly* inept) my endings nearly always meet with success. Naturally even without the astrological information I would likely have realized the same reality anyway. That would have occurred with life experience. But that takes time. Astrology has simply and effectively hastened the evolutionary process. And that is fine with me.

Reactions to birthchart interpretations vary because different people will gain different benefits. The range of variables is as infinite as human experience. One of the most significant contributions astrology has made to my life came in my earliest days with the language. It is a gift I would not have received through the event-oriented system of Hindu astrology. What I learned was the lesson that, based upon their psychology and inner workings, people have different paths to take. Put another way, "what is good for one is poison to another." This is a simple lesson, not a big deal. But through Western astrology I learned it immediately. I learned it with no qualms, quibbles, or pain. And I learned it in my gut.

While this lesson may, for some, seem simple to the point of absurdity for me it is a hurdle of immense proportion. My life, as indicated by my dominant sixth space, is one of service. It is also, because Pluto is the strongest and most influential planetary position in my chart, one inclined towards "universal welfare." For anyone with such psychological workings it is a cinch to pass through life never learning that each person has his or her own particular ways of progressing. In my quest for higher consciousness using various healing regimens and self-development techniques, I have always assumed that what worked for me would work for others. And the desire to share my discoveries was natural. Yet in my earliest days of analyzing Western birthcharts it became obvious that certain techniques and paradigms would be more comfortable, easy, and effective than others depending upon one's way of being. Further, different people have different life lessons to

155

learn. While some will gain much from astrology and this book others may gain nothing.

My eldest brother Herb, for example, is someone for whom astrology holds little value. According to his chart mysticism, religion, or any kind of "higher" philosophy are generally of little interest and benefit. This is because there is in his being a great propensity and attraction to disciplines more earthbound, more connected to the here and now, "what you see is what you get." Activities involving the universal, miraculous, or divine are areas of life that are to a great extent dead ends for my brother. Such activities have little, perhaps nothing, to do with the growth process he is engaged in during this life. This could be seen through the North node, which reveals the soul's "new territory," being situated in the house of earthly possessions and in the sign Gemini—the sign of narrowly focused analytical functions. Thus in this life there is, for Herb, more evolution in the discriminative process, the process of analysis, skepticism, and microscopic examination. All this I realized in a quick stroke when I learned Western astrology way back in my beginning days of study. I then understood why long before when I had attempted to teach him meditation, he had more interest in analyzing his dreams than repeating a mantra.

Most people know intuitively and from experience which areas of life to direct themselves towards. Occasionally there are discrepancies and that is when knowledge of one's birthchart is most beneficial. An occurrence of this sort takes place quite often in the lives of certain spiritual seekers whose lessons in this life happen to be connected to money, possessions, and earthly pleasures. The reason such people have difficulty is that they become torn between their own instincts and reality, and the general knowledge religion and spiritual leaders give out regarding material pleasures. When these individuals come to find that their fulfillment and evolution will be greatly enhanced by experiencing and enjoying the tangible pleasures nature offers a great burden is lifted. This is not the case for all spiritual seekers but for those whose specific paths involve earthly possessions.

The most difficult and tedious astrological placement involving individuals' courses occurs when a birthchart indicates two diametrically opposed life plans to follow. An example of this can be seen in the blueprint of Richard Nixon. One aspect (North node in the seventh space) reveals that he must learn cooperation and compromise with partners. That is an indication that in past lives he has likely been too much focused on himself without awareness of the partner. The other aspect (North node in the sign of Aries) means he must focus on his own interests and develop his own personality. It indicates that he has given too much influence and power over to his partners in the past. One may wonder how it is possible for both of these realities to have existed at the same time. Perhaps extremes of both activities were excercised. But that is not our concern. The point is that in this life a delicate balance is required. And that, I have noticed in my astrological practice, individuals find very difficult. It is as if during all their waking moments these people walk a delicate tightrope. This is the kind of insight Western astrology so wonderfully provides.

Western astrology can explain the meaning of an experience like nobody's business. Had I known Hindu astrology before early 1982 I might, possibly, have concluded that my father's life was coming to an end. The meaning that would have, without knowledge of Western astrology, I could not have begun to guess. But I did then know Western astrology and for me the Boss' death occurred while Saturn was "transiting my Sun." This means that Saturn during January 1982 occupied the same zodiacal position and degree in the sky as the Sun occupied in my chart. Saturn is the planet representing contraction, testing, and maturity. It was the planet indicating Anna's test of maturity as she was presented with the trial of loving two men at the same time. It was the Saturn-transiting-the-Sun influence that led Isabel Hickey to say "she will not be happy now no matter who she's with." My father's death was thus, for me, an experience to bring grief, maturity, discipline, and organization. It was to teach me contraction, form, structure, and responsibility. Following Boss' death I finally became accountable to myself for an action I had desired to take for ten years. That action, my trip to India, solved my questions and doubts about astrology and the free will issue. It also provided the form and structure for a career at long last. All this because of the *meaning* my father's death would have on my soul and psyche. All this was the psychological process underlying or responsible for my "predestined journey" openly communicated through the Western birthchart for anyone familiar with the language of the stars.

Boss' death took on a very different meaning, however, for my brother Charles, whose wonderful luck will later be described in this book. While I was going through one of the most depressing and contractive states I had ever known, he was busy having the first mystical experiences of his life. For in his Western chart, at the time of all this, the planets Jupiter and Moon were being transited by Neptune (in other words Neptune in the sky was in the same position as Jupiter and the Moon were at his birth). Jupiter is the planet of religion, philosophy, faith, and optimism. Neptune is the planet indicating the capacity for psychic and mystical experiences. When my father's casket was being lowered into the earth Charles was marveling over the fact that it was only the body and not actually the Boss that was being buried. For that morning as he lay in bed, some hours after Boss had expired, he had felt my father's spirit enter the room and for a few brief moments they had communicated. Boss told Charles that everything was fine and not to worry at all about his death. He repeated the message a second time and then said he had to go visit our mother who needed him. The meaning of my father's death for Charles was thus religious and philosophical in nature and was to affect his thinking and behavior along those lines. To come to realize that bodies die while souls live on was, obviously, a profound lesson. Meanwhile my testing continued. I pondered the fact that I had spent eleven years steeped in mysticism and the Boss visits my brother!

Aside from providing the means to move people forward in their lives, Western astrology had, from the beginning, a profound effect on my life as a spiritual seeker. Though I initially felt that to go from teaching meditation to informing people of their destinies might be taking a step downward I had no misconceptions about the effect the star language was having on my evolution. To study creation's communication, discern its validity, and then to give the information out to others was without question a path to God. This I mean not in the religious or devotional sense. Astrology does not, as far as I know, lead one to meet any personal aspect of the Creator. But it does lead to higher consciousness, to unbounded perception and the enlightenment mystics and classic literature speak of. Enlightenment is based upon unity, the experience of the "sameness" that underlies all of creation. Because astrology is a paradigm of such inherently wide perspective and because of the vastness of possibility within each individual birthchart, the boundaries of one's mind must expand simply to pick up the essentials and implied philosophy of the language. Expansion of mind by its very nature moves in the direction of unity or sameness. So although the practice of astrology does not affect the human nervous system as do physical forms of yoga or mind-altering meditations, it does so indirectly by culturing the mind to perceive a more limitless, infinite reality. The effect on one's personal evolution is the same.

To some spiritual aspirants of other disciplines it may seem strange to view the practice of astrology as a path to wholeness. Yet there is little difference in absorbing oneself in a paradigm so imbued with human reality, free will and predestiny, and following the traditional spiritual course of *gnana yoga. Gnana yoga* is a path to enlightenment that works by way of mental discrimination. It is a technique (really a way of life) whereby one attempts to discern the reality of experience and existence so as to finally attain liberation from the misleading illusion of separateness or duality which pervades ignorant consciousness. The literal meaning of *gnana* is knowledge. Therefore *gnana yoga* is the path or course of knowledge. While Westerners know this method as the "truth will set you free" philosophy, certain gurus or Zen masters using the technique may say they are working with their disciples to correct "the mistake of the intellect." In any case everyone has felt the freedom and liberation that arises when a closely-held illusion is dispelled by knowledge, knowledge corresponding with one's experience that is.

This is the way astrology illuminates. It does so for anyone with the slightest interest in self-discovery who is immersed in the language. Further, astrological practice is a perfect means of *karma yoga. Karma yoga* is a path to enlightenment based upon action performed without attachment. In *karma yoga* one works for the sake of the work rather than for selfish interest and personal reward. While almost any professional activity could be used for this evolutionary path, astrology is incredibly well suited to the cause. For its practice is above all a service to others. Unless one is extremely talented and innovative or has great financial karma, astrology is (take my word for this) by no means a path to riches.

160

One must, generally, love the work or leave it. And for those who are interested in such a field as this there is certainly no lack of excitement or challenge. In the quest for predictive perfection there simply seems to be no end. Although I have met some who have studied astrology and eventually laid the subject down because they reached a point, in terms of their own charts, where they felt they could go no further, these individuals were missing the other half of the picture—the Hindu system. And though, as already mentioned, the nature of Hindu astrology is no more complicated than the Western system, it is replete with techniques, methods, and detailed procedures. There are even numerous, completely different astrological systems within Hindu astrology (the author uses the *parasara* system).

At any rate, in my own life interpreting the star language has been greatly uplifting and evolutionary. If not by allowing me to enjoyably and excitingly serve others, if not by instilling freedom and detachment as a result of insight into the nature of experience, and if not by providing a *continually* widening viewpoint, astrology has propelled me forward merely by the inspiration I have gained in daily witnessing the order of the universe. Being able to examine and predict people's lives and their schedules based upon their entry into the world is, to me, no less than solid evidence of orderly existence, reason, and purpose. More than this I cannot desire.

Meanwhile back in Miami I used the birthcharts of both astrological systems for my clients. I was determined that their readings should be as complete as possible. I was determined not to simply provide the data revealed from the Hindu *chakra* without giving clients an understanding of their internal motivations and behavioral patterns as indicated through Western astrology. I had been to enough Hindu astrologers who, aside from knowing my spiritual and sensitive nature, knew almost nothing about who I was. That they had never truly known the person they were interpreting for had always left a part of me feeling empty and ignored. While on this subject I might add that whenever I attempted to share the beauty and profundity of Western astrology with Hindu astrologers most were extremely quick to dismiss the system as shallow and superficial. Though that was terribly saddening it was clear that in such cases there would have been a great deal to do to convince them otherwise. Even when I shipped Santhanam a copy of Isabel Hickey's wonderful astrological text he soon replied that he found the work to be "very general." The problem was that he was examining the Western system for its predictive value. That was, of course, missing the point.

At any rate, in my own work I realized early on that the most crucial point of astrologizing for others was to create a context for birthchart interpretations. For the language of the heavens takes no position or viewpoint of its own. It exists for the use of the listener. Nature, for better or for worse, does not in any way discriminate or censor its communication. Nor are there any built-in morals or ethics other than the extraordinary orderliness of it all which, to an extent, implies the law of karma—"as you sow so shall you reap." How the knowledge a blueprint reveals is used depends to the greatest degree on the astrologer and the context he or she provides. As easily as the information can be manipulated to uplift and enlighten so it can also be used to frighten, depress, or doom clients in their own mind. Indeed, there have been clients who have breathed great sighs of relief during our sessions. When questioned they would explain that they had, in the past, experienced scary or pessimistic readings by other astrologers. (As intensely difficult as certain lives are there is no reason for an astrological session to ever be a source of negativity or depression. These individuals had evidently been to inexperienced or "unconscious" astrologers, astrologers who were likely more concerned with their own egos than the human lives they were dealing with.).

Since my background, by the time of my practice, was mainly spiritual and philosophical and since the greatest reality of my life was the evolutionary process and man's quest for fulfillment, it was from this viewpoint that I naturally approached my astrological counseling. So although most clients coming through my doors wanted to know when their love lives would improve and their difficulties end, the birthchart information was always applied more intently to determine which activities would most effortlessly bring about their contentment and self-actualization. By analyzing the Western chart it is not difficult to ascertain such information. As a result of this people frequently left my sessions ready to sign up for all different kinds of self development courses and new age techniques. It was always extremely rewarding when, weeks or months after our meetings, clients would call to thank me for having moved them to take appropriate evolutionary action. Business, I must admit however, improved far greater when I was able to predict that someone's career or love life was about to greatly improve. Occasionally I would predict that some yearning woman would soon tie the proverbial knot. The next day, like the ticking of a fine clock, her friends would ring my phone off the hook making appointments. Such is human nature.

A Session of Prasna:
the Hindu Method of Horary Astrology

Astrologizing for the public has never been boring: weird, strange, exciting, crazy, fun, enlightening, frustrating but never boring. The variety of my experience runs, as they say, the gamut. From sessions with those who ascribe to the astrologer divine-like consciousness and wizardly ability to skeptics and conservative businessmen giving themselves an out-of-the-ordinary birthday present. From the most integrated, spiritual, self-responsible individuals worthy of being emulated to beings who would have done well to contemplate the difference between waking consciousness and deep sleep. There are those who are overly skeptical and dissecting, and those who would not think it strange if I advised them that their destiny was to head for planet Mars. I learned quickly that awareness, balance, and common sense was of extreme importance if nature's language was to be used effectively for strangers. I also learned the necessity to remain sensitive to people's specific agendas and not to assume *anything* about them whether relating to lifestyles, intelligence, or morals. I even found that quite often people seemed to care little whether my analysis of them was correct or not. Each person has his or her own reason for taking the time and spending the money for an astrological interpretation.

One day I received a call from a woman who wished to make an appointment for her husband Rick. As she provided the birth data I explained the importance of obtaining the correct birth time (at least within ten or fifteen minutes). And, as always, to emphasize the point I asked where she had gotten the information. For although people are told that the accuracy of their birth time is crucial they occasionally ignore or underestimate the fact. And while the responsibility for providing correct data is, of course, theirs, it is the astrologer whose work falls flat when the delineations of the chart do not match the person's experience. In any case Rick's wife responded that the birth time was correct because she *knew* it was correct. At that point I advised that she check the birth certificate or call the Bureau of Vital Statistics in the city of her husband's birth. She replied that the data was not on the birth certificate, but Rick's mother had told her the time and there were definitely no doubts or worries; the information was accurate. I was now relatively satisfied. It has been my experience that when mothers say they clearly remember their children's birth time they are usually accurate enough. I was now confident that I would not have to endure that most extremely irksome activity of spending several hours analyzing someone's birthchart only to find out days later that the work must be redone.

As mentioned previously certain birthcharts would change almost completely by a three- or four-minute discrepancy while others could be off by thirty or forty minutes without changing certain essentials of the chart. Rick's Hindu blueprint was one of those where a slight inaccuracy would change matters radically. If the birth occurred only a few minutes before the time he gave me, the first space of his chart would have begun in the sign of Pisces rather than Aries. The location of the first house is, if the reader has yet to surmise, quite critical. This is because the planets in their interrelationships barely change in half a day or a day (except for the Moon), so that it is the placement in the chart that distinguishes them. In other words it is the specific house placements, which are based on the birth time, that reveal the real details. Indeed the house placements reveal the differences of people who are, for instance, born on the same day. In such delicate cases as Rick's, whether the birth data comes from the mother or the birth certificate, it is generally my practice to determine the placement of the first house myself. The reason this action is taken even if the information comes from the birth certificate is that there is no way to be sure that the hospital attendants were precise in noting down the birth time (some astrologers, I am told, have studied the matter and found that attendants are often several minutes late in their clocking).

Rectification of a birthchart is done by explaining the most basic indications of the two possible blueprints and seeing which one matches the person's experience. The efficacy of the process depends, aside from the astrologer's interpretive ability, on the apparent differences of the two charts. If, as in very rare cases, both charts indicate similar destinies, then there are obviously problems. But that is rare. The rectification usually works quite easily and well for the simple fact that Hindu astrology is event-oriented. (I would not wish to engage in this process using the more psychological Western system even though it could, in fact, be done. The time and tediousness involved would be grueling. Neither, as explained earlier in this book, would I want the task of rectifying a chart for a person who has no idea whatever of their birth time.).

In any case when Rick, a rugged man in his mid-thirties, arrived I explained the problem and set out to solve the task at hand. I said that there was one particular space in his blueprint which was quite devastated and thus revealed great difficulties in a certain area of his life. From the chart based on the birth time he had supplied it appeared that hardships came on account of his younger siblings. Either there were none, I said, or they had suffered greatly or died, or there was great turmoil in his relationship with them. In other words the chart indicated, as the scriptures say "no happiness from younger siblings." He replied that his younger brothers and sisters were typical middle- or upper-class individuals whom he had always gotten along well with. This made matters easy. His birth time was, then, certainly wrong and the alternate chart that showed difficulties with his mother must have been the correct one. "Well no, not really," he said as he explained that his mother was in every way quite average and normal, and their relationship was relatively happy. Assuming one of the charts must be correct I attempted to rephrase and express differently my communications of the charts. There was no luck. Rick could not agree to any of my statements. Since this was a straightforward, no-nonsense sort of man it was clear that he was neither confused, unconscious, nor holding back. "Well, I think we have the wrong birth time. Where did you get it?" I said. "From my mother; it's accurate," he replied. "Well are you sure? I asked." "I don't think it is. Anyway it doesn't work, I think it's wrong."

Personally I wanted to simply send Rick home. I trusted Hindu astrology far more than people's assertions about their birth data. He obviously didn't want to leave because he maintained his position that the information was correct and asked me to continue analyzing the birthchart based upon the time he had given. By this point in my practice I had fairly well, though not completely, realized just how personal people's reasons were for visiting astrologers. Having chosen for my astrological practice the context of serving people in their growth process and quest for fulfillment I was fairly consistently altering people's lives by responding to their specific needs. Often enough, I was beginning to see, this could be done even without their astrological charts in hand. Often what people needed was guidance based upon plain common sense, an outside objective opinion, and most importantly a wider, more spiritual perspective if I may be so bold. So in the awareness that it was not my place to refuse Rick's request, for my context of service was still intact, and because Rick was obviously taking his own responsibility for gaining value, I agreed to go on even though I would have bet his birth time was hours off.

The more I analyzed his Hindu chart the more he consistently, yet without any sign of disturbance or bother, said, "Well no, not really: the way it actually was blah blah blah blah. . . ." Eventually the discomfort of this was enough to make me ignore his Hindu blueprint completely and analyze his personality and disposition from Western astrology. This I knew would be plenty accurate merely by using the information revealed from the interrelationships of the planets on the day of his birth. Now if Rick replied, "Well no, not really. . . ." I could simply assume the man was a great liar or psychotic. But about the Western delineations I made Rick agreed wholeheartedly. So I proceeded. However after ten or twenty minutes I realized that whatever it was that allowed this man to care not a whit that my Hindu analysis was so incorrect also influenced his interest in hearing about his psychological tendencies, talents, and behavioral patterns. So finally, with my best diplomacy, I simply said, "What I'm saying doesn't seem to interest you very much so why don't you just tell me: why are you here?" He replied, "I would like to know if I'm going to have to go to jail." Weird, strange, and exciting but by no means boring. Astrology is never boring.

I stopped my interpretation of Rick's life and began analyzing the *dasa bhukti* period of the present and near future. I also checked the indices revealed from his Western chart. From the blueprints of both systems there were no blatantly terrible revelations. However, this was not the end of the concern. For aside from the fact that every one of Rick's accomplices were being jailed, without exception, natal astrology is not the way to answer such a specific question as this. In an instance where one calls upon an astrologer to determine the outcome of a particular affair the method to be used is horary astrology or *prasna* as it is called in the Hindu system. As described earlier the procedure in this technique is to draw a blueprint based upon the exact time and place that the person asks the question. There is little in the way of logical explanation for why this works except to give the mechanics of the matter. It happens that when a person is so concerned about an issue that he or she is finally moved to take action (consulting the astrologer) then that is the time that the heavens reflect the life and energy, as it were, of the affair. In other words at the instant of creation of any activity (or question put to an astrologer) there is, to an extent, a complete life and schedule sprung into existence. For this reason there are actually some astrologers who will draw charts based on the time of their clients' appointments to ascertain why each person has chosen to visit. During my travels in India I had indeed made an appointment to visit an astrologer, Manik Chand Jain, who when I arrived proceeded to tell me about my depressed emotional state (over my father's death).

At any rate though I had little experience with horary astrology, I had played around fairly successfully with *prasna* which, because it is so similar to natal Hindu astrology, is not very difficult for the average Hindu astrologer. I had used it to determine the success of business ventures for others and in my own life for such "incredibly critical" matters as whether certain love relationships would work out. In fact once, although this was actually later in time, I drew a *prasna* chart to determine whether I would ever again see a woman I had previously been intensely involved with. We had broken up because she was, essentially, incapable of any kind of commitment. Because of the volatile and passionate nature of the affair and the obvious futility of it, I was resolved to move on without looking back. But, being human, I always hoped she would eventually get back in touch. The *prasna* chart that I cast revealed unquestionably that she would. Though there are, according to the scriptures, ways to determine the timing of the matter I was not so learned in that aspect. So I simply waited. It was I believe some three or four months after we had gone our separate ways that the phone rang and a familiar voice on the other end said, "I wanted to talk to you on the full Moon."

Back to Rick, I explained that he could have expressed his concern at the outset of our session to expedite matters. I could not, of course, be annoyed at him or myself for it was not up to either of us as to when his question was meant to reach my ears. That depended on when the heavens would reflect the life energy of the question on his mind. And that, I knew from experience, was right now. So I drew a *prasna* chart, examined it, and gave him the results. It appeared from the chart that the strongest likelihood was that he would not, like his partners, wind up behind bars. Though I asked him to inform me of the outcome of his trial it was some weeks or months away and I did not finally hear from him. I did, however, receive a message from his wife on my answering machine only a few days later. In an assertive, rather shrewish, voice she said, "Mr. Braha, I listened to Rick's tape (we had tape recorded our session) and I decided that you are either a lousy astrologer or his birth time was wrong. So I called his mother and it turns out his birth time was several hours later than what we told you. Would you please call me." "Bingo. So what else is new?" I thought.

Since Rick's question, which was the real reason for his visit, had been answered I had no intention of redoing his chart. I had no intention especially since he cared so little about anything I said other than the jail business. Rick's wife, however, felt differently about the matter. She wanted the chart done over. Before answering her concerns I asked to speak with Rick, who I was now perturbed at. I pointedly said to him, "Rick, do you remember how much time I spent telling you I was sure your birth time was wrong? Why did you keep saying it was accurate and refuse to further investigate?" His answer stunned me. "My wife wouldn't let me," he said. "I'm sorry, what?" I replied. "What did you say?" Here was a man I personally would not wish to tangle with, who in his actions evidenced little fear of the law, now revealing some terribly incongruent behavior in his married life. He explained that his wife said she was positive of the birth time and would—somehow, God knows how—not allow him to call his own mother.

Although I did not have another session with Rick, for my work with him was basically complete, I did calculate his birthchart based on the correct birth time to see his present and near future indications. Also, as an astrologer I was very curious to know which blueprint space it was that was so badly marred and thus which area of his life was so devastated by the malefic influences I had detected. It was, I should by now have been able to guess, the seventh house—the house of married life and the spouse!

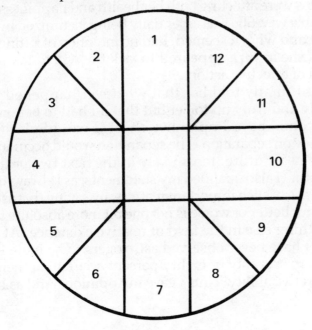

More Practice With the Public

And then there were more charts and more readings. There were readings with all sorts of people; confused people, happy people, curious people. There was one woman involved in a difficult marriage who continually pressed me to say whether or not her chart revealed divorce. Rather than answer such a delicate question with a yes or no, I did my best to give an honest and balanced interpretation of the blueprint along with the clearest discourse on free will and predestiny I could muster. Whether or not I, as an astrologer, am of the opinion that a couple will succeed or fail in their union the last effect I would wish to produce is for a person to give their responsibility and choice in the matter over to their birthchart; a birthchart they themselves have no ability to interpret! But the more the woman pushed for an answer the more I considered that perhaps giving something of a definitive opinion was in order. Her marriage difficulties were affecting both her health and happiness in a terrible way. She was essentially being victimized by her husband who, it seemed, had no intention of letting up. And she in turn appeared to lack the will to take any kind of effective action.

So I finally told her that whatever happened was really and truly up to her but that if I had to bet on the outcome, based upon her chart, I would place my money on separation. The separation would occur in the very near future, most likely in the next two or three months. I also qualified my statements, as I always do in the case of such important matters, by saying that astrology for better or worse is not one bit more absolute than anything else in the field of relative existence. At any rate I have never observed astrologers to be more than perhaps seventy or eighty percent accurate in their interpretive ability. Thus I gave my opinion. And as hard

Indian merchants selling dyes

P.M. Padia, my mentor on the second journey

R. Santhanam, my youthful first mentor

My uncle, a Kabala Rabbi

The author

Lions guard the entrance of a Nepalese temple.

The Boss, my mother, and a smelly camel driver

The author

With Tibetans in Lumbini, the grounds of Buddha's birthplace

A friend along the way

At Stonehenge, 1986

A temple on the grounds of Buddha's birthplace

The "burning ghats" of Benares on the Ganges River, where dead bodies are burned

as it was to be relatively definitive and for all the compassion the act required, for I personally believed the woman should have run—not walked—to the nearest divorce lawyer, there was in the end resentment as my reward. This woman, more than a year later, bumped into a friend of mine to complain that "James Braha said my husband and I would divorce and we never did. He shouldn't have done that."

At first I was only slightly bothered by the matter and chalked the whole thing up to "human-beingness." But the same exact occurrence between the woman and my friend happened more than once. Each time it brought me a greater sense of agitation. After all of my care and concern to employ the language of the heavens sensitively and with moderation, common sense, and tact I had obviously blown it. I had misjudged the woman's ability to hear what I was saying; not to mention that my prediction was wrong. Although decent astrologers never consider themselves infallible, each time my friend encountered this woman who related her story my frailty would painfully surface. After the fourth meeting, however, there was a different tune being sung. It seems the birth time she had provided was twelve hours off! She had in fact been born in the AM, not the PM as previously thought. Now she conveyed her intention to have her chart done again. "Not by *this* astrologer, I thought: "not this time."

Then there was the instance of an extremely domineering woman, one of the saddest cases I have ever seen (if most of my stories are about females it is because in my practice the ratio of women clients to males is about seven or eight to one), who wanted to know exactly why her daughter had committed suicide. This, however, was a case better left to psychiatry than astrology and so I told her. About the same time another manipulative mother called to make an appointment for her daughter. I somehow sensed that she intended to sit in on the session in an attempt to control or dominate the scene. Though there is nothing wrong with a person bringing a friend or loved one with them to a birthchart interpretation I clearly knew that this was not what was now happening. I therefore advised the woman tactfully but firmly that astrological sessions were quite personal and that since her daughter was twenty years old it would be more productive and appropriate for her to come alone. If her daughter wished to have someone else present then, of course, I would have no objection. The woman finalized the appointment and then, quite typically, cancelled it the next day.

These were some of the routines I faced in my daily practice. There were, also during these days, endless cases (or so it seemed) of women who were in love with married men and wanted to know if their lovers would ever leave their wives. In most of these episodes our discussions centered not around answering the question posed but of finding ways to repair the lack of confidence and damaged self-esteem that had caused them to create such unworkable situations in the first place. I was also frequently seeing individuals who were living their lives unreasonably in the past, suffering terribly because of it, and in obvious need of help. I, for the most part, enjoyed the astrological counseling process. It was extremely exciting to be involved so deeply in people's most intimate concerns so immediately, indeed in the space of only a few hours. It was exciting to see whether and how intensely people's birthcharts matched their stories and when they did not to try to determine why. As an astrologer this discernment process, difficult and frustrating as it is, is what separates the great from the average, the truly intelligent from the mere intellectual, and the humble from the arrogant. Most of all it was exciting to be able to use astrology and all I had learned throughout my "spiritual" years to alter people's thinking, to correct the "mistake of the intellect" wherever I was clear enough to perceive it. All of this was also, at times, painfully frustrating. I never ceased to be amazed at how difficult some individuals' lives could be. Having come to my maturity in the 'seventies, and been so involved in the self development, "me generation" it was hard to conceive of the extent of the lack of fulfillment people were willing to tolerate in their lives.

I remember one woman whose story was so incredible she wanted some day to put it in writing. She explained how her husband, who worked for the CIA, had left town just before president Kennedy's assassination never to return. She said he called from Washington to say he would be a few days late and that that was the last she had heard of him. There was a good deal more detail involved, of course: another agent had been made to look just like her husband, etc. But the point is that here we sat some twenty-odd years later and this woman, unbelievably, was still waiting for her husband to return, still suffering, and had not been with another man the whole time! I directed this woman to a particular new age movement where she could participate in the most powerful "be here now" type seminar I knew. The more I encountered clients in need of emotional or psychological help the more I wanted to obtain a formal degree in psychology. But I was preoccupied enough with my love of astrology, and there was plenty of work ahead simply to gain expertise in the interpretive process. Plus I hated school. God help me if I should have to take an English class.

Occasionally I would receive thank-you letters from clients after sessions they considered to be especially valuable or significant. This was something I genuinely appreciated since I was well aware that my sessions were often somewhat intense and confronting. For all of my love of astrology I had not chosen it, as a profession, for excitement, fun, or money. There was, and is, a commitment to make a difference in people's lives, a real and lasting difference. To do this, or even come close to doing it, in one meeting generally requires great and concentrated rigor. Despite our expressed desires to grow, improve, and evolve we can be extraordinarily lazy when it comes to taking responsibility for our lives and initiating appropriate action. Hence a good many of my readings with clients have not been the essence of comfort, especially from their point of view. And so their appreciation was rewarding to me.

Once, I sent out questionnaires to clients I had astrologized for to see some of their individual reactions and long-term results. A woman named Wendy very well summed up what many had experienced. She wrote that her session had a powerful effect on her psychology in that for the first time in quite a long while she was feeling at ease with herself. She explained that she had always tried to know and define herself by the world's response to her. Unfortunately she was never quite satisfied with people's reactions. Thus, Wendy concluded, there had to be something wrong with her behavior and way of being. However, having her birthchart interpreted and finding that her personality, motivations, and character traits were all as they were meant to be had a tranquilizing and liberating effect on her psyche. She wrote: "Throughout my life I've been a great help in solving other people's problems, but never knew how to solve my own. I often wished there was some way I could film myself in action so I could then look at my behavior and make the necessary adjustments. This was the experience that I had while in consultation with you. It was an experience I did not think was possible up until then." When asked if she felt any healing or harmonizing effect she answered that she gained a greater sense of confidence to be herself. As she put it, "It's like I got a message from heaven telling me that I am quite okay the way I am. There's a very good reason for me to be like this. . . . It's what I chose and evolved into. What a relief!"

Like so many others Wendy's confidence and sense of self had been injured in earlier years and she had spent tremendous energy trying to satisfy everyone else's expectations. "Now that I know about all the positive aspects and strengths in my chart," she wrote "I feel like I don't care what people may say. I will simply work on making these things a very real part of my life. I like them. I like me." Though Wendy's response was simple and not surprising what I most enjoyed about it, aside from the fact that she had obviously benefitted, was that her letter was written some two months after her session. The value she had gained had clearly remained with her. She had obviously heard what was said during her reading and made good use of it. Our session evidenced one of the great beauties of astrology—that it affords an opportunity, an especially unique opportunity which universal and spiritual disciplines of wide perspective so very well provide, to affect one's reality. In what other setting, what other packaging, can an advisor's words be so effectively heard, so taken to heart as when resting upon the interpretation of one's blueprint of destiny? It is, incidentally, for this very reason that I have always cautioned my occasional students to be careful, extremely careful when astrologizing. For one truth, over the years, has become crystal clear: for better or worse people rarely forget what their astrologer has spoken.

What I also enjoyed about Wendy's communication was the fact that value had been gained despite (actually, perhaps, because of) her session being an especially intense one. Wendy was a gifted woman, considering obtaining a PhD., who was apparently holding back her power. During our meeting I was seriously unleashing some "ruthless compassion." That is, I was saying whatever it seemed to take to move her to more responsible and fulfilling behavior. I was doing whatever it took to get her to own up to her ability. It was, to be sure, intense.

About this time I was lecturing fairly regularly on the benefits of the language of life. In my advertising I always used the term "real astrology" to try to distinguish birthchart interpretation from the nonsense in the newspapers and the genuine but all-too-general Sun sign books. Whether the term made any difference I do not know. Turnouts were usually small, from five to twenty people, but most who attended were serious. Because of my nonresistant attitude towards occasional skeptics and my lack of desire to "prove" astrology, I never had problems. I simply described my astrological experiences, answered questions, and let people draw their own conclusions. Any other way, I knew, would have bored me silly. Consequently people were frequently taking me aside afterwards to say they had never thought much of astrology or even considered it to be real until hearing me speak. Such compliments, though they did not pay bills, helped to make up for my impoverished status.

The theme of my lectures was always the same: An Introduction to Hindu and Western Astrology and the Need to Use Both Systems. Toward this end I would bring charts of friends or relatives and draw them on the blackboard to explain some simple rules of blueprint interpretation. I always brought my friend Emmett's charts for his life clearly demonstrated why both systems must be used. From his Western chart theatrical inclinations appear so incredibly strong (two benefics, Venus and Jupiter, well aspected in the fifth house—the house of art) that a Western astrologer would almost certainly assume he would choose a career in the arts. However, from his Hindu blueprint the most blatant and powerful indications are medicine or healing and any kind of public service work. As it has turned out Emmett was an actor in college and has just recently begun to dabble in theatre on the side, but his careers are: firefighter, paramedic, and nurse. Interestingly, both his Hindu and Western charts reveal the tendency towards numerous vocations.

Emmett's chart also is a good one to show how a Hindu blueprint could reveal great debts and expenses, a signification essentially ignored in Western astrology. The twelfth space is the main indicator of expenses in the Hindu chart and in Emmett's case the ruler of that house, the planet connected to it, is in the worst possible sign for its functioning. Therefore Emmett's karma with expenditures, though not as rough as movie director Francis Ford Coppola's (*The Godfather, Apocalypse Now,* etc.) whose twelfth house is almost completely devastated, is no enviable fate. No matter how much money he earns there is always something to spend it on, and quickly at that.

I would also bring to my lectures birthcharts of stars or politicians whose destinies were extremely simple to demonstrate the Hindu system. I, of course, never displayed blueprints which confused the daylights out of me. I never brought for instance Ronald Reagan's or Paul McCartney's Hindu charts which to my eyes still do not seem at all extraordinary. Such examples I would mention when people finally got around to asking what were the perplexities of the heavenly language. Believers in my audiences always tried to come up with explanations that perhaps these individuals were just "lucky" or worked very hard or are not in fact so special. Such answers I consider not only simplistic but far from addressing the crux of the matter. Both Reagan and McCartney are exceptionally well endowed in their earthly existences. And that is what Hindu astrology is all about. In any case, for now I simply think of such charts as rare puzzles which I must eventually solve with the help of more knowledgeable astrologers as well as with more intricate interpretive techniques.

As for president Reagan, there is a discrepancy in his birth data since there are at present two or three birth times for him in existence. Many astrologers believe that because Reagan himself uses astrology, he has given out differing information to confuse outsiders. Whether this is true or not is obviously hard to know. But it seems plausible since as Governor of California he chose to be inaugurated at an especially odd hour, some time after midnight. This gives good reason to surmise that an astrologer chose the time in order to ensure a positive destiny for his stay in office. It is also said that Reagan in his second presidential inauguration had an additional swearing-in separate from the formal public ceremony for the same purpose. At any rate no matter which of the popular birth times (obtained from astrological data books) I have used, I have never been able to connect the great career success of Reagan's life to the charts in hand.

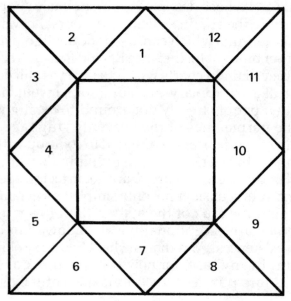

Astrologizing on Radio

Although during the two years following my studies in India I was unable to earn a decent living astrologizing I was definitely enjoying the positive effects of my Rahu *dasa* period. As already mentioned Rahu, though bringing on a good deal of grief and suffering, in my particular birthchart promises career success specifically regarding "swaying the masses." The reason for this is that the position of Rahu occupies the tenth space of my Hindu chart. The tenth space represents career, status, and the public. Rahu, which is not a planet but a calculated point in the chart (known as the North node in Western astrology), signifies power, cravings, and insatiable worldly desires. To understand just how effective the influence can be, depending on the individual blueprint position, the story of Rahu is worth describing. While some consider the account a reality others assume it to be mythological. But that is unimportant. Either way the message of Rahu's effect is well conveyed.

The story is that way back in time Lord Vishnu (one of the Indian gods) was giving *amrita*, a potion bestowing immortality on the beneficiary, to the planetary deities so that they would live forever. As the entities *Ravi, Chandra, Shukra, Guru, Buddha* (Sun, Moon, Venus, Jupiter, Mercury) and all the others drank the potion it so happened that a *rakshasa*, a serpent-like demon, entered the room and gobbled down some of the nectar. The Sun and Moon witnessed the terrible act and immediately informed Lord Vishnu who swiftly took sword in hand and severed the beast in two. However since the demon had already swallowed the liquid of immortality it could not, of course, be killed. Instead it now became two malefic or destructive influences ready to forever exert their effects on humankind. The top portion of the demon is called Rahu and the bottom is named Ketu. Although in most blueprint houses Rahu indicates problems and difficulties, in certain other spaces it promises great rewards. Since Rahu, in the story, is the head of a demon—an animalistic, hedonistic beast bent on nothing but power and sense gratification, its placement in the more desirable birthchart spaces reveals an area of life where a person may gain great power and worldly benefits.

Therefore Rahu's beneficial position in my career house produced warmly welcomed results almost as immediately as my astrological career began. I had been astrologizing less than three or four months before a newspaper reporter decided I would make an interesting article for the local section of the Sunday news. His piece was well written and captured much attention. I liked the reporter who was a fair man and a "nonbeliever" whose nonbelief was not so certain after our meeting. I was even more pleased with my Rahu in the tenth house which was now beginning to pay off with some serious publicity and notoriety and which, according to astrological schedule, should gradually increase in power over the next fifteen years or so.

Following the article, with no further effort on my part, I received a call from a local television talk show host who had seen the article and invited me on his show. This man, Don Webb, advised me before the live interview that he would be throwing some hard questions my way since he was not in the least bit impressed with the heavenly language. Between my understanding of his viewpoint (how could I argue with him; astrology as conveyed to the public through daily horoscopes and charlatan gypsies deserves all the scorn it gets) and my destiny to reach the masses, a good show as well as a future relationship emerged. Webb, who rather enjoyed poo-pooing Western astrology, found himself fascinated by what he was learning about the ancient Hindu system during the show. His interest was piqued and he wanted to know more. So he invited me to become a guest on his midnight-to-five-AM radio show where I answered questions for the first hour and astrologized for callers for the remainder of the show.

Unlike newspaper astrology, which is an almost total farce since no birth data is used except for the Sun sign, radio astrology can be done in a genuine, though somewhat general, way. Whereas each newspaper Sun sign forecast applies to one twelfth of the world, which therefore makes it an absurdity, astrologers on the radio use the planetary configurations of a person's actual birth date. Since the birth time is not used—there is no time for that since calculating a proper chart would take several minutes—one cannot get too specific about a person's destiny. And yet from the relationships of the planets to each other on the day of birth a certain amount of accurate information can be obtained, especially about a person's psychology and behavior, if the astrologer is experienced and astute.

The first time I was called onto the Don Webb Show I was uninformed as to what the hours were and I had no idea it was an all-night show. Consequently I had not rested and therefore wound up quite frazzled as we worked into the wee hours of the morning. I focused all my attention and energy on the neverending callers throughout the night. This being my first appearance I was distinctly aware of being scrutinized by the host— this practical and down-to-earth, yet highly perceptive, Mr. Webb. I did my best, which I assumed was fine since the phones never let up. Indeed I actually surprised myself at my occasional ability to correctly guess a person's vocation based upon their psychological workings. And then somewhere near four AM as I approached exhaustion I began to sense that my astrologizing was having some kind of effect on my nonbeliever talk show host. As I spoke into the microphone to the public at large, I saw through my peripheral vision an unwavering look of seriousness and contemplative consideration on Webb's face. I was also feeling rather content as the people I conversed with were fairly consistently validating my statements about their lives. This occurred as Webb persistently inquired into their reactions of my assertions. But more satisfying than their approval was the surprised look on Webb's face.

Just as I was feeling quite cocky that I had served the field of astrology well a man called up whose chart contained five or six planets in the sign of Taurus. At this point I was so tired that my usual tactfulness and sensitivity was somewhere fast asleep where I wished I could have been. The first thing that came to mind as I jotted down the planetary positions onto what is called the "natural chart" (meaning that the birth time is not taken into account) was that Taurus rules (or signifies) the throat and neck.

Now you must remember that while on the radio there is no time to sit and analyze. An astrologer in this situation must work very fast, in fact just about instantly. Without hesitation I simply blurted out, "Wow, you must have a fat neck!" There it was. Four hours of work down the drain as Don Webb looked at me as if I had lost my mind. "Come on James, what is that? What are you doing?" From his tone of voice and the look on his face my first appearance on his show would likely be the last. Anyway the damage was done and it was too late to care. Just then, as if God had taken my side, the caller interjected, "No Don, he's right. Every one of my shirts has to be specially made because the collars never fit." I have appeared on the Don Webb show regularly, every other full Moon, since that night.

I did little in the way of teaching during this time until I met a man, a Western astrologer, who asked me to show him what I knew of Hindu astrology. His interest was strong since he was involved in translating Hindu astrological scriptures. So I agreed to his request. Somewhere along the way he suggested that we write a book together on the subject. There was only one other written by a Westerner and that, to my eyes (and all my astrologer friends' eyes), was just about as difficult to understand as the Hindu texts. If anything was certain it was that Hindu astrology had yet to be presented in a simple, understandable way (for the Westerner that is; Hindu writings may be fine for one of Eastern origin). And if anything else was certain it was that I was born to teach. The only thing that stood in the way was my inexperience at writing. I had, incidentally, by this time completely forgotten the prediction made during my first Hindu astrology reading that I would write some books. That was, I suppose, how little sense the prediction made. Anyway I told my friend, who was as literary a person as I knew, that I would do the writing if he was willing to make it readable. This may have been no small task because when I finally sat down and put pen to paper and then brought the pages to him he simply never got around to reworking them. So I decided to do the job myself. With my usual compulsiveness I worked intensely during the day and night at my new pursuit. I began writing about the different natures of the two systems and the need to use them together. It was all very philosophical and I was terribly pleased with myself for my great, and previously undiscovered, literary ability.

After weeks of what I considered perhaps the most concentrated and tedious work of my life I proudly showed my friends the results of new efforts. I do not remember exactly what it was they said. Either the words were too flowery and the sentences way too long or there was redundancy or God knows what. In any case it was all I needed to hear. I tried, as diligently as I could, several times to fix the work but without any significant success. So I finally quit. "Maybe there is good reason that Hindu astrology never made it to the West," I thought. "Maybe writing is just too damn hard and the only way the subject will make it into easily readable print is if some great professional writer somehow gets bitten by the astrological bug." Thinking I would never again get such a foolish idea as writing in my head I washed my hands of the matter and resumed astrologizing for the public.

There is an old saying that nothing in the universe is static. Everything is either in the process of expanding or contracting, growing or decaying. After nearly two years of practicing Hindu and Western astrology together I experienced a strong dose of contraction. There came a point where I felt I had stopped growing in my knowledge of Hindu astrology and the inadequacies of my interpretive ability took on a glaring presence. At the time I began using the Hindu system for clients I was thrilled with all I knew. And it was great, really great for a long while. But the more time passed the more I was forced to confront what I did not know and could not predict. It was not that my work was very far off the mark. And it was not that I could not generally and fairly easily see the basics of a person's destiny. The problem was that occasionally, too occasionally I should say since astrology as practiced by humans is never one hundred percent accurate, there would appear huge discrepancies. Though I was constantly telling friends that I would someday soon be going back to India to study, I remember the exact moment I made up my mind to go. Never mind that I would be diving into debt to do so. Nature was now, with great clarity, telling me to get my act in gear.

As it happened I was interpreting the charts of an old high school friend I had not seen for ten or fifteen years. It was fun to astrologize for a friend and we both took pleasure from the session. There was a healthy blend of focus on both the events and karma of his life, and his psychological workings. All was relatively on track, moving quite smoothly until I proceeded to describe a *dasa bhukti* period he had recently completed. It was a period during which two well-aspected planets in his Hindu chart were holding sway. So I explained the specific implications and said that those two years or so must have brought fortunate times. He replied, "Really? That's when I tried to commit suicide!" His statement sent me straight back to India. I did not pass go. I did not collect two hundred dollars. I bought the smallest backpack I could find, stuffed four shirts, three pairs of pants, and about thirty or forty astrological birthcharts in it. I was on my way.

The sacred Yamuna River.

CHAPTER IV

STRICTLY PERSONAL
Returning to India and Meeting P.M. Padia

The plane landed in Bombay where I planned to rest for a day or two before beginning my search for an experienced astrologer to study with. I had no terribly specific plans of where to go except that I wanted to visit the southern part of the continent since my last journey was spent entirely in the north. I also knew that astrology is extremely popular in the deep south, especially Madras and Bangalore. That aside, I wanted at some point to visit Puri, a city near Calcutta on the east coast of India. For there, in that area, is a guru named Giri who took over for the great saint Paramahansa Yogananda and who is said to be a learned astrologer. Though I had no specific itinerary I was resolved to study with as many astrologers as I could over a period of several months. Because it had been my experience that astrologers excel in different aspects of birthchart interpretation—depending on their own interests, etc.—this plan made good sense. As fate would have it, however, I never made it to Puri nor the south, and I studied with only one man—P.M. Padia.

Indeed, my entire stay lasted only about one month, one intense month. Even though I was prepared for India's incredible assault on the senses I had, unfortunately, not been warned about the sanitary conditions of Bombay. I was careful of the drinking water but I had not been warned to avoid, above all things, cooked oil in that city. It was after my first meal off the plane that I found out. It was, sorrily, one meal too late. In any event I suffered the consequences of that food as my body instantly felt the same as it had almost two years earlier during the tail end of my first journey. And that was not good. I had, of course, known I would be having dysentery, powerful dysentery at that, but not the first day back! Westerners almost inevitably get sick from the unfamiliar elements, amoebae, etc. in India and Nepal. But during the first visit it had taken more than a month to begin. Not so this time. At any rate, I took the situation in stride and went about my business.

While my body suffered from its illness and the almost indescribable summer heat my spirit was in bliss. I was back in the most spiritual and charming land I have ever known. I was back in the country I knew would not deny my cravings for knowledge. One thing I had already learned about India was that the doing of any task there could be an enormous, but enormous, struggle. But if there was a desire for knowledge and if it was strong and the intention real, India would come through like nobody's business. Like Vito Corleone in *The Godfather* who could not refuse any favor asked on the day of his daughter's wedding, this immensely rich land of ancient mystical wisdom would never deny knowledge to a sincere seeker. It had not done so before and I knew it would not now. Of this I had no worries.

After a day's rest I decided to seek out a few local ashrams (sites where spritual masters teach their disciples) to see if I could find a guru who might direct me to some masterful astrologers. Since Bombay is a large, somewhat modern city, it has tourist information booths. I stopped at one of them to make my inquiry and was surprised that the woman in charge said she had a list of ashram addresses I could see. I then realized that if there was a list of ashrams there might just as well be a list of astrologers. And so there was. I happily jotted down addresses and phone numbers where they existed and began to plan whom to see first. The woman advised me that these astrologers must have achieved some status to be placed on her list. Therefore, she said, it would be wise for me to call before visiting any of them. I phoned two different astrologers and asked for appointments, which they granted. I explained that I was not interested in having my own chart interpreted but would be bringing over several charts I wanted to discuss together. I added that I would certainly pay for whatever time was taken.

One of the astrologers understood well what I meant. The other, I found out later, did not. For when I arrived at my appointment with him, after a long painful search which only one who has been to India could truly understand, I was sadly disappointed. The man, quite simply, insisted that he would not speak about several charts. He said for the sum of $20, which is no small amount of money in India, he would interpret any chart I put in front of him. I tried for five or ten minutes to persuade him otherwise, to answer questions I had about certain birthcharts, etc. and to charge me by the hour. But he refused, so I left. I could have had him interpret my chart but judging by this man's rigidity I had my doubts about his astrological ability. So I headed for my next appointment. Though by rights it probably shouldn't take more than a few minutes to find my next destination I knew it would likely take more than an hour or two. For some reason, about which I am still uncertain, Indians are almost completely unaccustomed to giving directions. Either that or they truly do not know where anything is.

I entered the abode of the popular astrologer Gunshyam Jyoshi and was startled by the fact that his place, which I believe was his office and home, was air-conditioned. This was both a great rarity and an incredible relief since it must have been over 100 degrees outside. I sat outside his private room for five or ten minutes until Jyoshi eventually emerged and ushered me in. Now I was even more surprised. For there in his room sat five or six elderly gentlemen whom Jyoshi introduced as local Bombay astrologers. Because I was a Western astrologer, Jyoshi explained, it was only fitting that we should all have a chance to meet and talk. I was amazed. My faith in India had been so quickly rewarded. I now had five astrologers from which to choose a teacher should one of them strike my fancy. And that occurrence was not at all far off.

We conversed together for some time and I was impressed by the fact that these were the first Hindu astrologers I had encountered who held Western astrology in high regard. Indeed, one of the men mentioned that he had met an Hindu astrologer, in another part of India, who was obtaining excellent predictive results using the Hindu and Western systems together. Although Gunshyam Jyoshi appeared to have achieved the highest status of these astrologers there was one man present whose passion for the heavenly language struck a powerful chord in me. All of the men were knowledgeable, of course, and perhaps to a similar degree since they were obviously a close-knit group that shared wisdom together. But P.M. Padia, P. for Poputlal, for my money stuck out like a sore thumb. While the others wanted to talk, this man wanted to get down to business — astrological business. He asked, as soon as etiquette allowed, to see my birthchart. Rather than search through all the blueprints in my knapsack I simply asked for pen and paper and quickly drew the chart from memory. Before mentioning anything of the general circumstances of my life Padia confidently exclaimed, "You got married when you were twenty-one or twenty-three." At this statement I was astonished. For

I had not yet given him the *dasa bhuktis*, the planetary periods, of my life and his statement was correct.

I had in fact married at the age of twenty-three and had no idea how he knew that. I immediately turned on my tiny casette recorder and asked him where he was getting his information. He explained that for marriage, pregnancies, and acquisitions of homes and cars he always used transits. Now I was completely confused. How the hell was he using transits, the current daily positions of the planets in the sky affecting the natal blueprint, without referring to an emphemeris, the book listing such positions? And what was he doing using transits anyway, which I thought were a strictly Western method and which Santhanam, my first mentor, had not mentioned? At any rate I made a mental note not to let this man out of my sight.

The Hindu method of transits, Padia explained, is somewhat different than the one used in Western analysis. The difference lies mainly in that the Hindu astrologer looks more for the general, rather than specific, position of a planet in the sky. For example Western astrologers note the exact *degree* of the zodiac a planet occupies at any given time to see what relationship it forms with other birthchart positions. The Hindu technique, on the other hand, is to simply note what zodiac sign the planet is in. In other words while Westerners are looking to determine a life effect or event that may occur during a particular day or week, the Hindu method reveals a tendency or occurrence that may result any time during an entire year and in some cases two or three years. In the case of my marriage Padia noted that in 1973 and 1975 the planet Jupiter, which indicates beneficial results, was in zodiac positions where it would form highly positive relationships with birthchart positions relating to my married life. Because Jupiter transits last approximately one year per zodiac sign it was simple for him to know what signs the planet transitted during those years by simply counting backwards in my chart one year at a time from Jupiter's present position. Padia also explained other differences in their use of transits too tedious to mention here.

My next question to Padia and the others regarded the length of my life. I was concerned about a *dasa bhukti* which, if I died in that two- or three-year period, would not surprise any Hindu astrologer. Indeed, to my mind the indications would make an excellent textbook example to show the predictive ease of Hindu astrology. Padia, as already mentioned in Chapter Two, said that aside from the free will factor the forecast of death was not a certainty. In fact the period itself could actually produce powerful benefits. Then again it could produce both great success and death. I was reminded of John Lennon whose Jupiter Saturn period brought him, after five hermit-like years, back to the top of the music charts as well as to the end of his life. All had happened in the same two-and-a-half-year *dasa bhukti*.

Since the period in my life in question was sufficiently in the future, my attitude toward the matter was appreciably more philosophical than emotional. And yet I was serious. In my own mind I had already decided the meaning of the period and resolved to take great precaution during such time that I might survive it. That, if nothing else, is the value of knowing beforehand about an oncoming bad period. Certainly if the weatherman predicts rain it is only wise to carry an umbrella. In my case, despite what Padia said, I plan not only to carry an umbrella but to also wear a raincoat, rubber boots, and waterproof my house. For as it happens the astrological indications in my Western chart during the same period are indicative of a similar intensely rocky road. So although padia's judgment threw a bit of positive light on the matter my handling of the situation, when it arrives, will differ little. Better, obviously, to be safe than sorry.

In the next hour or so it became clear that these men, of which I admired Padia most, knew certain things about Hindu technique that were totally foreign to me. Some of what they knew was the result of years of personal practical experience. Other information was simply basic scriptural knowledge that I had not yet been exposed to. As our meeting came to a close I told Padia I wanted to study with him. He said that there was simply no time. Between his two jobs, minding a retail store and his astrological practice, he was busy from early morning to late at night. I pleaded my case for a while in my typically determined way but seemed to get nowhere. Nevertheless my mind was made up that, somehow, Padia was to be my teacher. Finally Jyoshi came to my rescue. His words were music to my ears. He said, "Mr. Padia is too busy to teach you but if you will pay him one hundred rupees ($10) or so I am sure he will oblige you."

For the next three or four weeks Padia came to my room each night to pass on all he knew of my favorite subject. He would arrive at nine o'clock at night and stay till ten thirty or eleven (for which I paid an extra fifty rupees). Though he would arrive looking perfectly ready for bed and I would be languishing from my ever-worsening dysentery we always perked up from the excitement of astrologizing. Our energy seemed to feed off each other and spiral upwards until we would finish off the night with two or three glasses of freshly squeezed fruitjuice from the street vendor outside who always anticipated our request before closing. Because Padia worked in Bombay but lived outside the city he said it was easier for him to come to my room than for me to go to his. Though this defied the traditional teacher-student relationship it was clearly more practical.

The first night Padia arrived at my hotel room (if you

could call it that) I was fast asleep, dead to the incredibly noisy streets, Indian heat, and my stomach problems. I should have been downstairs at the entrance, looking for my guest, where I said I would be waiting. Instead I was under the covers! Now when a desk clerk knocked on my door to ask whether I was expecting company I felt about as embarrassed as I ever wish to feel. Here was this wonderful and intelligent man, with a family I might add, taking the last few hours of his day to teach me what I wanted to know and there I was asleep. I felt like a fool. As I apologized profusely my mentor brushed the matter off swiftly and gracefully. He said, "When you are coming from the other side of the earth for this knowledge I cannot doubt your sincerity. Anyway, since I am coming to you (to your room that is) I think you must deserve to get knowledge. Come, let us see." At that Padia looked at my Hindu birthchart and explained that when the ninth space is very well disposed, as mine is, it means a person will get higher knowledge very easily. It also means the knowledge will be genuine and there will be good fortune with gurus and spiritual teachers.

This was something Padia knew very well about. For he was a spiritual man, on the path of enlightenment, who for many years of his seeking had continually encountered false gurus and faulty knowledge, something certainly possible in India depending on one's karma and awareness. The reason for Padia's difficulties in this area was that the ninth house in his chart was in certain ways severely afflicted. Therefore genuine higher knowledge was hard to come by. This changed only when he entered a very beneficial *dasa* period which powerfully turned things around. At that point he came upon the knowledge of astrology as well as more effective spiritual techniques. By now he had been with the heavenly language for some fifteen or twenty years. And so this first night together Padia, in his deep humility and charming broken English, promised he would do his absolute best to teach me everything he could. "I will teach you all best secrets," he said, "so you will get perfect knowledge." He was as ready to teach as I was to learn. It was an exciting night.

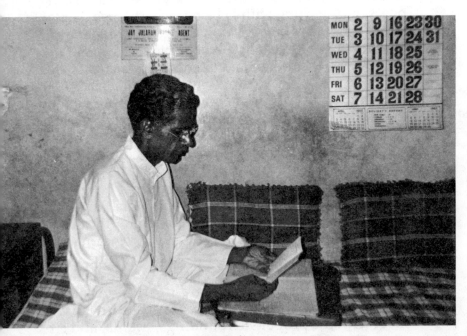

P.M. Padia

Although I had returned to India to improve my astrological ability my intention was, in fact, far more personal. I was actually agitated about my own life and destiny. There was an intensity and craving in the depths of my being to actualize my *dharma*, my life path. It was

197

now nearing the end of 1984, some four years after I had awoken to a sense of destiny of my life as a teacher. Yet despite my astrological practice, local lectures, and occasional TV and radio appearances I felt I was getting nowhere fast. Though I was clearly doing some good my range of influence was not nearly what I had in mind. Each individual knows intuitively, to varying degrees of intensity, what his or her life is meant to produce and mean. Indeed that is one of the greatest purposes of conferring with one's birthchart, one's map of destiny, to confirm whether one's instincts are on track or not. For the astrological blueprint represents in the truest sense the design and intention of a person's life. And while Astro-Logos presents the star science as a language of life, a language conveying nature's intent for its offspring, there is more, at least in our experience, to it than that. The astrological blueprint unequivocally signifies one's *own* particular intention and plan for his or her life.

Philosophically, the way this occurs may be considered religious, mystical, or even outlandish to some. This is because the logical explanation for the above statement lies in the theory of karma and reincarnation. That is to say that each person (as a soul or spirit, in the afterlife, in between births) consciously chooses his or her own time of birth and thus an astrological birthchart and life destiny. This the soul does to ensure that it will meet with the proper surroundings, events, and circumstances on earth necessary to facilitate its growth towards perfection. Whether or not such explanation is correct, since it is not at this time about to be proven, is irrelevant. That individuals so profoundly relate to the interpretations of their birthcharts is the significant point. That a person experiences contentment when his or her existence matches the direction and dictates of their birthchart (psychologically and behaviorally speaking) and is frustrated when it does not is of the greatest consequence. There is simply no difference between the reality birthcharts propose as paths to fulfillment and people's true heartfelt intentions for themselves. Therefore astrological blueprints reveal people's own plans for their own lives.

In my case the externals of my existence matched neither my powerful sense of destiny nor what my birthchart revealed as probable in the realm of career success. Therein was my disturbance. And therefore was I so plagued when the interpretation of the *dasa bhukti* period of my old high school friend, the one I had astrologized for before coming to India, had so varied from his actual experience. That occurrence brought powerfully home the inconsistency of my own situation. And if there was such an acute discrepancy between an aspect of my life and what my chart indicated, in terms of a reality I was truly trying to actualize, then there were indeed problems to be dealt with. If astrology was not working for me I wanted no part of passing it on to others. And so here I sat ready to deal.

The opportunity to address the issue arose during the second night of our study. Padia was analyzing the birthchart of my brother Charles and commenting on his practically unending good luck. "His *poorvapunya*," Padia said, "is very great." *Poorvapunya*, which means past life credit, was a new term to me. Thus Padia explained that while the entire birthchart is said to result, to a large extent, from one's past actions (in previous earthly lives) *poorvapunya* is the credit or debts one has incurred which must be rewarded, or punished, for certain in this life. "This man," Padia continued, "may have spent his last life caring only for others. Now he is being rewarded." "Bravo," I thought. "So this is why he has always had such abundance in his life." As a child I had felt very nearly cursed as I constantly contemplated our drastically contrasting fortunes. Of material pleasures we were given relatively little since money was so tight.

Yet Charles was always, and I mean always, bringing home some new found toy or bicycle while I looked enviously on. The most typical and memorable feat I recall occurred the day we both attended a spring training baseball game in Miami. Charles, who was ten or eleven at the time, fearlessly walked over to a Baltimore Oriole outfielder and nonchalantly said, "Can I have a bat?" The man said "sure" and happily handed him one of his own! I couldn't believe my eyes.

Now as Padia and I spoke, Charles was working in his three, count them three, retail stores in the shopping mall he had entered less than five years earlier. Before opening his own retail shop Charles had worked for others, always earning decent salaries. In November 1978 he entered a ten-year Moon *dasa* and his *poorvapunya* paid off like a Vegas slot machine. The Moon's position in Charles' Hindu blueprint occupies the fifth space, the space indicating past life credit. The Moon in his chart is incredibly well disposed, well aspected in relationship to other planets. So when the Moon period began, his entire existence took a turn straight upwards. He opened his store in early 1978 with all his assets at stake. By the middle of the year Charles could see he had made the right move. By 1979 he was calling me up north to say that money was raining from heaven.

Since the fifth house indicates one's past life credit it also reveals, by way of reason, one's sense of destiny. Simply put, people destined to achieve certain results in life quite naturally know it. While Charles is always optimistically expecting to receive what he desires, such as the above-mentioned baseball bat, I could not in my wildest dreams live the way he does. The karma is just so radically different. However, as for the ability to gain fame and affect the masses the only difference between Charles with his pleasures and me with my desire to influence was that he was realizing his destiny and getting what he wanted whereas I was not. I had now been waiting expectantly for four years with nothing in hand to show for it. It was now time, I realized, for some answers. And where better to find them than from nature's language as practiced by someone who, though not infallible, had already proved his interpretive mettle?

I told Padia of my previous spiritual and mystical experiences and the expectations they had created. Then I explained that despite the fact that absolutely nothing of any significance had been happening careerwise my sense of destiny seemed to increase in intensity every year. By this point the concern was not only extremely annoying but terribly paradoxical. The more time that passed uneventfully the stronger I felt that my knowledge, opinions, and thoughts should and would be heard. But nothing, dammit, was ever happening! My lectures never drew more than ten or twenty people. Advertisement offers to teach astrology, which I placed every six months or so, consistently brought very few phone calls of which even less were serious. And it was simply not of my reality to go about shouting that I was in possession of some vast storehouse of knowledge that everyone else direly needed. So if I was not going to take it upon myself to force my influence on the world and if the world cared nothing for what I wished to offer, how was this supposed destiny to occur? My thought now was that either such a destiny sat in my birthchart as a fated reality or it did not. My own judgment of my birthchart was that there was clearly a powerful career ahead. But experience had been proving that conclusion an exaggeration. In any case I was now ready to face the monster and, hopefully, once and for all be over and done with it.

Mind you I was not, intellectually anyway, attached to popularity or fame. For seven years I had been content to do nothing but meditate and think on God. I well knew the illusory nature and futility of worldly pleasures. Yet my instinct and personal reality was what it was and it would not, somehow, let me live in peace. So sounding almost arrogant, as if this man was in some way responsibile for my existence, I stated my demand. "Look in my chart. If I am not going to be known tell me and I will try to stop thinking this way. Because it's beginning to drive me crazy." There...finished. I had spoken my piece. I had expressed the most private and bothersome feature of my existence and what had truly driven me to put my life on hold, go into debt, and travel halfway around the world where I knew every meal would burn like hell and give profound meaning to the words Pepto Bismol™. The matter was now off my chest and onto his.

II ♃ 14°	12 ☽ 23°	I 2° /	2
10 ☊ 15°			3
9			4 ♂ ☋ ♀ 14° 15° 16°
8	7	6 ☿ 2°	5 ☉ ♄ 29° 14°

Poorvapunya *and "Maturity of Planets":*
Two Powerful techniques

"You will get fame in your life," Padia said. "You will definitely get it. But not until your thirty-sixth year, after your thirty-sixth year." In an instant, a slow-motion instant, I reacted to his declaration three ways. One was with joyous relief. My innate sense had been correct; I would have a signifcant influence on the world. The second was with skepticism. He's probably just saying what he thinks I want to hear. And the third was absolutely pessimistic. He must be wrong. How could anything really good happen to me? At any rate my thoughts were irrelevant since the one subject I was always good at learning was astrology, especially the Hindu system. Padia, he and I both knew, was certainly going to have to explain his judgment. I hoped it would make sense. I also hoped he knew something I didn't. But that already seemed likely since I had no idea as to why he had mentioned my thirty-sixth year.

Padia's basic analysis at first did not differ from what I already knew. But the feature that seemed to push him to make such an absolute declaration was related to this *poorvapunya* business. He said quite simply that because the planet connected to my career house (the tenth) was sitting in the space indicating past life credit (the fifth) and was well aspected, it was sure that in this life I would reap the rewards of career efforts I had made in past lives. There was, in other words, career credit following me around just waiting for the proper time to be redeemed. Since the planet involved was Saturn, Padia explained, my professional success, indeed even my "niche" in that sphere, would not begin to emerge until the thirty-sixth year (meaning age thirty-five). As for my *poorvapunya* being related to career achievement the concept made immediate sense. Why else was I always

203

thinking that I should have some large-scale influence, that my knowledge and opinions would be heard more than someone else's, as if God or the world owed this to me? I now reasoned that if there were certain effects of past-life actions I was meant to obtain, then it was perfectly logical that those effects would show up as my sense of destiny. Whether or not *poorvapunya* was for real I could not, without further astrological research, be sure. But the theory quickly gave reason to the madness I had been feeling for the past four or five years. Regarding Padia's statement about my career beginning around the thirty-sixth year I was totally in the dark as to this delineation. I therefore asked for an explanation.

What my new mentor taught is a basic astrological precept called "maturity of planets." Though only a very few Hindu texts (and none that I had read) mention the principle, each particular planet, as a representative symbol in a birthchart, is said to reach its "maturity" at a certain point in time. Saturn, which is typically described as a slow and elderly sort of influence, quite reasonably reaches its full development late in a person's life. When it is said that Saturn matures in the thirty-sixth year what is meant is that Saturn's "full effects," that is the "full expression" of whatever Saturn indicates in a particular Hindu birthchart, cannot completely manifest until that year. Also, it should be understood that the thirty-sixth year begins at age thirty-five because then one has lived thirty-five years.

At any rate, because Saturn in my chart is the planet connected to the career house the full effects of my professional life, both in terms of knowing and embracing my proper vocation and reaping the destined success or failure in that area, would not be realized until my thirty-sixth year. And since career accomplishment is connected to my past-life credit, it is also around that time (and to an extent the time of any Saturn *dasa* or *bhukti* period) that the expected *poorvapunya* results should occur. Fortunately for me, Saturn, though an extremely troublesome influence in my Western birthchart, is the absolute best planet in my Hindu chart. Therefore I now understood that I would soon, assuming this maturity of planets was genuine, be having some of my greatest desires fulfilled. I was now almost thirty-three years old, two months away from the thirty-fourth year of my life.

As Padia detailed for me the years each planet matures, my mind immediately began computing. I considered the effects a particular planet could be expected to produce, or indicate, in relation to its placement and condition in familiar birthcharts of friends, relatives, and public figures now in front of me. Jupiter, which gives its full results in the sixteenth year, is a very special planet in the blueprint of my eldest brother Herb. Not only is it one of the best planets for his chart (called a *yogakaraka* or union maker) but because of its relationship to a certain other planetary position (that of Mars) it forms what is called a *rajayoga* or "royal" union. This means that whenever Jupiter's effects are indicated to occur there will be enormously favorable life benefits. Regarding my brother's experience there was certainly no incongruity. Herb, as an actor, was practically a legendary figure during his three high school years. Aside from winning all the local drama awards and being voted "most talented" in his school, in the eleventh grade he took first place in a dramatic interpretation comprising students from seven southeastern states. Though he was gifted throughout childhood it was not until his sixteenth year (age fifteen) that he entered drama and his star began to rise.

Incidentally, concerning maturity of planets there are two points important to be clarified. One is that the maturity of a planet does not happen instantly on the day a specified year begins. Its planetary or life energy requires an integrating process which takes place during the entire year the planet is said to come of age. A sensitive person can generally feel this if made aware of the detailed astrological significations. Secondly, the year of maturity does not necessarily bring about drastic results. Much, of course, depends on the distinct chart in hand. But once the planet has matured, the significations it represents can come to fruition.

For example, take the case of Jimmy Carter. Saturn is the *rajayogakaraka* or best planet for his Hindu chart. It rules the fifth space, the space of politics, and its position in the blueprint occupies the first house, the house of the self, the personality, and physical presence (which therefore relates directly to leadership). However, although Saturn matures in the thirty-sixth year Carter did not enter politics the instant he turned thirty-five. The integrating effect, which occurred between the age of thirty-five and thirty-six, showed him what was possible. But he did not actually run for public office until age thirty-seven. The point is that at any time before age thirty-six, the year the maturation process was completed, his political and leadership abilities could not possibly have been fully developed. After that time, however, those same abilities were, so to speak, in place ready for active functioning.

Next, as I considered Mercury, the heavenly body representing writings and communications, which matures in the thirty-second year, I realized that it was exactly then that I had sat down for the first time to put some of my astrological thoughts on paper. This occurred in 1982 at age thirty-one on a mountain top in Nepal before my first encounter with Hindu astrology. I had just finished a full year of intensely contractive and depressing energy as indicated by three powerful Saturn transits. The astrological indications had finally passed and because I had learned so much about Saturn's meaning, within the heavenly language, I decided to write everything I knew or could decipher on the subject. The writing lasted about a week (five or six hours each day), not long by any means, but was by far the most serious literary effort I had ever completed. It was also during that time, about a month or two later, that the idea of writing for others presented itself when Shastri predicted I would author five or six books during my life. Perhaps a year or so later, in my thirty-third year of life I made my first serious attempt to write a text on Hindu astrology. Though that attempt failed (and it would not be until after my present stay in India that I would be back at work on a text that would succeed) it was not hard to see that my literary life, though sketchy, had begun during the thirty-second year of my life.

This maturity of planets precept, which worked separately from the *dasa* system of planetary periods, was quickly and powerfully bearing itself out. And that, for sure, was good. The more evidence I could find that this new (to me) astrological technique was real the more I could accept Padia's judgment and thus taste and smell my successful career looming fatefully in the future. At any rate, if I had any further doubts about the technique in question they were soon to be absolutely dispelled. For as I thought more about Mercury and examined its placement in the various charts before me, one blueprint provided the straw that broke the camel's back. It was the most dramatic and blatant case of just how significant and precise this rare, but quite traditional, maturity of planets business could be.

The chart belonged to none other than my friend who said he had attempted suicide in what I considered a very decent *dasa-bhukti* period. Mercury was the most devastated, the most negatively aspected, planet in his Hindu blueprint. Most significantly Mercury ruled (was connected to) the first space, the space indicating the personality, physical body, and self. Mercury's position in the chart occupied the eighth house, the house of death! Further, the planet was, as the Indians say, "hemmed in by malefics." In other words the zodiac positions of two planets (Mars and Saturn) known to represent terribly destructive elements in the Hindu system were flanking Mercury's zodiac position on either side. Here it must be said that although Mars and Saturn are capable of providing, or indicating, extremely positive results, as Saturn does in Jimmy Carter's case and my own, this occurs as a result of variables quite specific to our charts and to the particular methodology under consideration (i.e., *dasa* periods versus planetary aspects, etc.). But in my friend's case the two malefics were nothing more than disruptive, ruinous elements, to put it mildly.

At any rate the positions of Mars and Saturn were hemming Mercury in within a distance of only one or two degrees (out of a possible 360). They were therefore destroying Mercury in what is called a "planetary war." So, naturally, when my friend entered his thirty-second year of life and the integrating and maturing effect of that planet began to show its effects he was in for major trouble. Though he must have always experienced a significant degree of nervousness, psychological troubles, or depressions by virtue of Mercury's afflicted condition, it was not until then that he came to know what his mental functioning was truly capable of. To me, here was Hindu predictive astrology at its best. The planet representing the mind, connected to the house of the self, sitting in the space of death annihilated by planetary aspects and the man attempts to take his own life when the planet comes of age. I was impressed, damn impressed!

Aside from my new awareness of the significance of my thirty-sixth year, only some twenty-six months away, there was another reason to count my blessings. In a matter of three months I was to enter my Saturn *bhukti*, the Saturn subperiod of my present *Rahu dasa*. Once the subperiod began it was scheduled to last a good two and a half years. As it was, the whole eighteen-year *Rahu* period promised career success since it occupies the tenth space of my chart. But now I was coming to the subperiod of Saturn, easily the best aspected planet in my Hindu blueprint. I knew from past experience just how fortunate my life had been during such times. (I had never had a nineteen-year Saturn *dasa*. That occurs in the year 2013 for me.) Anyway Saturn *bhuktis*, I learned through retrospective analysis, had always been the harbinger of tremendous pleasures and achievements. Because Saturn relates to my past life credit, which was clearly abundant, and is connected to career, as well as religious and philosophical significations (since it also rules the ninth space of my chart), those were the life functions that served to benefit.

During the last Saturn subperiod, in 1975, I enjoyed the greatest, indeed the most blissful, *dharshan* (grace and presence of the guru) with my spiritual master ever in my seven most devotional and mystical years. The experience, though entirely nonverbal, was the most intense and sublime personal contact with my preceptor I had ever known. Because of its extremely subjective nature, I will not convey what occurred in writing. I will say, however, that when our ten- or fifteen-minute meeting ended, my fiercely logical mind could only conclude that either of two things had occurred. Either I had just been spiritually initiated *for real*, meaning my guru had now taken responsibility to see me through to enlightenment no matter how long (how many lifetimes) and how hard it would be, or I was somehow never to see him again. Or both. My sense of the affair was that I was, by his grace, being granted a profound experience of our relationship that I would never forget. As it has happened our paths have indeed been separated and I have not seen him since. At any rate what happened that day in June 1975 was the most holy state of surrender, of Godliness, I have ever felt. Perhaps because my eyes were open, the experience surpassed any of the previous metaphysical or "supernatural" occurrences I had gained in meditation. Careerwise, at the time, I found myself teaching meditation in the New York City center of our movement, a distinct improvement over the smaller, less prestigious centers I had known. 1975 was also the year I got married. Thus between the fulfillment of my relationship with my guru, my career success, and marriage to a woman I very much loved I always considered 1975 my favorite year.

The preceding Saturn subperiod, occurred in the Moon *dasa* during my eleventh grade of high school. That *bhukti*, also being a great one, brought on my first leading role as an actor. I was cast as Tom Sawyer in the play by the same name. Though that now seems of extraordinarily little importance, it was to me the best recognition I had ever received. In fact, it was during the rehearsals of that play that our director announced in front of my peers that if my ability continued growing I should consider a life in the theatre. Although I had already decided to be an actor on my own I was at that point too shy to say so. What her statement meant was that for the first time in my life I had done something right. It was clearly a high point. Saturn *bhuktis*, for me, were always a high point.

As an astrologer I have seen, if I am to be honest, enough cases where a *dasa* or *bhukti* has not matched the quality or quantity of experience I would have expected. The reasons for this are, obviously, numerous and debatable. The field of study is vast. Perhaps some astrological knowledge is lacking as it was in the case of my friend whose afflicted Mercury matured in the year of a favorable *dasa-bhukti*. Perhaps free will comes into play more so with some than with others. Perhaps more spiritually-evolved individuals have more power over their life schedules than those who live their lives according to every sudden whim. And occasionally, of course, people's birth times are just way off. I do not know. In my own case, however, for better or worse, the Hindu *vimsottari dasa* system works as dependably as death, change, and taxes. (There are, believe it or not, forty different *dasa* systems in existence. *Vimsottari* is the most widely used, followed by *asottari*, followed by thirty-eight others astrologers rarely mention.) I therefore had great cause for excitement as I awaited this oncoming Saturn subperiod.

Also, aside from its occurring within the career-oriented *Rahu dasa* and aside from the fact that it would be lengthier than any other Saturn *bhukti* I had ever experienced, it was running all the way into my thirty-sixth year—the auspicious year Saturn would mature. Saturn *bhukti* was not set to end until I would be thirty-five-and-a-half years old. Here, it took little to realize, came into play the old adage: "See an astrological indication once and it is a possibility. See the same indication twice and it is a likelihood. See it three times and it is a certainty." Here were several significant clues as to just how positive a period of life I could expect shortly on.

Throughout the next three or four weeks with Padia I spent the nights absorbing his teachings. Though he taught certain techniques I was previously unfamiliar with the main part of my learning came from simply analyzing birthcharts together. Like all astrologers his delineations were not perfect. But they were close, often extremely close. In fact I constantly found myself distrustingly probing Padia's reasons for his assertions. Sometimes the statements he made were so accurate I was sure they were the result of intuition. Not that there is anything wrong, mind you, with using intuition and psychic ability to gain accuracy in an astrological reading. There is not. It just does not interest me personally and is not what I had in mind when entering the field of the heavenly language. While I have occasionally gone to professional psychics and found them sometimes valuable I do not wish to practice that art myself. I rather more enjoy and trust the objectivity involved in using the birthchart of one's destiny. In any case, every time I thought I had caught Padia intuiting his judgments he would, almost annoyingly, simply explain his purely astrological reasoning. When he was done explaining he would always finish with his usual masterful advice: "You must look at the entire chart; you must develop a computer mind." Other times when I would ask incrediuously how he managed some extremely accurate prediction or analysis he would answer "my dear friend, *chai* (a very special-tasting Indian tea) is not simply made of water, sugar, and milk. It is a mixture of many herbs and spices, all delicately balanced."

"Many indeed," I thought one night after Padia startled me with an uncannily astute statement. I had just handed him the chart of a girlfriend who wanted to marry me and whom I knew from the start I never could. To my mind there just was not enough passion or commitment in her life, to anything, to powerfully capture my interest. Padia, who I never said a word to about any chart before showing it to him, took a minute or so and then put the blueprint down proclaiming, "This chart is boring. There is not much to say." It was true. He had hit the nail on the head despite the fact that, superficially, the chart appeared fairly special. That was indeed the reason I wished to discuss it in the first place! As he explained his reasoning for the pronouncement I was sure was intuitive, I finally realized his ability was astrological—always astrological. His judgments, quite simply, were the result of fifteen or twenty years of interpreting the language of the heavens. Precision and accuracy were the rewards of his experience and dedication.

So it was that my testing of Padia was not only somewhat arrogant (who was I to question him?) but also inept. Throughout our weeks together I regularly returned to my own chart, especially to this career business and my sense of destiny. Having examined my own Hindu chart for the last year or two and having made the incredible effort it took to return to India I was not going to accept Padia's opinions about my life so easily. I would not believe them easily even if they were supported by logic. Healthy skepticism, or discrimination, had always played a major role in my search for knowledge and higher consciousness. It had served me well in a field as perilous as mysticism and I had no intention of dropping the practice now. Somewhere along the way I therefore asked Padia whether, in the fame he said I would have, I would be known in other countries as well as my own. This was a test, and nothing but a test. If he said "yes," I thought, he would have failed. Then I would know he was simply saying what he thought I wished to hear. My ego, you see, was big. But it was not, thank you very much, that big. I wanted to have some significant influence, but the possibility of my name reaching foreign countries seemed absurd to me; not just out of proportion but absurd. I was, after all, a "fringe person." Mystics and monks may be considered eccentric but astrologers... well, enough said.

At any rate, reaching people in my own land was sufficient to complete my sense of self and fulfill my needs. Therefore, after Padia looked at my chart and answered my question saying, "You will be known in other countries too," I was shocked and, truthfully, disappointed. His words did not match my expectations and for that reason they did not inspire my trust. But as I considered the matter I realized that every other time I had challenged Padia, asserting that he was using intuition rather than astrological technique, he had been right and I had been wrong! Now, it hit me, I had really no way at all to judge. I felt backed up against a wall and intellectually out of control. Some thinker I was. I therefore dropped the matter without further ado and surrendered myself to Padia's teaching as best I could. I had not the slightest idea I would, within three months, be working on a Hindu astrology text that would receive rave reviews in America, Europe, and believe it or not my favorite spiritual country—India.

The Himalayas

Developing a Computer Mind With Padia

One month, I am well aware, is not a long time to spend with a teacher as experienced as P.M. Padia. It is not long even if I had been at the practice for nearly two years when we met. And yet it was within that one concentrated month that I truly grasped the crux of Hindu astrology. Padia's teaching, added to what I already knew, provided my work with an element of subtlety and wholeness that had been lacking. When my studies ended I felt extremely complete. Though I knew there were years and years, indeed lifetimes, of more learning ahead I had at least begun to develop the "computer mind" Padia always spoke of. I found this out for sure during my first astrological session with a client back in America. I also understood, experientially, how it was that padia's seeming intuition was actually astrological ability. For in my first consultation at home I was making statements I would have previously considered quite impossible.

I told a new client of mine, a woman in her mid-twenties, that she was likely to develop a hearing problem in her right ear (the third space of her Hindu chart was totally devastated). She was, in one way, not the least surprised as she replied that the problem already existed. She was however, in another way, both surprised and relieved. The reason for this was that her doctors insisted the defect was in the left ear while she knew the right ear was the afflicted one. The birthchart confirmed her personal experience. Also within that first reading I said that the two strongest career posssibilities I could determine, as evidenced through her birthchart, were nursing (or anything in the medical field) and any "technical" work involving mechanics or surgery, etc. She replied that her desire was to become a "surgical nurse."

I had not heard that term before but I immediately understood that Padia had taught me well.

Though I left India and my mentor in fear that I might actually die of dysentery (it was that bad and people do die from it) the greater truth was that my brain had absorbed all the knowledge it needed, and perhaps was capable of, for the time being. In my heart of hearts I knew that, sick as I was, I would have gutted it out and remained longer had my questions not been answered. That was simply the way I was raised. But there was no need. The teaching had been there. Following our nightly sessions I spent each day going over my notes and listening to the taped sessions made with my trusty miniature recorder. Because of what Padia had said about my own life and destiny, based upon his analysis of the fifth space of my chart, I spent at least as much time studying the fifth house of every birthchart I had in my possession. Whenever I found a chart indicating some specific *poorvapunya* or past life credit that had not manifested in the person's life I brought it to my teacher and asked why. But this happened rarely. Fortunately *poorvapunya* proved to be one of the most reliable astrological indications.

I noted that in the blueprint of an actress friend of mine the planet signifying art, Venus, occupied the fifth space. This meant that her artistic talents were a result of efforts made in past lives. The reason this was significant was that this woman was easily one of the most talented actors in my college and that was no small accomplishment. I found the chart of another actor friend of mine from college who had since given up the theatre to become a writer. His chart, if the reader has not yet guessed, contained Mercury, the planet of communications, in the house revealing *poorvapunya*. Perhaps what satisfied my mind the most about the matter was that every chart of a famous person I examined, almost to a person, contained an extraordinarily powerful fifth house. The more I analyzed such charts, including those of several United States presidents, the more I understood that no matter how hard these people may have worked in this life to achieve their goals it was their past life credit that ultimately (at least from the astrological paradigm) made it all possible. Concerning fame I came to see that, aside from *poorvapunya* what is necessary is a strong and well-disposed first house as well as a significant tenth. The first space represents confidence, self-esteem, and the ability to put oneself forth (or be recognized) in the world. The tenth, as already mentioned, indicates status and career in general.

Usually in the case of famous personages all three of these spaces are very well disposed. But not always. In cases such as Steven Spielberg and Roger Maris (now deceased) for example, the first space is very weak while the fifth and tenth houses are enormously strong. Therefore there is great career success and plenty of past life credit but a shy personality. These individuals are, for that reason, best advised to focus energies strictly towards career efforts rather than self promotion. Their destinies simply do not include much in the way of self recognition. What benefits in this area do come their way do so as a by-product of professional success and status, and are disproportionately small in relation to their achievements.

This is the reason that Roger Maris had such trouble with fans and the press and was not inducted into the Baseball Hall of Fame. It also explains why Steven Spielberg has been ignored by the Motion Picture Academy. In other cases one may have an extremely beneficial first space, such as Marilyn Monroe and Marlon Brando, and the wisest course of action is to focus on one's powerful presence and prove the worthiness to be emulated. All in all, however, the entire chart must be examined and synthesized as a whole since it contains so many variables. And that was, aside from discussing basic tech-

217

niques in more depth, what I learned from Poputlal M. Padia. Also, of course, the more I studied and contemplated different people's *poorvapunya* the more confidence I had that my own past life credit was genuine.

As I had done with Santhanam, my first mentor, Padia and I together analyzed as many birthcharts and human destinies as time allowed. Padia's statements covered a wide and interesting range: "This man will go on *moksha marg*" (the path of enlightenment, where most of my friends seemed to be going). "This man will be charged in court cases" (the chart actually belonged to a woman who indeed had quite a story to tell about being unjustly accused). "This man has no luck." "This woman," Padia enthusiastically announced, "may own her own car and her own home! She will also easily get good educational degrees." "This man will make money ... but slowly, very slowly." "This woman was born to a wealthy family." And then came my favorite: "If you sleep with this woman," Padia exclaimed of the chart of an ex-girlfriend of mine, "she will invite you back for more and more." "Oh no," I thought, "Here we go again with his intuitive ability." The twelfth house of this chart was nothing to brag about and since that is the space indicating sexual pleasures there was no apparent reason for Padia's judgment. He had, though, zeroed in on just about the strongest feature of this woman's existence. This I knew because she was the second most sexual woman I had ever been with and the only one with whom I had ever maintained a *purely* physical relationship. Padia explained: "*Shukra* and *Chandra* (Venus and Moon) are in a *kendra* (an angular relationship) from each other. I have noticed that when this happens the person is very sexy (meaning sexual). If you sleep with her once she will come back for more and more." I confessed that he was right and laughed while Padia grinned.

At that point I thought of the most sexual woman I

had known, actually the one most "skilled in the art of sexual pleasures," as Hindu scriptures put it, and wondered if her birthchart also contained the same aspect. It did. Later I found out that somewhat similar Venus Moon aspects existed in the Hindu charts of Marilyn Monroe, Hugh Hefner, and John F. Kennedy (such aspects, incidentally, may exist in these individuals' Hindu charts even though not necessarily in their Western ones. Aspects and their orbs are calculated differently in the two systems.). As I considered the matter I realized just how valuable this Hindu astrology could be. I had no trouble committing this Venus Moon aspect and its meaning to memory.

Finally as my illness progressively worsened, despite medical treatment, there came a night when I could not acquire any sleep whatever. And that was, after four weeks of the absurd Bombay heat, noise, and filth, all I cared to endure at the time. I returned home to the States, ate a ton of brown rice and vegetables (sans curry and amoebaes), and began to gain back the fifteen pounds I had lost from my already slim 135 pound frame. Apart from the joy of eating clean food and having some control over my environment, I was quite happy on two accounts. One was that I now had a far better handle on Hindu astrology. The other was that I was at last content that my *dharma*, my work and destiny, was relatively soon to unfold in a way that would satisfy my expectations. Although the future might bring more career changes (I will never forget Padia once saying to me, "You have had many careers! And you will have more after this one, ha ha ha ha.") it was certain that a favorable professional life lay ahead. I had studied a sufficient amount of birthcharts and seen enough to know whereof I spoke. Because of all this, this belief born of astrological knowledge and experience, my life changed.

It changed simply but profoundly. For somehow once

back in familiar surroundings I noticed that my desire to be known and recognized, which had been a source of annoyance for so long, had in a certain but very real way disappeared. It disappeared because in my mind the reality of the event had already occurred. Now all that remained was for the physical, the earthly, phenomenon of it to follow. To my mind this aspect of my destiny, being known, had finally actualized—*it was only separated by time!* Therefore I finally began to take some responsibility for the matter. I began to "speak my dream," if you will. I told my brother and a few close friends what I had been thinking for several years. I said, without shame or self consciousness, that I would be famous in some way and that it would begin somewhere around the thirty-sixth year of my life. This, for me, was a breakthrough. A big one.

Upon returning from my first journey to India I was not quite sure what I wished to do with the knowledge I possessed. I could easily see the possibility of Hindu astrology being misused in the West and therefore had my doubts. But by now I had become absolutely comfortable with the ancient Hindu method of interpretation making its way into Western society. I realized that wherever there is potential for profound good there must also exist the possibility of disastrous misuse. Such is the nature of life. At any rate if I did not spread the teaching someone else would. Obviously I was not the only Western astrologer knowledgeable in the field. From my point of view the world would be lucky to have the discipline presented by someone of a spiritual background. So here I was.

In the next three months as my body healed itself (it took at least that long) I considered how to make best advantage of the auspicious two-and-a-half-year Saturn *bhukti* about to begin. Since Saturn is the best planet in my Hindu chart and in the past had always brought on great success, I had no fears or doubts about setting my sails and setting them in a grand way. As I pondered what the Saturn subperiod indicated, my brain functioned in its usual logical fashion. Reason implied that if I had previously been a local astrologer with a regular practice, occasionally stirring up the airwaves via TV or radio, then success meant more, much more, abundance within the same realm. So I naturally assumed there would be more television and radio appearances, bigger and better newspaper articles, and a flock of astrological clients beating down my door to make appointments. And of course there would be hordes of people begging me to teach the interpretive methods of the language of life so that they could themselves decipher their destinies and those of their loved ones. What else could my success mean?

I pondered opening up an astrology business, a retail store out on a main street or an outdoor mall where real astrology could become a possibility for the public. Though I was in debt from my recent travels I did have a piece of savings tucked away in an ailing investment made several years earlier. Cashing in on the venture meant losing almost half of the original capital but that was not a deterrent since I was weeks away from a Saturn *bhukti* promising to be one of the best career periods of my life. This was a delineation (an astrological interpretation) not made from the psychologically-oriented Western astrology. I personally would never stake my assets on a prediction made through its use unless the matter somehow depended entirely on an internal state or mental outlook. But this was different. Therefore I began to search for an appropriate location. I, of course, had no intention of putting the plan into action until the Saturn *bhukti* actually commenced. I also wanted to remain open to whatever possibility nature might offer and to see whether the Saturn subperiod would find me feeling differently.

The current *bhukti* now coming to an end was that of

Jupiter and as far as I was concerned "praise God for that." Though the last few years had included two trips to India and been filled with abundant higher knowledge it was without question a terrible period for material and worldly success. Other than learning and making some important contacts none of my actions bore serious fruit. Making ends meet through my chosen trade was an uphill struggle. Jupiter, in my chart, though occupying a good sign for its functioning is badly aspected by three malefic planets, two of the aspects being of enormous intensity. So naturally I was glad its *bhukti* was ending.

I never opened the astrology store I had in mind. Two days before Saturn *bhukti* began an old friend of mine asked about the Hindu astrology book I had begun to write before my last trip to India. Feeling slightly embarrassed at the failure of that writing stint I quickly set her straight in such a way that she would not mention the matter again. "No, no, no," I stated, "I'm not a writer. I tried. It was miserable. Maybe someday I'll get hold of a writer and have him or her organize the teaching." As if she hadn't heard a word I said she replied, "Well, I'm sure you'll write the book as soon as you're ready." "Fine," I thought, "as long as she doesn't ever mention writing to me again." I had not forgotten wasting a solid month of my life laboring at the most tedious work I had ever confronted. And to think people consider interpreting the heavenly language difficult.

As instantly as our conversation ended, I realized that while writing a book was not an option, organizing my astrological knowledge was a fine idea. Only two and a half months earlier I had learned *and integrated* so much of the Hindu predictive system thanks to P.M. Padia and my serious intent. I was still highly charged, still studying birthcharts of politicians, sports figures, and superstars found in astrological birth data books day after day. And I was still, five years into my passion for the wonderful language of life, analyzing, contemplating, and scrutinizing my own astrological blueprint. So with eagerness I began, for me and only me, to systematically compile all I knew and could deduce of the specifics of Hindu astrology. I say deduce because the heavenly language speaks exclusively through symbols—elaborate, in-depth, representative elements namely the planets, stars, zodiac positions, and the relationships between them. Therefore the interpretive process is not one of simply memorizing static empirical findings, rules, and regulations. Though that is obviously a significant part of the procedure the greatest factor depends upon adroitly applying one's intelligence, wisdom, life experience, and most of all consciousness to the task.

As I worked on my text I kept a few hundred birthcharts of friends and people whose lives I knew intimately (people tell astrologers alot!) and famous personages at my fingertips. Thus as I wrote about each astrological blueprint factor I examined who, amongst these individuals, had a particular aspect and what the effects were in their own lives. And, aside from drawing on past experiences within my practice and the teachings of my two mentors I considered, for each and every interpretation, the opinions and views of as many Hindu astrological authors and sages as were available. Then of course I drew my own conclusions. The work was painstaking. It was also fun and richly rewarding.

Within only a few days of the start of my task I began to observe that something about my work was different. Something had definitely changed. For no explanation, rhyme or reason, other than the fact that I had entered the long-awaited, highly beneficial Saturn subperiod, my writing suddenly seemed perfectly readable. Instead of the laborious, longwinded sentences that had filled the pages of my first writings my expressions were now succinct and clear. The proper words and phrases, when I needed them, were forthcoming. While I myself had no objectivity, no way to truly judge, for I had of course believed my first writings were effective, there even appeared a flow or gracefulness to the work. So I decided to show my efforts to a friend, Lilly La Paz. If Lilly, a Colombian woman who had been in America for about five years, could understand my writing then perhaps the teachings could finally make their way into legitimate print. There was, in my mind, no question that a Hindu astrology text, if it was accessible, informative, and readable would be highly appreciated by Western astrologers. So I went to Lilly, who worked in one of my brother's retail stores and begged her opinion.

Fortunately, she approved and even encouraged. Therefore I persisted in writing and continued every few days to show her the progress. Of course being innately skeptical I tested Lilly to determine whether her opinion was an honest one. At some point I, apprehensively, handed her part of my old writings from the year before, the ones everyone said were difficult to understand, to see her reaction. Like the others she complained. Thus I came to trust Lilly's judgment. And thus I soon understood that my Saturn *bhukti* was to be far more rewarding than what I had previously concluded. I was not, in the next two and a half years, to merely enjoy an expansion of astrological practice. I was to finally breathe life into Shastri's prediction that I would someday write books. I was also performing the actions which would create the possibility to actualize Padia's declaration that I would "get fame" in my life. If there was a way to utilize the miraculous language of life for all it was worth then I was doing just that. The difference between my current existence and the one in my mind, the one I intended to create, was dissolving. I could literally feel it. At last I was taking responsibility to realize my destiny and dream. I was making it happen.

Rewarded Efforts

Reviews were good. In fact they were great. Greater, I now realize, than anyone creating a body of work for as many different opinions as I was, should have a right to expect. Yet I did anticipate the raves I received. The book was clearly the first easily understandable instruction on Hindu astrology for Westerners. It was the first time this wonderfully practical and profound interpretive system would be presented in a palatable and appropriate form. And I knew it. But more than that, much more than that, I understood my karma. Throughout the nine months (of seven-day work weeks) it took to complete the text, it became obvious that I was blowing the lid off something that Western astrologers had been awaiting for a long, long time. And it was obvious that this was due less to any vast intellect of mine than to my exceedingly fortunate career ability. The professional success, ability to affect masses of people, and past life credit connected to public life which appear quite openly in my Hindu birthchart were all essential ingredients to the success of my endeavor. Of this I was aware very early on during the writing of *Ancient Hindu Astrology for the Modern Western Astrologer.* My only fear, actually, was that I might be beaten to the punch. Perhaps someone else would produce a similar text before I could. For it was plain as day, to my logic anyway, that the time was ripe, nearly overripe, for the predictive system of heavenly interpretation to make its way to the West.

Therefore, after my book made its way into public hands I was not at all surprised to occasionally receive letters from Western astrologers saying that they had wanted for years to do exactly what I had done. Some, apparently, were even presently engaged in the process.

225

The last paragraph of one book review (from an astrological association) read as follows: "I write this review with mixed feelings, for this is the book I have had on the drafting table for the last year, and which will now not see the light of day. James T. Braha's book deserves to become the classic reference on Hindu astrology for Western readers. A better book could not be written." The words confirmed my belief that the time for Hindu astrology had arrived. It also gave me to understand what Sir Laurence Olivier may have felt when Sir John Gielgud folded his concurrent production of *Othello* because he felt Olivier had just delivered the "definitive performance." I slept well that night.

My book came out in early 1986 and coincided with the reappearance of Halley's comet. For advertisement purposes I had an artist design a poster with a picture of a comet flying through the book. Written above was the copy: "Arriving with Halley's comet—what Western astrologers have been missing out on for two thousand years." While it undoubtedly seemed, to some, little more than an attempt to cash in on the current fad of the day there was good reason for my presentation. Astrologically, the sightings of comets (major ones) are associated with two particular effects. One of them, irrelevant to my purpose, has to do with the deposing of national leaders. The other is the alteration of the status quo through radical innovation. So it was that I was making the statement, to those astrologers who would understand, that with this new (or should I say ancient) method of interpreting the heavenly language the field of Western astrology was about to undergo a major advancement. The status quo of the astrological field, at least in the Western world, was now being powerfully altered. As for politicians that year, the Swedish president was killed and the longtime leaders of Haiti and the Philippines were ousted.

My sense of destiny to be known or famous was not

satiated, particularly, because of favorable reviews. It was fulfilled because of a stream of appreciative letters I received from all over the world, which incidentally still persist. How the book came to sell overseas is an interesting tale. Since I decided in favor of self publishing, mainly so I could control the quality, my hands were quite full from the start. Therefore I had no inclination to think about distributing outside the US for a while, at least until I knew what I was doing and things would calm down. As for being known in other countries I still rather assumed Padia was overdoing it with that prediction. Regarding the possibility of selling the text in India, a perfectly intelligent thing to do, there was one problem standing in the way. Where the hell was I supposed to obtain the audacity to do so? Who, after all, was I to tell Hindus about *their* system of astrology? This time I had underestimated the extent of my karma as witnessed through the tenth house, the career space, of my Hindu blueprint. As fate would have it, it took less than three months for my book to reach the hands of astrologers all over the world.

There was, in an astrology class I was teaching, a stewardess who every so often flew to London. One day I handed her a few copies of my book and asked her to bring them to some metaphysical bookstore owners over there to get their reactions. I did not, at that point, know how I would deliver the books in any cost effective way if indeed they wished to purchase any. But I assumed that could eventually be worked out. The woman returned about a week later practically in a frenzy about how badly England wanted my book. She said a few of the merchants she had visited would almost definitely take ten copies. Further, one storeowner asked if he could sell the book exclusively and even distribute it himself to outer areas of the country. Beyond this, because the British have a special sort of appreciation for literary works, everyone who saw the book was extremely impressed with its elegance and physical beauty (my self publishing had paid off). And then she said the magic words "*James, in London there are bookstores everywhere.*"

Like a wild man who had just won a million dollar lottery I got very nuts very fast. "My book overseas," I thought. "Now, that's for me, that's definitely what I want." So in my usual intense and compulsive way I made plans almost immediately. As I saw it the most feasible and financially efficient way to achieve my goal, which was to put as many of these books on England's bookstore shelves as possible as fast as I could, was to board a 747 jumbo jet and carry the books with me. Now 400 copies, understand, of an eight-by-ten-inch, two-and-a-half-pound hardcover means twenty-five good-sized cartons weighing forty pounds each. And that, plus a week's worth of clothing, was my luggage (for which I, of course, paid extra).

It was crazy, truly crazy. And I knew it. But I also loved it. It was just my style. Mind you, I could not in the least afford a disastrous monetary blunder. My first printing had already consumed my life savings, a generous loan from my brother Charles, and the peace of mind people free from debt take for granted. Moreover, I had just moved into a normal, more expensive apartment leaving at long last the closet-sized room I had, almost unbelievably, lived in for the past year while writing my book. So I honestly did not need to be wasting $1500 I did not have on a miscalculated venture to England. But I wanted my books over there—badly!

When it comes to making decisions what can one do but rely on logic, experience, wisdom, intuition, feelings, and available data? Nothing really. One must do all he or she can and then as they say, "take a shot." Having grown up in retail business and the theatre, one lesson I learned early on is that after doing one's very best the rest is, like it or not, in God's hands. Or the rest depends, if you like, upon one's luck. Idealistically, even spiritually speaking, we are responsible for and in control of every aspect of our life. Realistically however, we simply do our best and take the leap. That is just the way of things, the "Tao" of life if you will. Astrologers, however, if it is not by now thoroughly obvious, have an edge. Not an absolute edge, for the magic does not (for whatever reason) *always* work. But a very decent, formidable edge. In my case it was that particular element, the astrological edge, that was the dominant factor in deciding to follow through on an action even I knew was risky at best. But in the past sixteen months of my auspicious Saturn subperiod everything, truly everything, of significance relating to my career had gone the right way. Events and circumstances had clearly surpassed my expectations.

First of all from the moment the *bhukti* began my literary life took on a mind of its own. Seemingly complicated astrological ideas shaped themselves into proper, accessible, legible form. Phrases and expressions, often quite alien to my vocabulary, eased themselves into awareness when I squeezed my brain in a sufficiently vigorous way. As for the enormous discipline and organizational ability necessary to complete a reference text, those qualities manifested in superabundance because Saturn, whose subperiod was now underway, is the planet representing such life functions. Then, once the writing was finished and I seached for a typesetter I could not have made a more intelligent choice. The local ISKCON center (International Society for Krishna Consciousness), known for their award-winning, quality publications, charged less than commercial companies and turned out art work and a format more beautiful than I had envisioned. When I was baffled over what to do about prohibitive printing costs a friend brilliantly proposed the idea of doing the job in Hong Kong where the price would be far less. The printer there charged nearly half of what local printers asked and the quality of his work was superb. More than that, the integrity of the owner's word was absolute.

Employing this overseas printer—with whom, incidentally, I had no familiarity other than one hardcover sample of his work and three or four phone conversations—was in itself a risk and a half. For he, of course, demanded half of the payment before beginning printing and the other half the day the books left the Hong Kong docks. But, thank God and Saturn *bhukti*, it had all worked out fine. Better than fine. Indeed the previous Saturn subperiod of 1975 was beginning to lose its status as the best year of my life. This Saturn *bhukti* being more than twice as long, and so much closer to my auspicious thirty-sixth year, as the last one was now gaining the distinction. So naturally I reasoned that even if there were risks involved in bringing 400 books to England, albeit with no prior commitment on anyone's part, I still had a good chance of succeeding. There was still more than a year of Saturn *bhukti* ahead. The career credit I had earned through efforts made in previous lifetimes was still, like a healthy tree, bearing abundant fruit. So I gambled. I crossed my fingers and took a shot.

The idea that I could bring 400 copies of my book to a city, even if there were bookstores everywhere, and sell them in a week or even two, was absurd. Absurd enough that a college graduate like myself eventually figured this out before leaving America. However, by such time there was no amenable way to turn back. The plane ticket had already been purchased and was one of those nonexchangeable, nonrefundable, "you have no rights—don't even think about it" tickets. So I left and tried as much as possible (which for me is not much at all) to think as little about it as I could. Shoving twenty-five cartons in my friend Harold's van (Harold, the one who excels at heavy work) and then into the airport, then back into a rental car and into my hotel room was not the worst part. Neither was the fact that customs held my cartons for three, count them three, out of my alloted seven days in England. The worst part was that from the time it took for a bookstore salesperson to retrieve his or her manager to the time it took to complete a deal for the two or three books the manager might decide to carry an hour or more would have gone by.

Thus during the first morning in London, with 128 books in my car (the rest were in my hotel room), I acquired a very sick feeling in my gut. Only this time it was not dysentery. I spoke to some store managers to try and "sus out the situation" as the British would say. One of the very first stores I had visited was Finch's, an extremely large bookstore. That was the one store my astrology student, the stewardess who had originally brought the book to England, was almost sure would take ten copies. Though she had not spoken to the manager himself, a salesperson in the metaphysical section of the store had said that the book was so beautiful and unique that she was almost positive her boss would buy ten of them. She had also intimated that the man could be a rather "moody" person and that it would be wise to be mindful of his potential wrath.

Unfortunately for me the odds were heavily in my favor to witness exactly what the salesperson had warned about. The reason for this was that the day I arrived happened to follow a national holiday that occurred on the heels of a weekend. So, when I reached the basement of the store, where such dealings take place, there was a line of fifty eager men and women. perhaps more than fifty. I did not stay to count. Instead I left and made my way to other, smaller, stores. When I returned to Finch's for the last time (it took two return trips before the line thinned out) three or four hours had passed. By then I was tired, hungry, and disgusted at my predicament—the one I and no one else had created. I had also already witnessed the intensity of the manager's emotions and the sternness with which he could censure those around him, including people trying to sell him books. Especially people trying to sell him books.

But what did I care about upsetting his mood? Taking ten, out of 400, books off my back was not going to save my hide. Not by a long shot. So, unlike everyone else around this man who seemed to call the shots, I was not intimidated. When my turn came and I handed him a copy of Ancient Hindu Astrology, some favorable book reviews, and an advertising poster he glanced at the material and took his best shot: "I don't believe in astrology," he said as provokingly as he could. "People make their own destinies." Without the slightest hesitation I addressed the statement rather than his combativeness, which to my perception seemed to mask a rather kind-hearted nature anyway. I said, "You're right, we do make our own destinies." And I meant it. Sure astrology is real, and sure our destinies can, to whatever extent, be perceived before they occur. But at the same time we are ultimately responsible for everything, at every moment that happens to us. Spiritually speaking, there are no two ways about it; we are responsible. And I had trained spiritually for alot more years than I had trained astrologically.

Quite suddenly the man, whom I was now beginning to enjoy for his straightforwardness, took on a very different demeanor. First he called over a subordinate and directed him to take the few remaining booksellers upstairs and to keep them busy. The manager now began to speak in an extremely friendly and jovial, even somewhat intimate way. It was a welcomed relief from my highly stressful morning. Because my mind was as preoccupied as possible I do not remember much of the specifics of our conversation. But I do recall that the man started asking highly intelligent and sincere questions about astrology, my spiritual experiences, and trips to

India. And I do remember liking him for his warmth and humaness, and explaining what a silly thing I had done in bringing 400 books to England and expecting to sell them to storeowners in a week. But most of all I remember, even as if it were yesterday, a very unexpected phrase emerging from his lips. "How many books do you have in your car," he asked. "Eight cartons of sixteen to a case," I replied. "Well", he said, "pull your car up to the side of the building and then come up to my office." After this deal I would still have over 250 copies to unload but the sale to Finch's covered the cost of my plane fare. I was at least out of the dog house.

My background being what it is I had no difficulty identifying a miracle when I saw one. For all of the logical reasons the Finch's manager bought $2,000 worth of books on a subject as distinct as Hindu astrology, to my mind none of them *really* justified the act. I therefore did not search for more miracles. Having only three days left (one of which was not a working day) till my return to the States I decided to approach a book distributor and convince them to sell my work. That, anyway, had been the advice of some of the store managers I had already spoken to. When I inquired into the matter I was informed that there were two major distributors of occult and metaphysical books. One of them was in London but that information went in one ear and out the other because the man advising me said that in his opinion the best distributor was a company a few hundred miles out of town. Since the stars were in my favor and it was time for success I set my sights on what appeared the most successful company. I phoned them as soon as I could and explained my situation. They said that of course they were interested but could I please mail them the book rather than deliver it in person. Distributors rarely wish to deal with a one-title publisher. The effort and paper-work involved is not much less than what it would be for a company supplying numerous books and therefore greater profits. Thus the secretary I spoke with was well aware that the likelihood of this distributor taking on my work was extremely slim. The rejection, should it have to occur, would be far simpler by mail. Also, this particular week the decision-making executives of the company were unusually, extraspecially, "just my luck" busy!

My problem, of course, was that time was absolutely of the essence. Bringing them the book myself would take all day, leaving only one more to seek out the other distributor, should this one refuse. If I could not achieve my goal within these two days I would have to buy a brand new plane ticket, added to the further expense of another week's worth of food, rental car, and hotel which I was truly hard pressed to afford. Therefore I wanted to handle the matter quickly. So, for the opportunity to deliver my book in person that I might obtain a swift reply, I convinced the secretary that I would simply bring in the book and leave. And I was sincere. With that she said that perhaps they could allow me five minutes, assuming there were no unforeseen tragedies during the day. Gratefully, I thanked her. Cautiously, she warned me not to get my hopes up.

Kathy Halligan, a saving grace of a woman, whose boarding house I had stayed at on my way to India three years earlier, was the only human being I knew in England. Being one of those wonderful people who live only to serve others, Kathy insisted, when I asked for directions to the book distributor, that she accompany me so I would not get lost. The drive took three or four hours and was the kind that even with a native navigating caught us making wrong turns every so often. Finally when we arrived in the town of Shaftesbury, I phoned the secretary to obtain final directions as she had directed me to do. "Mr. Braha," she said obviously upset. "I thought you were coming Friday. The directors are leaving for a meeting in ten minutes. You'd better get here immediately!" I did.

The meeting was amazing. The chief director seemed instantly to fall in love with my book (the English can do that). He said he had been wanting a text on Hindu astrology for some time now. But, unfortunately, every time he had come across one the quality had been poor and the writing unreadable. He pressed me for an exclusive to sell the book everywhere outside the United States, especially India. I agreed—happily. And felt joyous relief that I would not have to carry seventeen cartons of books back to America. We shook hands and the deal was done. It was thrilling. It was also quite a heady feeling to know that my knowledge, opinions, and convictions would very soon be reaching astrologers all around the globe. Things could not have worked out better. There was only one slight, bothersome hitch, which I revealed to no one, not even to Kathy who appeared even happier than I did over the events of the day. Each time the director mentioned India and how that country might be our best customer I winced.

Of course I was confident about my book. I loved it, knew it was great, and even made a regular routine of thanking God for having it appear that I had something to do with the fact. But Indian astrologers could, with very little effort, be my harshest critics! I was after all playing on their turf. As traditional and conservative a book as I had written there was no way to avoid stating hundreds of personal opinions and conclusions. An astrological reference text filled with specific interpretations is, after all is said and done, mainly the result of an author/astrologer's personal and practical experience. At least that is what the book is *if it is of any value.* Because in India the heavenly language is learned mainly through the writings of ancient sages and seers it is considered a relatively audacious act to write a text on the subject. If it is audacious for Indians, what should be said about an outsider muscling in? One part of me adored the idea of my work reaching a land as distant as India. I had for some time now wanted fame. Indeed, had I not always dreamed of playing in the majors—astrologizing with the "big boys?" I had. But this was scary. In any case there was clearly nothing to do but keep quiet and hope for the best. Certainly I had no intention of spoiling the director's fun. Here he was solving my dilemma and doing it in a way that would fulfill my dreams of so many previous years. So I kept my thoughts to myself.

Although the directors were indeed on their way to a meeting when we arrived they went late and apologized intently that they could not spend more than the half-hour we enjoyed together. As Kathy and I went outside to retrieve the 250 books, the director dashed briskly to his car to leave. Then suddenly he stopped, turned around and came over, and heartily thanked me for allowing his company to distribute my book. It was grand. All of my life luck had been such a damned scarce commodity. Now, despite any of my strangest "Brahilian" actions, it seemed I could do nothing wrong. I thought to myself, "Everyone, once in his or her life, should have a Saturn *bhukti* like mine."

The next six or eight months, believe it or not, was a fairly depressing time. Though I was praised for my work and it was loved even in India (a distributor there was negotiating to buy 500 copies, which to me was the ultimate validation) psychological changes were occurring. People began treating me differently, with more respect and occasionally with awe, which took some getting used to. My family, none of whom could understand my book since it is written for astrologers, began to perceive me as a serious intellect rather than merely their new age, counter-culture loved one. And that, even though far more acceptable consciously, was in a subtle way disconcerting. There was an adjustment to make. Also, I had achieved something of a lifelong goal and nothing, really, had changed. I had finally gained the fame I wanted (not to be "street recognizable" but to have a bit of an influence—to make a genuine difference) and life was in fact not very different. I was still me, still innately shy, socially stiff, extremely kind, as spiritual as ever, and still basically a loner (or shall I say overly sensitive).

During the nine months of my writing I had gone to sleep each night with the distinct thought that if I did nothing else with my life but make Hindu astrology available to Western astrologers that I could, when the time would arrive, die a happy man. Content that I had accomplished something worthwhile, that I had contributed my share. One part of me had known I was to be successful. It was obvious. Another part of me could not believe I would ever wind up with a published book in hand. With my lack of literary training and a background in theatre and mysticism there just was not great evidence for such a reality. Success in the endeavor therefore lived for me as a remarkable feat, a victory over an almost impossible task. Now that the future had arrived and I had won, had beaten the odds and made my mark, why was everything still the same? I had expected something else. This hurt. Now I knew what George Bernard Shaw meant when he wrote, "There are two tragedies in life. One is not to get your heart's desire. The other is to get it." At any rate I gave thanks that I had never craved real stardom, realizing that the crash of achieving that might be horrendous, and contemplated the strangeness of human existence. I also kicked myself a few times for not having realized that the greatest joy had been in the work, in the struggle to succeed, rather than the results—the praise and favorable book reviews. Who, after all, should have known this better than a student of mysticism?

Added to these "downer" influences was the question of what to do next. Sure the astrological critics and reviewers thought I was some wonderful writer to disentangle the complications of Hindu astrology and present it in understandable form for Westerners. But I, of course, knew better. I just had God and Saturn *bhukti* on my side! Now that I had completed this endeavor, which all along caught me feeling like I was in the midst of a "huge karma," a predestined, unalterable event designed by the *real* powers that be, where did this leave me? So instead of feeling great gratitude to have had, for once, a hand in something beyond my own petty existence I feared my future would never exceed, or even equal, my present. I had recently received a letter from Robert Hand, one of the most famous, prolific, and successful authors of professional Western astrology books alive. A terribly brilliant man and one for whom I had, for years, nothing but tremendous admiration. While scores of astrological reference texts sit on my bookshelves the really worn ones can be counted on two hands. Several of them are Robert Hand's tomes. In his desire to support my book he sent a letter with comments I could use for the bookjacket of future printings. He generously wrote: "This book is not only the best introduction to Hindu astrology that there is, it is a superbly written astrology book in its own right." And then, at the end of his kind and lengthy communication, especially for a man with his schedule, he wrote, "I think you may have written something of a masterpiece here. I look forward to more of the same from you."

Masterpiece. More of the same. I loved the masterpiece part. As for the "more of the same" business I wanted very badly to think the man was crazy. Just who was he to have the nerve to expect more masterpieces, as if such work grew on trees; as if such a phenomenon was actually within my conscious control? The answer was that he was Robert Hand, the Western world's foremost astrologer/author. He was the man whom for years I had respected, admired, and learned from. He was also someone who had been interpreting the heavenly language for more than twenty-five years. If he expected more work like this from me, then in my mind he had a damned good right.

A Second Book

I had an idea. An idea for another book. It was something I had been thinking about for a long, long time. The thing to do was to address, head on, the problem of society's ignorance and terrible misconceptions of astrology. Unfortunately, every time I sat down to write, difficult business in its own right for me, I was possessed by an awful occurrence which, not being a writer, I had only heard about. It is what is called "writer's block." No matter how hard I tried I simply could not set down in writing what existed in my heart and mind. Indeed I could not yet even discover a schema, an organizational format and plan, within literary boundaries suitable to my intention. As weeks drifted into months and the "block" continued so did my attempts at writing. I spent many tedious hours and many tedious days. I did not get far but so what? What else was there to do? So what if the idea took a long time to formulate—five months for an introduction and foreword (the foreword eventually being deleted!)? If I had learned anything from completing my first book it was that there is, ultimately, nowhere to go and nowhere to get to. So I was relatively patient, considering my intense nature.

Perhaps the most worrisome factor was what a writing teacher I had met at a local restaurant said to me one night. Thrilled at having run into an actual writer, and a teacher at that, I inquired as to just what this writer's block was all about. He, not knowing that I was a nonwriter who had just finished a first book, nonchalantly said, "There's really no such thing as writer's block. That only happens to people who write one book in their life." "Oh Lord," I thought and asked, "Why is that?" He replied, "Certain people have one book inside of them which has been waiting a lifetime to come out. When that's over so is their creativity." "Well it's a good thing that doesn't pertain to me," I joked to myself, "I have Mercury, well aspected and as ruler of the second and fifth houses, posited in the sixth space. Shastri distinctly declared that I would write some books. He did not say one book, he said *some books*." So I did my best to ignore the writer's words. Willfully, I returned home and "blocked" at my typewriter for more days and weeks. I was, however, still in Saturn *bhukti* and would be for another eight or ten months. So nature and the odds were still, I figured, heavily in my favor.

By the time the writer's block decided to knock itself off and allow me to see that an autobiographical approach was a perfectly workable starting place, I had just barely turned thirty-five years old. This meant I was finally beginning my auspicious thirty-sixth year, the year I might begin to locate and embrace my professional "niche" in life. Gaining fame and creating an impact had already begun some few months earlier when my book reached metaphysical bookstores around the world. That occurrence was more a result, or validation, of Saturn *bhukti*, the subperiod, than anything else. But now what was happening was something different. Something truly profound and clearly the result of reaching my thirty-sixth year, the year Saturn and everything it represents in my particular Hindu birthchart would mature. Quite plainly, I was experiencing a quantum leap in relation to my *dharma*, my duty and life's work. I finally began to realize exactly what I wished to contribute and accomplish with the language of the heavens. Not just in a general, vague, or obscure way but *exactly*.

Thankfully, for one who has had so many different careers, it was something at which I could spend, God only knows, the rest of my life doing. The stronger the understanding of this *dharma* became the more frequently I would hear Padia's steadfast reply to my career

241

questions echo in my brain: "Not until your thirty-sixth year, James. Your career begins after your thirty-sixth year." Indeed now Saturn's integrating effect was occurring and it was coinciding with a life commitment so specific that if I ever again complained about my *dharma* I deserved to be tarred and feathered. Mine was a huge commitment that seemed to have existed in the depths of my being for all of eternity, but of which in the past I had only been partially aware. The intention was to clarify for the public, the masses, indeed for next door neighbors everywhere, the miraculous language of the stars that exists for all as a *natural birthright* (in the truest sense of the word). And at the same time to make available the highest quality birthchart interpretations possible, which in my mind means having astrologers employ both methods, Hindu and Western, for blueprint readings. Like this, in my thirty-sixth year I had found, as Padia predicted, everything I had been seeking professionally. In this arena I had at last come home. It was far more fulfilling than simply gaining recognition.

During my writer's block, I found myself sitting in a spiritual seminar of sorts with Emmett (the one with great expenses). Emmett and I have been best friends since as far back as I can remember. We have acted in plays together, shared apartments during college, gone into business, taught meditation, engaged in week-long fasts and all kinds of evolutionary diets. The one subject we have not shared with real intensity, oddly enough, is astrology, the great passion of my life and that which gives meaning to my existence. Emmett, you see, does not speak the language. So although we often speak *about* astrology, we do not really share it. Emmett, like most people, is just not that much interested. As my mind wandered from the lecturer's words I tried to discern the reason for my friend's apathy and to discover whether there was any way to influence the situation. Not only for him but for those like him. Immediately I was confronted by the realization that in today's society there is almost no reason whatever to take interest in astrology. The fact is that at present there is almost no way for anyone, *other than those who already interpret the language*, to gain an accurate view of what astrology is and what it is not. It is not so much that the discipline has been poorly presented; it is that it has not been presented at all, not successfully and so all could hear. If a presentation has ever been made it must, I assume, have occurred thousands of years ago, when the knowledge became public. Now unfortunately, because of centuries of misuse, exploitation, and amateurish practice astrology is unquestionably a prisoner of its own thoroughly defamed reputation.

As my thoughts continued I contemplated what one could do to create an interest, not an interest but an opening—a receptivity, towards the possibilities, potentials, and basics of the heavenly language. How could one introduce a fair and accurate view of the subject that the recipient could hear, without ear-piercing past impressions bursting forth in the mind? To my mind there was only one answer: change the name. Change the name so people, at the very least, would be guided to a clean slate, a relative openess. Control the quality of birthchart interpretations, train astrologers to use both methodologies, speak intelligently on the subject, and drop the bloody, and I mean bloody—even suffocating, name: astrology. Let that word mean what the masses already take it to mean: the nonsense in the newspapers, the Sun sign business, and the work of gypsies and charlatans. Present the language of the heavens for what it is: a language of nature—of life itself, conveying destiny, purpose, psychological behavioral patterns, ways of being, and cycles of becoming. Control the quality of the work with a vengeance and enjoy the rebirth and development of a beautiful paradigm as old as Methuselah. Renaming astrology: the problem is huge, the task enormous. But perhaps that is not the drawback. Perhaps that is the fun.

Thus ends Chapter Four of the book *Astro-Logos, Language of Life*. For some readers this could be, at least for a while, the end of the line regarding our relationship. What you have just read has been a truthful account of how one man, through listening to the language of life, self actualized a significant aspect of his existence. The narrative has included a smattering of teachings presented, I hope, in a more than enjoyable form. The following material, take heed, is not at all of the same nature. Nor should it be. What we are engaged in is a revolution: an overthrowing of present conditions, a war against ignorance in a designated field. Revolutions are not pretty—especially to authority figures and those set in their ways. But they are sometimes necessary, even crucial. We are renaming an old discipline and charting a new course. We are declaring war against present powers and taking matters into our own hands. This is a starting from scratch with nothing, save purity of heart, balanced intellect, resolve of will, and a relentless commitment to the benefit of individual human life. The responsibility is great. In fact it is everything. There is almost nothing to lose and a new world to gain. In the words of Santhanam: "It is not a joke."

BOOK II
Workbook

CHAPTER V

WORKBOOK
PARTICIPATION

The following pages are for those who wish to partake of an Astro-Logos™ birthchart session. Until certified practitioners are available in local areas, interpretations can be done by telephone. Sessions will be tape recorded for your benefit.

For further information please send a self-addressed, stamped envelope to:

ASTRO-LOGOS
P.O. BOX 22-1961
Hollywood, Florida 33022-1961
Name –
Phone –

Please Include Birth Data
    Date –
    Local time –
    Place –
    Source of data (mother, birth certificate, etc.) –

QUESTIONNAIRE

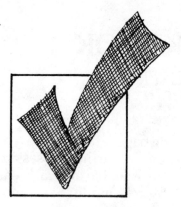

The following questionnaire will aid you in using your Astro-Logos™ session valuably. Please ponder the questions for a few days before answering them. This sheet must be completed before the birthchart interpretation session. These questions may be referred to by your interpreter. They may also bring up issues you will want to discuss at the *start* of your meeting.

1) What is your immediate reason for this consultation?

_____

2) In order to utilize the star language to its fullest one should have a strong intention to gain value. What do you specifically intend to gain? In other words what areas of your life do you expect to influence? _____

3) Increased clarity and intellectual understanding is a powerful benefit of the Astro-Logos process. However, this is not the final goal. Generally the knowledge realized is the basis for future actions, which lead to greater fulfillment and happiness. Would you be willing to undertake new activity in your life based upon revelations of your birthchart that match your own intuitive and instinctive reality? Are you willing to take action even in

the face of struggle or the possibility of short-term failure? Please answer with as much certainty as possible. Any further questions or comments? _____

4) What do you consider your dream in life to be? What passions, accomplishments, and desires did you fantasize about as a child? If you suddenly became a billionaire how would you spend your years? _____

5) Issues of a sensitive or emotional nature sometimes arise during interpretive sessions. Are you willing to discuss such matters if they come up? Any questions or comments? _____

6) It is generally through responsibility, the act of perceiving oneself as the cause of all aspects of one's life, that a person gains a degree of power and mastery over the conditions of personal existence. Therefore in dealing with troublesome areas of your life the job of the Astro-Logos practioner is to support you in understanding your part in the creation of any such difficulties. Are you willing to inquire deeply into matters you would like to improve from the viewpoint of self responsibility? Any questions or comments? _____

7) Are you aware that planets and stars do not necessarily cause anything but are symbols of a language conveying direction, likelihood of experience, and inbred ways of behaving? Do you realize that although interpreters often predict events or scenarios accurately that the practice is not absolute fortune telling? Any questions or comments? _____

8) The star language in its entirety is a vast system of intense complexity. Even without the possibility of free will no interpreter is likely to achieve absolute predictive perfection. Therefore the only sane way to approach a birthchart session is with as much common sense and discrimination as possible. Are you willing to be responsible for that? Are you willing to remain genuinely

open to the interpreter's findings while at the same time maintaining healthy skepticism to interpretive elements that contradict your instincts? Finally, will you rely on your own life convictions and consciously make up your own mind as to which details of the interpretive session you will allow to influence your life? _____

9) What do you believe would make you happy? _____

10) Everyone generally wishes to contribute something in life. What do you feel is your contribution? What, if anything else, would you like to contribute? _____

11) What kind of activities would you need to be doing and what kind of success would you have to have in order to conclude that your life makes a difference—a difference to you and to others? _____

The Twelve Spaces

THE FIRST SPACE

The first space of your birthchart represents, or relates to, the following areas of your life.

- the personal self, ego
- appearance, face, head
- character, disposition, tendencies, conduct
- will power
- dignity, self-esteem, confidence (Hindu system)
- ability to be recognized, fame, etc.
- birth, early childhood, start in life
- vitality

During your Astro-Logos interpretive session the first house will be analyzed and explained as it describes the state of your affairs regarding these issues. Please place a checkmark next to any concerns you would like extra help or clarification on. Contemplate your present ways of behaving in these areas and how you would ideally like to function.

251

It is not necessary to memorize all the various meanings of the first space. However, it is important to grasp that this part of your blueprint (along with certain other features) "corresponds" to your success and behavior in these realms. The birthchart is a symbolic map of the heavens at the moment you took birth. It represents nature's announcement of the purpose and destiny of any of its progeny created at that time; in this case—you.

NOTE—Attributes of the houses in the Western system are not always the same as those of the Hindu system. For the sake of Western astrologers, those that vary are indicated in parenthesis.

THE SECOND SPACE

The second space of your birthchart represents, or relates to, the following areas of your life.
• money, wealth, finances
• values
• knowledge, education, educators (Hindu system)
• orators, poets (Hindu system)
• truthfulness, tendency to lie (Hindu system)
• imagination (Hindu system)
• family life, domestic happiness (Hindu system)
• food one eats (Hindu system)
• dress (Hindu system)

THE THIRD SPACE

The third space of your birthchart represents, or relates to, the following areas of your life.

• the lower mind (Western system)
• brothers and sisters
• communications, journals, writings
• relatives (Western system)

- travel (short journeys)
- education (Western system)
- courage (Hindu system)
- ability to fulfill daily desires
- fine arts of music, dance, and drama (Hindu system)
- actors, directors, producers, (Hindu system)
- hearing in right ear (Hindu system)
- energy, enthusiasm, excitement

THE FOURTH SPACE

The fourth space of your birthchart represents, or relates to, the following areas of your life.

- mother
- family and home life (Western system)
- real estate and other fixed assets
- endings of all matters
- homes
- happiness (Hindu system)
- jewelry and other luxuries (Hindu system)
- the heart, emotions and passions (Hindu system)
- cars, boats, planes (Hindu system)
- academic degree (Hindu system)

THE FIFTH SPACE

The fifth space of your birthchart represents, or relates to, the following areas of your life.

- children, childbearing
- arts, creativity, self-expression (Western system)
- speculation, investments, gambling
- love affairs
- play and amusement
- intelligence and mind (Hindu system)
- rewards or credit due from previous lifetimes (Hindu system)
- government, rulers, politicians (Hindu system)
- religious-mindedness, morals (Hindu system)
- spiritual techniques, mantras, hypnotism (Hindu system)
- sports (Hindu system)

THE SIXTH SPACE

The sixth space of your birthchart represents, or relates to, the following areas of your life.

- health
- daily work
- service
- self-improvement
- pets
- ability to defeat enemies and competitors (Hindu system)

- appetite (Hindu system)
- doctors and nurses
- litigations, tendency to be charged in court cases

THE SEVENTH SPACE

The seventh space of your birthchart represents, or relates to, the following areas of your life.

- married life
- the spouse
- all partners
- sexual passions (Hindu system)
- residence in foreign countries (Hindu system)
- lawsuits

THE EIGHTH SPACE

The eighth space of your birthchart represents, or relates to, the following areas of your life.

- length of life
- sexual experiences (Western system)
- virility and sexual vitality (Hindu system)
- reproductive system
- death
- mysticism
- wills and legacies
- money from unearned means, insurance companies, lotteries, etc.
- occult subjects, intuition, psychic ability

THE NINTH SPACE

The ninth space of your birthchart represents, or relates to, the following areas of your life.

- religion and philosophy
- travel (long journeys)
- law
- higher mind (Western system)
- luck and solutions to problems (Hindu system)
- associations with foreigners
- the father (Hindu system)
- gurus
- higher knowledge

THE TENTH SPACE

The tenth space of your birthchart represents, or relates to, the following areas of your life.

- career, professional activities
- dharma
- fame, status
- holy pilgrimages (Hindu system)
- government officials

THE ELEVENTH SPACE

The eleventh space of your birthchart represents, or relates to, the following areas of your life.

- friends and groups
- major goals and dreams in life
- eldest sibling (Hindu system)
- opportunities

- gains and profits (Hindu system)
- supplemental monies

THE TWELFTH SPACE

The twelfth space of your birthchart represents, or relates to, the following areas of your life.

- expenses (Hindu system)
- moksha—enlightenment (Hindu system)
- self-undoing
- karma from past lives (Western system)
- hospitals and monasteries
- sexual pleasures (Hindu system)
- hidden enemies
- which of the seven planes of existence one goes to after death (Hindu system)
- travel to remote foreign lands (Hindu system)
- hearing—the left ear (Hindu system)
- vision—the left eye (Hindu system)

Personally Prescribed Gemstones

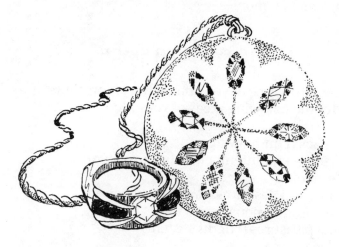

The Hindus have employed gemstones to alleviate discordant birthchart effects for thousands of years. The way this is done is to ascertain which planets in a blueprint are afflicted and then wear the stone corresponding to that element. The result is said to be a "strengthening" of the affairs represented by the planet and a reduction of negative influence in the life. However, care must be used in prescribing gems. Strengthening some features in a chart (malefic houses or planets) can cause certain harm to an individual. During your Astro-Logos session stones will be prescribed to help alleviate negative effects and adverse periods likely to occur. Gems that create greater confidence, harmony, and benefit in your life, whether needed or not, will also be advised.

The ideal size of the gemstones is two carats or more. However, smaller stones will most definitely have good effects. It is best if gems can be set in rings, bracelets, or necklaces, such that they slightly touch the skin. Choose quality over size.

The following information is given only as a point of

interest. It is not necessary to memorize or even comprehend the material. Gems will be prescribed for you by
an experienced practitioner.
*Note—Western astrologers are cautioned not to apply these
prescriptions for use within Western delineations.*

The gem for the Sun is red ruby.
The gem for the Moon is pearl or moonstone.
The gem for Mars is red coral.
The gem for Mercury is green emerald.
The gem for Jupiter is yellow sapphire or yellow topaz.
The gem for Venus is diamond.
The gem for Saturn is blue sapphire.
The gem for Rahu (North node) is gomed or hessonite
    (honey colored form of garnet).
The gem for Ketu (South node) is cat's eye or chrys-
    oberyl (not tiger's eye).

SOME RULES REGARDING GEMSTONES

It is traditional for individuals to always wear what is
known as the "birthstone." This is the gem representing
the planet connected to the (Hindu chart) ascendant. It
specifically increases confidence, vitality, and the ability
to be recognized and promoted in life.

Aries ascendant (Mars) wears red coral entire life.
Taurus ascendant (Venus) wears diamond entire life.
Gemini ascendant (Mercury) wears green emerald en-
    tire life.
Cancer ascendant (Moon) wears pearls or moonstone
    entire life.
Leo ascendant (Sun) wears red ruby entire life.
Virgo ascendant (Mercury) wears green emerald entire
    life.
Libra ascendant (Venus) wears diamond entire life.

Scorpio ascendant (Mars) wears red coral entire life.

Sagittarius ascendant (Jupiter) wears yellow sapphire or yellow topaz entire life.

Capricorn ascendant (Saturn) wears blue sapphire entire life.

Aquarius ascendant (Saturn) wears blue sapphire entire life.

Pisces ascendant (Jupiter) wears yellow sapphire or yellow topaz entire life.

Note—The ascendant is *not* the same as the Sun sign. It is the first space of the blueprint and is determined by the time and place of one's birth. Furthermore, the stones mentioned are for the ascendants of the Hindu chart only, not the Western one. Take heed.

DASAS AND BHUKTIS

One may always wear the gemstone corresponding to the *dasa* planet. However, unless specifically advised otherwise that stone should be removed upon termination of the period.

During Sun *dasa* wear red ruby.

During Moon *dasa* wear pearls or moonstone.

During Mars *dasa* wear red coral.

During Mercury *dasa* wear green emerald.

During Jupiter *dasa* wear yellow sapphire or yellow topaz.

During Venus *dasa* wear diamond.

During Saturn *dasa* wear blue sapphire.

During Rahu *dasa* wear gomed or hessonite.

During Ketu *dasa* wear cat's eye or chrysoberyl.

Jargon

Interpreters of birthcharts often use blueprint language, technical terms, with even the most inexperienced clients. This is not done unconsciously. It is an attempt to convey to you the basis for, or the reasoning of, the detailed statements and explanations being made about your life. The human mind learns, and constantly functions, by analogy. For example, when approaching a new parking space we do not first measure the actual length and width of the car and the space and then deduce whether the car will fit or not. We merely analogize that since the space resembles previous ones that fit the car, this one shall most likely do the same.

Analogy, in all aspects of our lives, is extremely useful. It is especially so in the birthchart interpretive process since the blueprint is a "symbolic mirror" of a person's life. Therefore, the surest way to communicate the deepest essence and meaning of part of one's destiny or makeup is sometimes to simply take that person through the interpretive process of the particular birthchart element involved. By doing so an additional way of explanation, and a most powerful one at that, is produced. Another vital reason for using star language terms is that the symbols of the system are extraordinarily rich in significance. The oral expression of one simple representation may conjure up innumerable meanings, images, and impressions if not in the conscious mind then certainly within the sub- or superconscious. Expect to hear tidbits of birthchart language during your Astro-Logos session whether the terms are familiar to you or not.

Listed below are some common phrases of the star language. They need not be analyzed or studied. However, if by glancing over this material you can bring even the slightest awareness of their meanings to your session you will be that much more an active participant in the interpretive process.

Afflicted: a negative or adverse condition of a birthchart element. If a particular feature is "afflicted" then the affairs it represents or corresponds to *in your life* are harmed. For example, if Mercury in your chart is "afflicted," then you most likely have problems with speech and communications.

Well disposed: a positive or beneficial condition of a birthchart element. If a certain feature is "well disposed," then the affairs it represents *in your life* are favorable. For instance, if Venus in your chart is "well disposed," then you most likely have enjoyable and beneficial love relationships.

Strong or powerful: same as well disposed.

Weak or devastated: same as afflicted.

Aspects: aspects are spacial relationships between different planets within the birthchart. These relationships can be either positive or negative.

Good aspect: two planets in a beneficial relationship to

each other. Causes both planets to be "well disposed." The affairs those planets represent in your life are thus rendered favorable.

Bad aspect: two planets in a negative relationship, thus causing difficulties in the areas of your life which they symbolize.

Benefic: a planet is considered benefic if the affairs it represents are of a generally fortunate nature. Venus, which is the significator of love, wealth, and beauty is a typical benefic.

Malefic: a planet that symbolizes the more serious, challenging features of life. Saturn, which reveals one's sense of restrictiveness and discipline, is a natural malefic.

Fallen: a very bad condition for a planet to be in. Means the planet is "afflicted."

Exalted: a very good condition for a planet to be in. Means the planet is well disposed.

Dasa: (pronounced dasha) a period of time during which one's life corresponds to the representations of a particular planet. For example in a twenty-year Venus period a person is likely to experience more sensitivity, romance, and artistic endeavors. During a nineteen-year Saturn *dasa* the focus is on more serious, disciplined concerns such as career and worldly accomplishment. Explanations of *dasas* become more specific as relating to each individual's birthchart.

Bhukti: (pronounced bookti) a subperiod within a *dasa*. There are nine *bhuktis* within each *dasa* period revealing more detailed data about each year or two, etc.

Retrograde planet: Occasionally planets appear, from our viewpoint, to move backwards. This occurrence is called retrograde motion and is significant in birthchart analysis.

Natal: refers to the birthchart; the chart which is calculated based upon one's exact (or near exact) time of birth.

Transits: a predictive technique based upon the effects of the *current* daily motion of planets in the sky on positions in the natal, or birthly, chart.

Progressions: a predictive technique whereby the positions of the planets each day after birth reveal information about the corresponding year of life. For instance, the planetary positions approximately thirty days after a person's birth express the conditions of existence for the thirtieth year of life.

Ascendant: the sign of the first space, or house, of the birthchart is called the ascendant. Relates to a person's tendencies, disposition, and personality.

The Sun: the representative element of the star language symbolizing power, ego, authority, the soul, father, etc.

Your Sun: the zodiac position and birthchart condition of the Sun at the moment of your birth. Indicates your power, your ego, your father, your soul, your sense of authority, etc.

The Moon: the representative element indicating emotions, mother, females, breasts, the public, comfortableness, etc.

Your Moon: the condition and zodiac position of the Moon at the moment you took birth. Conveys your emotional nature, your mother, females in your life, your sense of comfortableness, your public life, etc.

Mercury: represents intelligence, speaking ability, nervous system, writings and communications, education, etc.

Your Mercury: indicates your intelligence, your speech, your nervous system, your communicative ability, etc.

Your Venus: corresponds to your experience of love matters, married life, wealth and prosperity, beauty, artistic ability, happiness, etc.

Your Mars: describes your agressiveness or lack of it, your sex drive, courage, mechanical or technical ability, talent in sports, temper, strength, etc.

Your Jupiter: corresponds to your religious and philosophical nature; long distance travel; wisdom, luck, and opportunity; wealth and fortune; gurus; etc.

Your Saturn: represents your conservatism, sense of discipline, restrictiveness, perfectionest tendencies, difficulties and challenges, leadership, longevity, etc.

The Responsibility of the Client— Gaining Value

Individuals interested in consulting their blueprint of destiny, which is for most people today a delving into new and uncharted territory, should fully understand that such actions are, *whether realized or not*, serious business. Entering this domain, even as a client, is more like signing up for a rigorous physical workout than boarding a cruise ship for the weekend, as a friend of mine once very aptly put it. What shows up in birthcharts are all sorts of challenges, demands, talents, abilities, problems, possibilities and favorable seasons to take advantage of. How can this be anything but a serious and "quintessential to life" undertaking? It cannot. Stepping into this arena, this detailed map and schedule of one's existence, even though perhaps done to ascertain very specific insights and information, is bound to open up new concerns and affairs previously unaddressed, dormant, or unrecognized. Like a child on the way to a library to gain some particular bit of knowledge who is soon to be overwhelmed by the incredible amount of books there are on other subjects, so it is with the potentials and details of our lives.

In an Astro-Logos interpretation session what transpires is not merely a presentation of interesting and somewhat useful information. What happens is a dialogue, a working conversation between two individuals both committed to correcting whatever misunderstandings of life the client may possess and to that person's gaining an experience of greater capability in future existence. But this does not occur by the practitioner's intention alone. It is the definite and prescribed task of the client to treat the session as such. At the same time the recipient must utilize the practioner not just as an interpreter and speaker but as a kind of intermittent counselor and committed listener; as someone who cares and is dedicated and willing to discuss finding appropriate and suitable options to whatever areas of life are in need of regeneration. It is, then, the client's responsibility to intend at the outset to gain real and lasting value from a session.

Clearly it is in a person's best interest to invest something of oneself, over and above the time and money, into the birthchart interpretation experience. Apart from how the custodians of this great field of knowledge have failed over the centuries, it has been the recipients' lack of personal commitment to *their* star language interpretive experiences that has perpetuated the subject's superficial use and disallowed its proper functioning. What this has amounted to is individuals relinquishing their discriminative powers and common sense and approaching the star language simplistically. This must end. Clients must no longer consider this work absolute fortune telling and interpreters of the language all-knowing, magical seers. There is much to be gained from the interpretation of one's life blueprint. But, we can only get out of something what we put in. More, much more, benefit occurs when the client actively and committedly participates in the Astro-Logos process. This extends even beyond maintaining the proper attitude in the birthchart session. It includes possessing a rudimentary (extremely rudimentary) knowledge of the mechanics of the interpretive process, the terms of which have been constantly mentioned throughout this book (the symbolism of the blueprint houses, and some concept of the representative meanings of the planets, Sun, and Moon).

In a traditional master-disciple relationship so much is gained by blindly and faithfully accepting the master's dictates. But actually the greater growth occurs when seekers gain for themselves a conscious and intelligent understanding of the whys and wherefores of the evolutionary process and the necessary behavior towards such end. For one can then embrace and own up, quite organically, to one's responsibilities. In every field of endeavor it is by virtue of personal responsibility, the act of perceiving oneself as cause, that evolution and benefit take place. So it is with Astro-Logos.

Chanting Astrological Mantras

Mantras are Sanskrit sounds or phrases, the effects of which (when chanted) are beneficial. They are used, like gemstones, to alleviate birthchart afflictions indicative of specific life difficulties. For those willing to spend fifteen or twenty minutes a day chanting, the appropriate mantras and pronunciations and procedures will be prescribed during your Astro-Logos session.

1) MANTRA FOR THE SUN—to be chanted 7,000 times (not necessarily in one sitting).

Japa   kusuma-saṅkaśaṁ   kaśyapeyaṁ mahā-dyutim
tamo-riṁ sarva-pāpa-ghnaṁ
 pranato 'smi divākaram

PRONUNCIATION

Japa koosooma sankarsham kashya-peeyam maha-jutim, tamorim sarva pahpagnam pranato smee deevahkaram.

Let us chant the glories of the Sun, whose beauty rivals that of a flower. I salute the greatly effulgent son of *Kasayapa* who is the enemy of darkness, and destroyer of all sins.

2) MANTRA FOR THE MOON—to be chanted 11,000 times.

> *dadhi-śaṅkha-tuṣārabhaṁ*
> *kṣīrodarnava-sambhavam*
> *namāmi śaśinaṁ somaṁ*
> *sambhor mukuta-bhūṣanaṃ*

PRONUNCIATION

Dadee shanka tusha-rabam ksheero darnava sambhavam na-mahmee shasheenam somam samboor mookuta booshanam.

I offer my obeisances to the Moon, whose complexion resembles curds, the whiteness of conch shells, and snow. He is the ruling deity of the *soma—rasa*, born from the Ocean of Milk and he serves as the ornament on top of the head of *Lord S'ambhu*.

Note: In the mantra translations the "feminine" planets (Moon and Venus) are referred to as "he" or "him." This is simply the way of the Hindus.

3) MANTRA FOR MARS—to be chanted 10,000 times.

> *dharanī-gharbha-sambhūtaṁ—*
> *vidyut-kānti-samaprabha*
> *kumāraṁ śákti-hastaṁ ca*
> *mangalaṁ pranamāmy aham*

Daranee garbha sambootam vidyut-kahntee sama-prabam koomahram shaktee hastam-cha mangalam prana-mam mya-ham.

I offer my obeisances to *Sri Mangala*, deity of the planet Mars, who was born from the womb of the earth goddess. His brilliant effulgence is like that of lightning, and he appears as a youth carrying a spear in his hand.

4) MANTRA FOR MERCURY — to be chanted 4,000 times.

priyaṅgava-gulikaśyaṁ
  rūpeṇa pratimāmbudam
saumyaṁ saumya-guṇopetaṁ
  taṁ budhaṁ praṇamamy aham

PRONOUNCIATION

Preeyangava guleekash yam roopeyna prateemahm budam, sowmyam sowmya goono-peytam tam boodam prana-mahm mya-ham.

I salute *Buddha*, deity of the planet Mercury, whose face is like a fragrant globe of the *priyangu* herb and whose beauty matches that of a lotus flower. He is most gentle, possessing all attractive qualities.

5) MANTRA FOR JUPITER — to be chanted 19,000 times.

devānāṁ ca rsīnāṁ ca
  guruṁ kañcana-sannibham
buddhi-bhūtaṁ tri-lokeśaṁ
  taṁ namāmi bṛhaspatim

PRONUNCIATION

Deva-nancha rishee-nancha gurum-kanchana saneebam boodee bootam treelo-keysham tam namamee brihas-pateem.

I salute *Brhaspati*, deity of the planet Jupiter. He is the spiritual master of all the demigods and sages. His complexion is golden and he is full of intelligence. He is the controller of all three worlds.

6) MANTRA FOR VENUS — to be chanted 16,000 times.

hima-kunda-mṛnalābham
  daityānām paramaṁ gurum
sarva-śāstra-pravaktāraṁ
  bhārgavaṁ praṇamāmy aham

PRONUNCIATION

Heema-kunda mri-nala-bam deyt-yanam para-mam gurum sarva-shastra pravak-taram barga-vam prana-mam mya-ham.

I offer my obeisances to the descendant of *Bhrigu Muni* (Venus), whose complexion is white like a pond covered with ice. He is the supreme spiritual master of the demoniac enemies of the demigods and has spoken to them all the revered scriptures.

7) MANTRA FOR SATURN — to be chanted 23,000 times.

nīlāñjana-samabhasaṁ
ravi-putraṁ yamāgrajam
chaya-mārtāṇḍa-sambhūtaṁ
tam namāmi śanaiścaram

PRONUNCIATION

Nee-lanjana sama-basam ravee-putram yema-grajam chaya-martanda sam-bootam tam na-mahmee sanee-charam.

I salute slow moving Saturn, whose complexion is dark blue like *nilanjana* ointment. He is the elder brother of Lord *Yamaraja* born from the Sun-deity and his wife *Chaya*.

8) MANTRA FOR *RAHU* — to be chanted 18,000 times.

ardha-kāyaṁ maha-vīryaṁ
candrāditya-vimardanam
siṁhikā-garbha-sambhūtam
taṁ rāhum praṇamāmy aham

Arda-kayam maha-viryam chandra ditya veemar-danam seeng-hee-ka garba sambootam tam rahum prana-mam mya-ham.

I offer my obeisances to *Rahu*, born from the womb of *Simhika*, who has only half a body yet possesses great power, being able to subdue the Sun and Moon.

9) MANTRA FOR KETU—to be chanted 17,000 times.

palasa-puspa-sankasam
taraka-graha-mastakam
raudram raudratmakam ghoram
tam ketum pranamamy aham

PRONUNCIATION

palasha-aushpa-sankasam taraka-grahu masta-kam rowdram row-drat makam goram tam keytoom prana-mam mya-ham.

I offer my obeisances to the violent and fearsome *Ketu*, who is endowed with the potency of Lord Shiva. Resembling in his complexion the flower of a palasa plant, he serves as the head of the stars and planets.

How to Use Astro-Logos:
Faith, Action, and a Lifelong Relationship

To succeed in anything one must have faith—much of it. For faith is what keeps one going in the face of obstacles and adversities. Those who possess the gift seem to perform miracles. Those who lack it continually fail. Mahatma Gandhi once said, "I have not the shadow of a doubt that any man or woman can achieve what I have, if he or she would make the same effort and cultivate the same hope and faith." Almost any successful person, with a degree of humility, can relate to his statement. But faith is not everything. In fact it is almost useless without action to back it up. The remainder of Ghandi's statement went like this: "What is faith worth if it is not translated into action?" Exactly. It is not worth much.

Astro-Logos, our new way of presenting the star language and making available interpretive sessions, exists for healthy, progressive-minded people, for those who would like a "boost" in their lives. It is generative more than curative, even though the healing element is prevalent. Therefore the birthchart, as we are employing it, represents a call to action, a guidance system of possible choices and *things to do* in order to contribute, gain fulfillment, and evolve in life. Clearly, one should leave a birthchart interpretation session with action on one's mind. But in the same way faith is nothing without action, action is nothing without faith. Actions are almost never instantaneously successful. One must have faith —again alot of it—to "keep on keeping on" or there will be no success. As an interpreter/practitioner of the star language it truly never ceases to amaze me how quickly people relinquish their instinctive and intuitive lifelong dreams, passions, and purposes because they do not seem (and some would say "are not") "easily fulfillable". Never mind how boring it would be if they were. What sense would a life destiny make if it took only four or five years to achieve? Furthermore, what else is there worth doing other than what one came to life to do in the first place? What else could possibly bring fulfillment other than following one's natural, inherent direction be it difficult, extremely difficult, or even extra jumbo size difficult?

At any rate, one of the most consistent results of interpreting blueprints for individuals is confirming, based upon the chart, that their instinctive ultimate dreams or visions are correct (assuming, of course, that they are) regardless of whether the outer world has immediately conferred great success upon their activities. Then, because of this process of validation and re-connection with one's dream, there arises a great deal of inspiration for the recipient. Unfortunately, it appears that inspiration will lead to action. This is, generally, a falsehood. Inspiration does not necessarily lead to action. Action leads to action. And action then, at some point, if we are in our proper *dharma* or life path, leads to inspiration. And that inspiration, combined with more action, produces *"inspired action"*—which results in success.

Because inspiration (and only one dose of it at that) does not always generate action, some individuals may wish to arrange a series of meetings with a birthchart interpreter. By doing so there is greater possibility of using the birthchart knowledge to its fullest and the opportunity to go into greater depth of understanding of one's psychology and experience of life. Such a process facilitates a program of positive reinforcement whereby a person can learn, through repetition, to begin to trust and follow one's instincts, drives, feelings, and ambitions. For it is through repetition that the subconscious learns, absorbs, and draws its conclusions. There is then more chance of putting into action what has been, at first perhaps, only intellectually understood.

People often ask practitioners "how often should I come to see you?" The answer is that it is not a matter of how often one "should" return. It is a matter of what exactly the client wishes to gain and how much he or she is willing to invest in time, energy, and money. Ultimately, all who are interested in Astro-Logos should maintain a lifelong, perennial association with the discipline. Whether clients consult with a practitioner once or twice a year, or for extended sessions at certain points in their lives is of course a completely personal consideration. But the blueprint of destiny and the knowledge it reveals is as consistently relevant throughout life as different periods may be pressing or urgent. The person committed to growth, progress, and fulfillment always wants to know the general directions of the seasons and what evolutionary purposes they serve within the context of the entire destiny. It is always beneficial to be aware of what kinds of opportunities are worth pursuing and which are not, at different times in one's ever-unfolding journey. Therefore a lifelong association, to whatever extent the individual desires to participate, is the logical conclusion.

Even more than this, a lifelong relationship is necessary because it gives rise to a new and better way of using nature's language; a way of responsibility and ownership. Rather than perceiving each successive birthchart session as an isolated episode exclusively designed to serve some current need, the discipline should be considered an ongoing experience. In the same way people relate to the medical and law professions, by holding their doctors, dentists, and lawyers on retainer, maintaining awareness of their own past histories, and continually learning and absorbing more about the subjects over the years, so it should also be in the relationship between a person and his or her Astro-Logos blueprint. There is no need, as already mentioned, to master the interpretive process. But it is definitely in one's best interest to come to understand whatever basic aspects of one's birthchart a person can. This occurs naturally when individuals realize that their involvement with the star language is an ongoing experience.

Notes and Goals
(to be Filled Out After Session)

Use these pages to record goals, ambitions, and other matters of particular interest discussed within your interpretive session. It is to your benefit to complete this section even though you will receive a tape recording of your consultation. Because the birthchart is a blueprint for life there is value in learning as much about it and maintaining a continual commitment to its available opportunity. One reason for recording the knowledge and information gained is that benefits will be cumulative. The more you understand your own chart, destiny, and internal makeup the more you will gain from birthchart sessions year after year. Also, it is important to note the similarities different practitioners will conclude about your life. You may use these pages of reference for all your blueprint sessions whether interpreted by regular astrologers or practitioners of Astro-Logos. Aside from consulting the star language during specific periods of crisis, it is probably wise to do so at least once a year in any case. Reviewing these pages from time to time, as well as the original questionnaire you filled out, will be both interesting and insightful.

Date of birthchart session - _____
Name of practitioner - _____

1) What did you and your interpreter talk about mostly? _____
2) What is your reaction to the advice or guidance you received during the session? _____
3) What are your goals for the current year? _____
4) What are your goals for the next three to five years?
5) How sure do you feel of achieving these goals? ___
6) List any positive statements or predictions that your interpreter made about your life which stand out.
7) List any interesting but far-fetched statements worth remembering. _____
8) What would your life have to look like one year from now for you to conclude that this session made a significant impact? _____
9) Do you intend to undertake any new or special actions or commitments based upon your session? If yes, describe. _____
10) How do you feel, at this point, about your birthchart? Good, very good, just so-so, great, lousy, perfect? _____
11) Do you believe that despite whatever difficulties exist in your chart and destiny that fulfillment is possible? If not, say why? _____
12) Any other personal comments or notes about your present state and the session just finished? _____

Please read your answers to these questions just prior to your next interpretive session.

Defining Astro-Logos™

Practically speaking Astro-Logos™ is a proposed organization, a network of trained and certified practitioners interpreting the star language in a specific and relatively standardizd way. Really, however, Astro-Logos represents a new possibility, a specific "distinction" which has not yet existed. Moreover, it is a discovery appropriate and tailored to the need of the times. And in a certain sense it is simply a gift, one which has been a long time in the making, waiting to be received.

The creation of Astro-Logos is a timely one (for reasons discussed further on) and for my part exists solely to support and promote the understanding and practice of the universal, natural language of life. Such an intention will be realized when the average person can genuinely appreciate that there exists for the listening a natural language conveying destiny, purpose, and meaning, and which is spoken by nature or creation itself. That is the essential intention of Astro-Logos, and the reason for its conception.

The Possibility of Astro-Logos

Astro-Logos is the possibility of the masses possessing an authentic understanding of what the star language is and can do and what it is not and cannot do. It is that simple. Not easy but simple. In order to understand something, "to grasp the meaning or reasonableness of" (Webster's definition), a certain amount of intelligent and accurate information is needed. And in this case, because confusion and misunderstanding already abound, proper presentation is crucial. Hence the proposition of Astro-Logos, whose aim is to provide what is required in a carefully monitored and relatively standardized way. Individuals can then determine for themselves whether there is any meaning or reasonableness to nature's language of life.

At present there is an enormous gap between what the average person perceives about the star language and what the individual learned in the subject knows is correct. The discrepancy is so vast that practitioners, even amateur ones, are in a sense part of an exclusive or secret society. And yet membership need not be declared. We are members by default, by virtue of the fact that the public and the media are so far off in their understanding of the discipline that there is no common ground whatsoever between us.

The way we remain separated is simple. First of all, we who study the star language share our experiences and most exciting findings predominantly among ourselves, where our words can be readily understood and appreciated. Conversing with other practitioners is incredibly stimulating. It is also something of a relief, much like meeting a fellow countryman when traveling in some remote land. It is wonderful and enjoyable, and so we do it—and there is exclusivity. Furthermore, our books, the genuine and detailed interpretive texts, are sold mainly in occult or metaphysical bookstores, practically a secret order in themselves. As for astrological conferences and conventions where experienced and knowledgeable practitioners give out their teachings, most people have no idea that such happenings even occur. The media, merely an extension of the public, has no inclination to cover such events. So we are aliens. In terms of sharing and imparting our knowledge on a significant level, we have simply been impotent. And since interpreters of the language have found no way to alter the situation we are a kind of undeclared secret society without wanting to be. Indeed, while desiring the opposite.

Astro-Logos is the possibility of going public. Really going public—which means closing the *gap of understanding* between the expert and the layperson. It can be done as long as intentions are pure and the concern is to educate rather than to gain philosophical agreement and praise for our wonderfulness. It can be done because the time is ripe; people are ready and want to hear. Also in our favor is the fact that Astro-Logos is a "generally inclusive" creation, willing to recognize and confront all different points of view with understanding rather than resistance. We are tolerant of individuals' existing realities whatever they are. Furthermore, Astro-Logos is not a replacement for astrology or astrologers, though to some it may appear so. It is merely a way to accomplish certain long-standing goals, which astrology cannot begin to achieve except through a process of evolutionary reconditioning that would take several hundreds of years.

Astro-Logos is not an attempt to alter, change, or deny astrology as practiced today, even in its misused forms. We merely distinguish our new development as something distinct from astrology. In this way power of expression is gained as preconceptions do not yet exist. Whoever hears of Astro-Logos cannot easily assume anything about the subject. This is quite unlike astrology which is something *"everyone knows about,"* even though most have never experienced a professional birthchart interpretation or even spoken to a real astrologer. Actually, from one point of view astrology could be defined as a belief system that individuals either accept or don't accept based solely upon newspaper and magazine horoscope sections, and Sun sign books. Not so for Astro-Logos.

Aside from our new creation having a clean slate, Astro-Logos is the possibility of *intrinsic* quality control. Whereas anyone today can call themselves an astrologer and set up shop, practitioners of Astro-Logos must complete a training program and gain proper certification. This is vital for two reasons. First, the poor quality and sometimes fraudulent work that so distorts the field of astrology must not exist within Astro-Logos. Studying the subject from books alone for a few months will not suffice. Second, there are an infinite number of ways to practice the language of the stars, especially in terms of how to give out the knowledge and deal with clients. Some astrologers serve people profoundly well, while others manage only to frighten, criticize, and depress clients. Then there are those who call themselves astrologers and yet only use the birthchart to gain a tiny fraction of their information, relying almost entirely on psychic ability. And of course there are those who use no intuition at all. Further, there are interpretive techniques upon techniques upon techniques, in both Hindu and Western systems, of which certain ones appeal to some and not to others.

The ways to interpret the discipline are very many. And certainly no one system or way of working is *the* right way. But with Astro-Logos, a standard, reliable, and consistent kind of practice, at the very least, is ensured. Although interpretive procedures are not absolutely rigid and fixed, they are sufficiently structured and organized to achieve very specific results. The main purpose is to provide uniformly high-quality birthchart work that individuals can rely on without any fear or trepidation. Thus Astro-Logos can, most definitely, be considered a certain brand, or type, of star language interpretation whose qualities and characteristics can be readily known by our presentations, writings, and word-of-mouth referrals. So, Astro-Logos is the possibility of built-in quality control.

In providing a definition of star language practice—as is being done throughout the explanations, viewpoints, and techniques given in this book—limitations obviously result. Discipline and structure always close the door to certain options while supporting and validating others. Because the field at hand is as vast as it is any kind of definition may strike some as offensive. Therefore, Astro-Logos, like anything else, will not appeal to everyone. What are lost or rejected are various differing viewpoints, beliefs, and perceptions about the subject which are not necessarily wrong or inconceivable.

For example, Astro-Logos defines the star language as exactly that—a language or communicative system. Such an explanation, from our standpoint, excludes the conviction that planets *cause* effects. Not everyone may agree with this. Perhaps not everyone should. Also, while the magical and miraculous nature of Astro-Logos is in no way to be denied, there will be no promoting the subject as secretive, mysterious, or incomprehensible. Finally, some may not like the idea of using Hindu and Western astrology side by side. Different opinions and approaches to the star language are people's rights, and yet they are lost or denied, within our framework, if they do not fit into Astro-Logos as it is defined and structured. However, what is gained by our definitiveness and willingness to impose limitations is the possibility of bringing the language of nature back to the average person and restoring its ancient respected status.

Astro-Logos is a viable way of presenting our subject in an understandable, nonthreatening, and acceptable form. Moreover, it is the possibility of doing so *by raising, rather than compromising, the quality of practice.* Astro-Logos is the possibility of using the Eastern and Western systems together to achieve greater wholeness, balance, and accuracy than ever before. It is a way of reaching the people.

What does this mean ultimately? It means that individuals will be better able to understand themselves through the language of nature. It means parents will really know their children, spouses know each other, and friends understand friends. The use of our knowledge means employers can take advantage of birthchart analysis to discover the most natural talents and affinities of their employees. It means increased ease and success for psychologists and social workers who choose to use birthcharts within their practice. Likewise for vocational guidance counselors. And it means individuals can recognize potential health hazards before they occur in order to take preventative measures. Public acceptance of the star language means a list of benefits that goes on and on and on and on. This is the possibility of Astro-Logos.

The Need for a New Name

Astrology today is in a terrible state. It is fallen from honor. Whether or not this should have ever occurred is irrelevant. The fact is it has occurred. There was a time, history teaches, that astrology was held in public favor, in high regard. Unfortunately, such days have passed.

The time is nearing, however, when the language of life as spoken through the heavenly body system of symbols as words will become an accepted and prevalent discipline. This is not something a nonastrologer could know. But it is sufficiently clear to those capable of interpreting the language of the heavens that such a condition is in the making. For according to nature's communication we are approaching (some interpreters say we have recently begun) the age of Aquarius: the approximately 2,000-year era of knowledge, inventions, enlightenment, and the prevalence of the star language.

But how can this new, "celestially relevant" age come about when the discipline at hand, such a positively complex one at that, bears a name so blatantly stigmatized? Although the term "astrology" has for years served me and many astrologers well, because of its defamed reputation it has done nothing but injustice to the

287

promotion and potential acceptance of the language. It has also done an injustice to the masses who, incidentally, do their best to survive in a world where gullibility is a costly and debilitating error. The fault, clearly, does not belong to such unwitting individuals. Indeed, the public very much wants, and is constantly seeking, to find new avenues of practical, workable paths to orderliness, self actualization, and understanding of personal destiny. Shall we interpreters of the language make their process of discrimination so ghastly difficult by continuing to call our genuine and rigorous birthchart work and healing accomplishments the same name given to the newspaper horoscope nonsense, overly general Sun sign books, and carnival gypsies? Doing so is not only absurd but nearly ensures overlooking the greatest portion of the populace.

It is time to create a new name for what astrologers mean when they speak of the natural language of life and the interpretation of that language. The need of the times demands taking, at last, some responsibility for our knowledge and chosen field. There is, perhaps for the first time in centuries, a vast amount of intelligence and consciousness in our field. What has been significantly missing, however, is responsibility and courage: responsibility to accept society's lack of acceptance of astrology *as currently presented,* and courage to take matters in hand. A change is desperately in order. It is almost humorous, were it not so self-defeating, that astrologers have for so long been waiting for the public and the authorities to relinquish their claim to the word astrology. Give them the damn name to use as they wish! Let us adopt a new name, package and control the quality of our work and once and for all take back the wonderful, immensely useful, and sublime field of knowledge nature has given us.

Dictionaries define the word crazy as "mad, insane, erratic, impractical, and distracted." Rita Mae Brown once had a different definition for the word. She said a crazy person was one who continued to perform the same action while expecting different results. Calling the interpretation of the language of life "astrology" and expecting anything but misunderstanding, as you can see, is *crazy*!

CHAPTER VI

Practicing Astro-Logos

For Astrologers and Those Who Wish to Practice Astro-Logos

How and Why the Star Language Works

"The heavens declare the glory of God; and the firmament showeth His handiwork. Day unto day uttereth speech, and night unto night showeth knowledge. There is no speech nor language where their voice is not heard."

The 19th Psalm.

The following is an explanation regarding how and why the star language works. It is not proof, mind you, but explanation, food for thought. And just the tiniest bit at that. Within existence there is, necessarily, language. Within language there is, necessarily, existence. The two, language and existence, cannot be separated. While this concept is, for most people, far more difficult to grasp than our friend "Mr. Paradox" it must be addressed for it is truly important. Moreover, the precept is one of those now being expounded (quite consistently) in spiritual and philosophical circles and will inevitably come to be commonly accepted. Within existence there is always language. Within language there is always existence. The term language includes not merely communicative ability but that which is the basis of the phenomenon—quasi verbal distinguishability. In other words language includes the ability to consciously distinguish and label different items accordingly whether communicated to others or not. This must be understood.

Regarding the intertwining and interdependence of existence and language one must attempt to comprehend the reality first as if from one particular viewpoint. This does not mean that the connection between language and existence is true only from one viewpoint, but one must first see it as such before perceiving it in any other way. For the principle is so jarring and uncomfortable to our limited, "what we see, taste, and feel is what is real" perception of life that a start must be made somewhere. What the concept referred to implies, in no uncertain terms, is that *without language there is no existence. And without existence there is no language.* Helen Keller intimates that it was exactly when she awoke to language that she became human. She writes, "Suddenly, I knew not how or where or when, I awoke to language, to knowledge of love, to the usual concepts of nature, of good and evil." Of her life before "languaging" ability she relates: "For nearly six years I had no concepts whatever of nature or mind or death or God. *There was not one spark of emotion or rational thought. . . . I was like an unconscious clod of earth* " (italics added). In other words Helen Keller's human-beingness, to herself, during those years was clearly questionable even though most people would say she was human but did not, perhaps, know it.

But reality, please consider seriously, is just not that simple. Reality, according to enlightened yogis and gurus, is different in different states of consciousness, different states of beingness. Notice that they do not say "perception" of reality is different in different states of consciousness. They say reality itself is different. This fact, which would not likely influence scientists or any who are convinced that life is simply one giant objective reality, is, to my mind, absolutely relevant. Concerning Helen Keller, from one point of view, *perhaps the only real one—hers*, she was not yet human. Likewise can there be to a living entity such a thing as existence before that entity has the power to distinguish life in language (symbol corresponding to perception)? According to certain spiritual thinkers and philosophers of the day there cannot. There cannot even though it *seems* that there can.

This concept can be compared to the koan: "If a tree falls in the forest and no one hears it does it make a sound?" The difference, however, is in the significance of the matter. No one cares whether the tree in the forest makes noise or not other than the person who loves a mental puzzle. The fact that existence, for a human, cannot exist without language, without some form of distinguishability, provides some reason or logic to the heavenly body system of stars as words. It is, by now, almost commonly accepted that we are tiny microcosms of the universe. If language is intrinsic to us, so it must also be for the macrocosm. While it would be wonderful to explain the language of life as a product of God's infinite compassion; a desire to give humankind something of a built-in guide or blueprint to our lives it is, perhaps, more notable that existence is simply not possible without language. Hence the universal system of stars as words, the star language.

The logical question, then, is just why does the macrocosm speak? Why does it "language" (why does it possess the ability to distinguish)? The universe is, after all, inanimate. What can it possibly gain from this basically mechanical procedure?

It is perfectly reasonable that humankind, which is said to be made in God's image, has the ability to distinguish. Humans, by possessing "language" (distingushability) get to perceive existence—get to actually exist. From their point of view there would be no existence otherwise. But what, exactly, does the universe get out of being able to "language?" The same thing— existence. The universe, in a peculiar sort of way, exists by virtue of its "language." The universe is, believe it or not, "languaging" (distinguishing) us! That is what the macrocosm does when, quite naturally even if mechanically, its planets and stars form a mirror or blueprint of our individual human lives.

To grasp this concept we must clarify what we mean by "language" (or the ability to distinguish) and its relation to existence. That existence depends upon "language" or "the distinguishing factor" can be easily seen by analyzing a picture puzzle nearly everyone has experienced. Certain portraits or drawings have been created in such a way that they actually present two images, one of which the majority readily perceives and one which very few can at first make out. In one of these —a well-known picture of a balding man (I believe it is Sigmund Freud) and a nude woman—at first glance only the man's head is discernable. One notices the appearance of the woman only after being told to look very closely, or after being given hints that there is more to the drawing than meets the eye. After being told what to look for the viewer soon sees what in the beginning was not there. Quite reasonably, we can say that *from the viewer's standpoint* the nude woman did not exist until the viewer could distinguish her. In this sense the viewer brought the nude woman into existence—into the viewer's existence—by perceiving her, distinguishing her, "languaging" her.

Notice, for it is absolutely crucial, that the terms "language" and distinguish are used interchangeably. This is not a slip up in logic, nor an oversight, despite the fact that the human mind desperately wants to separate the two, as if there is no connection between language and existence. The human mind, designed to keep us playing in the field of illusion, or *maya* as the Hindus call it, wants to argue that life can be experienced without first being perceived in language. Sorry. It cannot. It cannot even though it seems to us as if it absolutely can. Once this is understood, as completely as we can understand it, we can see what the macrocosm gains by "languaging" us. For that is indeed what it is doing. The universe is "languaging" us, distinguishing who we be psychologically and circumstantially, through its (to us mirror-like) star language.

Here is the key to the free will issue and also to the plaguing concern of whether planets *cause* effects or not. Before proceeding, it is worth noting that throughout the writing of this book I have been perplexed as to how it could be that the heavenly body operative could, as a language, manage to have us *feel* that planets cause effects. Like all astrologers, I have during my years in this discipline literally felt the (seemingly planetary) energies which my brain has first, or sometimes afterwards, perceived through intellectual, astrological interpretation. So while I have in the preceeding chapters of this book asserted that Astro-Logos is a language and not a cause-and-effect construct it has not been until now that I have understood why or how. It is only in understanding why the macrocosm "languages" (distinguishes) that the answer is known. In distinguishing humans, in detailing our lives, through its star language the universe gets to exist by virtue of a kind of dance it creates with us. In the same way we have brought into existence, through language, the nude woman mentioned above (an inanimate creation), the cosmos—the macrocosm of humans as microcosm—has created into existence something which, like itself, is also capable of "languaging." This is the significant point regarding the cause-and-effect matter. The universe "languages," distinguishes that is, entities able to communicate and therefore it comes to exist. For it has created into its existence beings able to communicate back, to return the communication.

How do humans respond? We respond in two ways. The first is by simply distinguishing ("languaging" or acknowledging) the cosmos. The second is by our handling, our actual living, of the energies—the realities of our lives the universe has delineated/"languaged," in the way *we choose.* We reply by living the realities we bring into existence by *our* "language," our interpretation and process of distinguishing. In other words because we also possess this "language," this calling things into existence by distinguishing, we are not simply at the effect of what the star language has declared. Now if this is so then why is it that interpreters of the heavenly language can make predictions that come true so very often? Because the macrocosm, the universe, "languages" certain aspects of our being with such precision, such extreme definitiveness and clarity that there is from our vantage point almost no way to "language" (create) ourselves differently.

This may be difficult for many to understand, especially nonastrologers who have never seen firsthand how the heavenly language expresses its dictates through percentages, through greater or lesser intense birthchart aspects, etc. The concept is, no doubt, quite abstract. But the reality of being at the mercy of the universe's description of certain features of our being is no different from being around a person, often a relative, who is so absolutely positive of how we behave that we are very nearly powerless to act any other way when in their presence. There is in such cases an interplay, a dance if you will, between two created, "languaged," realities. There is conversation between two entities. The conversation exists, understand, even if no sounds (words) are made.

It is a conversation between two already distinguished, "languaged" realities (in the mind—not spoken out loud necessarily). One reality is created by the person mentally (therefore "languageably") anticipating certain behavioral patterns from the other person. The other side of the conversation is the actual behavior of the other person, the behavior based upon that person's own language and distinguishing ability. So it is exactly the same in the relationship between the cosmos and the individual. The universe "languages" us (our behavior and our lives). We "language" back. We behave according to our declarations, our language. In this way we, the microcosm, get to exist. And in this way the universe, the macrocosm, gets to exist.

In analyzing this interaction, this *interdependent* functioning of the individual and the cosmos, we can finally see the mechanics of how free will and predestiny exist simultaneously. For it is now evident that the universe and the individual depend upon each other for their very existence. Could the individual exist if there was no universe to distinguish, to perceive? It could not. There must be something (some thing) for humans to distinguish in order for them to exist. Otherwise there is only the perceiver without object of perception. And that is no existence at all. Or shall we say that is not existence as we know it. There is actually a certain kind of existence involved in "perceiving without an object of perception." It is what people in the metaphysical world like to call real existence, or pure consciousness, being, absolute, all, void, God, etc. But that is another whole reality. That is not the existence we are speaking of. We are dealing with the physical, manifest, material, worldly existence everyone daily experiences. For that existence to exist there must be a universe, an outer objective creation for the individual to distinguish. Likewise the universe cannot exist without us humans—us distinguishing, "languaging" human beings who "language" back (by living freely) to the cosmos its existence, its "languaging" ability.

In fact the universe's "languaging," its distinguishing (of us) is what we experience as predestiny. Our "languaging" to the universe, our living our lives as we choose—as we "language," is the basis of free will. The two realities are obviously interconnected. They depend upon each other. One cannot be without the other. If humans did not have the ability to "language" ourselves in a different way than the cosmos "languages" us, the universe itself could not exist. It would not then have us communicating back to it and thereby giving it existence. Its being, which is essentially its distinguishing of us and which shows up in the world as predestined human life therefore depends upon our free will. If our free will ceased entirely to be then the universe, theoretically anyway, would disappear. It would cease to exist.

The universe's process of "languaging" (which for us is the element of predestiny in our lives) cannot be without the simultaneous presence of our free will. We in turn could not exist if we did not have a universe, something to perceive. In other words we, who ultimately (from our point of view anyway) represent free will, could not exist were it not for the element of fate. Free will and predestiny depend upon each other for their very existence. They are interconnected, bound, if they are to exist, by each other's possibility. There can be no fathers without children. There can be no darkness without light. Neither can there be free will without fate. And the two must occur simultaneously or they simply cannot exist. The big question, it is now clear, is not how can free will and predestiny exist together. The question is how could we have ever thought one might exist independently of the other. What an absurdity!

There is another relevant issue worth addressing. If free will and predestiny must exist simultaneously for there to be existence, it now becomes apparent as to why twins, who are born extremely close in time, are not exactly the same. Or more importantly why the same aspect in two people's charts does not always (and in one sense can never) produce the same effect. The obvious and already understood reasons—that twins do not take their first breath at the same instant, that two people with one similar aspect may have otherwise contradictory charts, etc. —need not be dwelled upon. These explanations are commonly known.

By our newfound understanding we now realize that humans are engaged in a conversation, a back-and-forth "languaging" (distinguishing) process with the universe. Both parties, we and the universe, depend upon each other for the conversation to exist. The reason for this is that free will cannot be without predestiny and vice versa. Most significant is that from our viewpoint the universe's distinguishing shows up as our predestiny while our "languaging" shows up as our free will. And remember, of course, that the universe depends upon our free will in order for it to exist. For the universe had to distinguish beings also capable of "languaging"/distinguishing so it could be. Therefore twins *must* not be the same. Twins, or any two people who possess the same birthchart factor, must react to the distinguishing that the universe has made of them in their own individual way. They must, after having felt the "predestined" energies, the universe's "languaging," or whatever one wishes to call it, "language" themselves in their own chosen way. This they must do in order for the universe to exist. For the universe cannot be without our "languaging" ability, our free will. Therefore every particular birthchart (star language) aspect, though having a precise and exact meaning or effect, would necessarily show up differently for different people once the individuals involved completed their side of the conversation; their "languaging" process of the moment, of the experience.

The birthchart aspect itself, the "languaged" item of the cosmos, might of course be experienced (internally) in the same way for all who possess the aspect. However, that could never be known for certain because human beings are intrinsically "languaging," ever living freely. By this it is not meant that a person is *consciously* distinguishing at every moment. Yet we are, whether we are aware of it or not, always under the influence of such process because once language has begun for the human (somewhere during babyhood) his or her experience is to some extent being affected by that previous, or original, distinguishing. Thus, once a person has begun distinguishing he or she is necessarily always, to some degree or another, "languaging."

An entire book can perhaps be written to clarify and expand upon what has been said above. The philosophy of language and existence being interconnected, not incidentally, is an accepted reality for anyone who knows much about the Sanskrit language. Sanskrit is the language of the (Hindu) Vedas, which predates religion and is said to have been cognized by enlightened beings. It is, as already described in the pages on mantras and *yagyas*, a "name and form" language where there is said to be literally no difference between (the essential vibration of) a particular object and its true (Vedic) name. Since different names always invoke different forms, it is perfectly appropriate that as the star language is given a new name (Astro-Logos is not astrology) a new understanding, such as just presented, now appears.

At any rate what the reader has read is the author's attempt to explain the language of life, Astro-Logos, in view of what is already known about language and life. The reason I am so keenly aware of how difficult the philosophy may appear to most is because it took every bit of a rigorous, weekend seminar given by philosophers, real experts on the subject, to persuade my mind to give up its previously rigidly held beliefs and boundaries and see objectively what was being said. In fact, getting the philosophy, and I mean GETTING it—not understanding it, for like paradox it is not quite understandable—was an enlightening experience: a spiritual breakthrough of sorts. However, let it be absolutely clear that the person who wishes to take advantage of Astro-Logos, either through a birthchart reading or through practicing the interpretive process, need not be concerned about agreeing with these pages. What should, simply, be understood are the benefits of the Astro-Logos birthchart interpretation; what it can provide and what it cannot. That is most important.

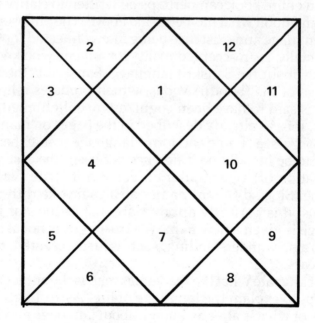

The Name

Throughout this book the discipline at hand has been continually referred to as the star language, the language of the heavens, the heavenly language, for that is precisely what Astro-Logos is—a language of life, or nature, which uses stars and heavenly bodies as its words. There is, then, very little explaining to be done. Astro, in Greek, means star. Logos means word. Astro-Logos translates literally into: STAR WORDS. Or to take some liberty: STAR LANGUAGE. It is not at all complicated. The name works perfectly because Astro-Logos is close enough to the word astrology that people, when hearing it, will quickly sense that what is referred to relates to the stars and somehow to our lives. Yet it is new and different enough that they must, no matter what, ask for a genuine explanation. Thus a real and powerful opening for our teaching is ensured. The rest is in our hands. The name also supports the speaker in describing the discipline as a language rather than anything else. When a person asks what Astro-Logos is it will always be appropriate to explain that astro means star and logos means word or language. How better to convey Astro-Logos as a communicative system than to teach that the name itself means star language?

Hindu and Western Methods—Why Both?

Polarities, differences, exist to make life interesting and exciting. Eventually, however, because opposites attract and because of evolution (the orderly force of nature) polarities must merge to create harmony. They always have and they always will, despite those who think that life moves randomly or in the direction of chaos. This is the real, underlying explanation for the advent of Astro-Logos—an interpretive system employing two very opposite methodologies. There is at present a great, worldwide harmonizing effect taking place. It is coinciding with what is called, as already mentioned, the Aquarian Age. This new age is something very different from the last 2,000 years of Pisces, a time characterized by religion, devotion, and intensely held belief structures somewhat independent of logic. It is to be an era of understanding and reason. Especially, it is an age of metaphysical and higher knowledge. Perhaps because of this fact, perhaps not, the time is predicted to be one of peace, harmony, and (spiritual) enlightenment.

The peoples of the earth are scheduled to enjoy a unity of purpose such as has not been seen for thousands of years. Indeed, the world is already undergoing massive change towards greater alliance. The process is, no doubt, long, arduous, painful, and fairly well concealed but it is definitely occurring. Eastern and Western nations are, quite amazingly and for the first time in aeons, borrowing from each other's cultures, philosophies, and economic practices. Weaker, Third World nations are commanding more power and presence thereby lessening the more obvious differences between themselves and superpowers. Even male and female stereotypes are breaking down. This is all, *ultimately*, a move towards more balance, unity, and agreement. The differences of life, during this metamorphosis, will be hard pressed to maintain their separateness. And in some cases, at least in the short term, there will be pronounced difficulties to be worked through.

For example, as cultures borrow from each other's philosophies and religions many very fine, indigenous traditions are being mercilessly tossed away by natives of their respective lands. Also, the merging of masculine and feminine traits has produced confusion, uncertainty of role identities, and distressingly high divorce rates. But ultimately this is part of a purification process that must accompany the integrating of natural forces. It is most definitely for the better. For the result will be a world of people more unified, tolerant, and infinitely more able to understand and embrace each other's dissimilarities.

As for Astro-Logos employing both the Hindu and Western methods of star language interpretation the gains are tremendous—truly wonderful. It is not simply that between the two methodologies twice as much information about a person is revealed. It is that the birthcharts of the systems are counterparts of each other: they reveal complementary information. The Hindu chart provides details of what, for no apparent reason, seems to be routinely missing from the Western blueprint. And vice versa. That the Western system reveals the inner workings and behavior while the Hindu system tells of the actual life circumstances clearly requires that the systems function as two halves of one whole. Even the underlying contradictory cultural philosophies when joined together make for more balanced living. Easterners would do well to realize just how much their free will, their present attitudes and actions, affect their lives rather than attributing so much to karma and past lives, etc. Westerners can avoid a great deal of tension, frustration, and wasted energy in accepting that certain features of their lives have essentially been predetermined from birth and that fierce resistance is not always an appropriate tactic. Life is, after all, more rewarding and successful in working tolerantly and patiently within one's given (actually chosen before birth) boundaries. Using the two systems in tandem is definitely advantageous.

Aside from greater accuracy and the many other reasons already discussed in previous chapters for using the Eastern and Western systems together there is another very powerful one. It concerns the counseling or healing process that occurs within birthchart readings. Human beings, until enlightened spiritually, emotionally, intellectually, and physically have needs. That is, generally, what brings them to consult the heavenly language in the first place. The job of the interpreter/practitioner is to meet those needs through any and all available means. There are counseling techniques to be used and there is the basic content, or the underlying medium, the star language birthcharts.

All existence is made up of two contrasting forces, two opposite energies. They are called yin and yang. Yin and yang are characterized as feminine and masculine, expansive and contractive, lunar and solar, relaxation and tension, centripetal and centrifugal. Illness, described by Webster's as "an unhealthy condition of body or mind," is due in whole (ultimately) to an imbalance of either one of the forces—yin and yang. Regarding physical illnesses the body can be said to be a kind of harpsicord. If the strings get out of balance, too tight or too loose, the body becomes susceptible to sickness. And the illness itself is said to be caused by excess yin or yang energy. The same is true of the other human levels—emotional, intellectual, and spiritual. For instance a person may be too emotionally or psychologically contracted or restricted (yang). On the other hand one could be too scattered and "spaced out" (yin).

Ailments caused by different imbalances require different treatments. Individuals overly yang in nature, overly tense that is, need a therapy consisting of abundant yin: relaxing, comforting, or soothing input. Those who are too yin, too weak, lazy, and fearful need a powerful dose of yang, or direct, forceful, confronting energy. It is the task of the Astro-Logos practitioner to deliver, in as effective a way as possible, the yin or yang input a particular client is lacking and to guide them in the appropriate direction. In other words the practitioner must act as a conductor or transmitter of energy within the interpretive session. And he or she must advise and counsel the recipient to take future actions which will lead to balance.

Obviously no two people are the same. Furthermore each person is yang in certain respects and yin in others. Everyone, also, is on the whole, more yin or yang. Perfect balance is extremely rare, if not impossible. In order to meet the terribly varying needs of different clients one must be sensitive, astute, and perhaps more than anything else flexible in the ability to transmit either kind of stimulus. Having both Hindu and Western birthcharts at hand supports this humanistic process perfectly. The reason is simple. The systems are opposites; one is yang and the other yin. The Hindu system

—being prediction oriented, objective in nature, and based on strict rules and regulations—is yang. The Western methodology is yin. It is behavior oriented, psychological in nature, and requires the use of intuition or a kind of meditative blending. Practicing both systems in conjunction develops the two energies within practitioners and therefore gives a client greater and more ready access to either yin or yang energy. It also leads practitioners themselves to balance.

In terms of the treatment of a client the Western chart, because it reveals the client's psychology and humanness in such detail, enables the interpreter to deeply empathize with that person. There is then great potential for sympathy, care, and compassion: something, I can say from experience, is often lacking in birthchart interpretation sessions with Hindu astrologers. The Hindu chart, on the other hand, unravels the reality of circumstance; it provides hard and fast data with which a counselor may confront the client or move the person to action. The Hindu chart generally contributes more concrete information: that which is so very necessary to gain a person's trust and confidence. At any rate it is both interesting and wonderful that if the practitioner is sensitive to allow nature to take its course, each birthchart session will focus predominantly on one particular chart interpretation, either the Hindu or the Western. In other words after the basic meanings and explanations have been given and the client and counselor get down to the nitty gritty—the real reason the person has shown up for the session—one chart often jumps out, as it were, as the main tool to use in order to provide guidance. Psychologist Abraham Maslow once wrote, "If the only tool you have is a hammer, you tend to see every problem as a nail." Possessing both systems marvelously increases one's options and thus the likelihood of success in the counseling process.

Above all, to the interpreter of the heavenly language

what the ability to use both methods of chart interpretation provides is confidence; confidence in one's ability to deliver a complete, whole, portrait of a life satisfying both the client's psychological and circumstantial needs. This is no small accomplishment. It is indeed no small accomplishment for a person brave enough to have taken on the enormous task and responsibility of interpreting the language of life for others. Confidence, I dare say, is absolutely essential. In fact aside from that, and of course intellectual talent, there is only one other human attribute so necessary to success in this field of endeavor. And that, contradictory though it be, is humility—the ability to reflect, to remain always open to possibilities unknown and indefinite. And it must be present in equal abundance!

To interpret birthcharts, life destinies, for others requires absolute confidence as well as absolute humility. Confidence without humility in this field is dangerous. The discipline is simply too delicate and consequential for a practitioner lacking sensitivity, flexibility, open-mindedness, and the ability to admit unknowingness (when necessary) to serve the purpose well. Such a person could, with precious little effort, cause harm, fear, and unnecessary expectations to unsuspecting and unwitting clients. Anyway, those who are greatly confident but lack humility stand little chance of ever achieving profound interpretive ability. The star language is much too complex. It is far too commingled with the possibility of creating our own futures: the paradox of simultaneous free will and predestiny, etc.

On the other hand humility without confidence is wasteful, or worse—useless. Practitioners unable or unwilling to own up to their abilities, while they do little harm, are generally impotent to do much good. Aside from often driving themselves out of business by charging insufficient fees for their work, they may also lack the required strength of conviction to effectively convey what the recipient needs to hear. Without confidence it is nearly impossible to move others to make use of the information revealed in a birthchart reading. Interpreters of the language of nature simply must possess absolute (or as much as can be mustered) confidence and absolute humility. Using the Hindu and Western systems together for each interpretation so enhances one's accuracy, as well as the level of understanding about the entire subject, that greater confidence is a natural result. To say this is a profound benefit is an understatement.

It is tempting to assert that much of the reason, or basis, for the star language being maligned for so long is that it has been practiced in a fragmented state; a state of incompleteness. Whether that is so or not is, at this point, merely intellectual entertainment. For the process of using the two systems side by side has already begun. That it will become commonplace is a foregone conclusion. What is significant is that tremendous strides are bound to occur as this happens. While some might argue that over the past few thousand years there have been those who have been extremely adept in their work with the "mystical" language, using only the Eastern or Western method, such fact is of no consequence. For it is just those practitioners, the ones who have managed to succeed so well with only half of the available tools, that stand to make the greatest advances. These are the ones for whom Astro-Logos is the most thrilling proposition.

At the risk of being terribly redundant I must again say that in just practicing one system, in my case the Western, it was obvious within a mere few years that something quite basic was missing. Here I do not simply mean that predictive ability was lacking. Even within the Western methodology one could study and develop more intricate, detailed predictive techniques, probably till the end of time, and achieve considerable success. Of that there is no doubt. But in practicing either the Hindu or Western systems, systems emanating from cultures so thoroughly favoring an exclusive philosophy of life (either free will or fate), something great is necessarily lost. That something is wholeness; wholeness and therefore balance. What is lost is the opportunity to determine the complete picture of a person's life and thus counsel one properly; with wisdom and perspective. It is the ability to have some power, some actual impact during the counseling process, over the free will issue *as it relates to a person's actions;* their "fixed" destiny as revealed from the Hindu chart and their internal struggle or "creative will" as detailed in the Western blueprint. Wholeness of chart interpretation means the ability to determine when a client's attitudes and habits are in perfect working order but their karma is, somehow, deficient. Or vice versa.

Finally, the wholeness resulting from dual-system chart interpretation means answers; answers to long-standing interpretive questions. From a platform of wholeness and broad viewpoint certain interpretive problems disappear quickly and without fuss. The most basic dilemma, and one which has plagued Western practitioners for centuries—"the problem of the houses" —vanishes immediately when one finally understands the distinct purposes of the predictive and humanistic systems of East and West and begins to experience the more traditional house method of the Indians. (Two techniques are available, one more recent and one traditional.)

In using Western techniques it generally happens that after two, three, or four years, depending on the interpreter, one comes to realize that the houses, the twelve spaces of blueprint, produce somewhat inconsistent results in terms of revealing objective life effects. Yet they do work extremely well if one uses them exclusively to ascertain a person's psychology and behavior.

When analyzing a Hindu chart while using the more traditional method, the houses—which now become organized in a very different way (meaning that planets in a particular house in the Western chart may occupy a different space in the Hindu blueprint, etc.)—are far more reliable predictively speaking. Thus in using the two methods there is complete orderliness. The most common house method of the Western system (Placidus) provides the exactness of a person's inner life while the traditional method of the Hindus (equal house system, i.e., planets in *any* degree of a sign occupy the corresponding numerical house) tells of the actual life effects. In this manner many frustrating discrepancies of the interpretive process resolve themselves as the wisdom and experience of East and West are combined. What is most exciting regarding this evolutionary process is that we are, at this point, merely in our infancy in addressing such matters.

The case for Astro-Logos, for employing the Hindu and Western systems together, should be understood in perspective. Having both charts of a client at one's disposal is a breakthrough—a wonderful quantum leap. It is, most definitely, not everything. Practitioners who use the Western or Hindu chart exclusively can do amazing things, as has already been exhibited through the various accounts in the first four chapters of this book. Possessing both systems is simply, in the author's opinion, much better.

Proving Astro-Logos

We are not in the business of proving Astro-Logos. Astro-Logos is, after all, a language. In the same way people do not set out to prove English or French neither is there any need to do so with Astro-Logos. We are, of course, responsible to educate and teach those who wish to understand and decipher the language. From that position the individual may come to his or her own judgments and conclusions as to its effectiveness. Naturally one may like or dislike the means of communication; consider it difficult or easy, pleasing or displeasing to the mind, etc. And one may consider it to work well, fairly well, or poorly in its intended (or allegedly intended) functioning. But such opinion depends upon direct experience with the language itself, not anyone's speaking *about* it. It would be absurd to try to prove that certain symbols within a complex system represent specific meanings without actually teaching the decoding process, the meanings and manners themselves. There does exist, of course, the possibility of simply demonstrating the language. But that would never suffice as proof. For the very nature of language and communication is that it is heard through individual ears, subject to different interpretation. Therefore the decoding and deciphering of nature's communiqué will always vary according to the interpreter's level of consciousness, not to mention experience, astuteness, and intelligence. This is not to say that nature does not speak or convey its own exact and specific utterances. It does. But that fact is not as quintessential as the reality that Astro-Logos as we experience it is a language and not a cause-and-effect construct.

Even more significant, perhaps, is the fact that Astro-Logos is not an ordinary language. It is one we can hear and interpret but not speak! Therefore, Astro-Logos is a one-sided conversation. There is no way to question, or reply to, nature about its expression. Imagine one entity speaking an intricate, lengthy, and highly spirited discourse to many individuals all of whom listen though their own individual makeup and who possess no means whatever to probe or clarify their understanding through questioning. Could there really be any other result than a mass of different interpretations? Would there be any way to prove what the speaker truly meant? Probably not. One could know what was said but not necessarily meant. To those who would seriously ask for proof of Astro-Logos we do best justice to all in simply suggesting that they experience the language firsthand. By this we mean actually learning the interpretive process or some degree of it. We do not propose that they merely obtain a birthchart interpretation. For even this, no matter how exemplary, no matter how profound, meaningful, or objectively accurate is still not "proof" of the language. Birthchart readings are not absolute in any sense of the word. Therefore proof, in the current scientific community's accepted meaning, would definitely be elusive.

For those who wish to determine whether nature has created an effective means of communication or not, there is only one way to do so and that is to begin to learn the interpretive process. As for the organization of Astro-Logos, much of its purpose is to provide just such teachings. Further, for the benefit of society, birthchart interpretations are available for all who wish to partake. However, it must be said that practitioners of Astro-Logos have no desire or intention to thrust upon, or to alter or convert, people's ideas about anything. Neither are we bent on turning noninterpreters of the heavenly language into interpreters. Practicing Astro-Logos is, for obvious reasons, not for everyone. Our purpose is simply to educate and make available the knowledge of the natural language of life both in its theoretical and practical aspects. In this mission we are neither resistant nor assertive. We are merely sharing what we have experienced as a tremendously functional and essentially irresistible gift of nature. A gift whose time, we declare, has arrived.

While we do not offer empirical proof of Astro-Logos, it would be folly not to provide something enticing for people to relate to as an incentive to participate. We are, to be sure, engaged in a monumental course of action supported by evolution and destined, by our commitment, to prevail. Therefore we offer the simple stuff that alters history. Ourselves. Astro-Logos thrives entirely by virtue of the people who benefit from its use. There is, in moving fellow men and women, nothing greater than the genuine, heartfelt sharing of human experience. Thus in relating to others, specifically, coherently, and logically how we have profited for ourselves and managed to serve others through nature's language we will accomplish our goals and spread our word. The success of Astro-Logos will then, ultimately, depend upon individuals achieving rewarding and favorable results from their association with the discipline. And that is absolutely as it should be. In expressing our experiences through lectures, TV and radio appearances it behooves us to speak intelligently and in a manner which illuminates the *basic teachings* of the language of life. We should especially demonstrate and share, whenever possible, our own birthcharts and those of famous personages. That which is real and genuine to us we can with clarity, power, and integrity convey to others. Personal experience is the ultimate tool we possess to excite others to the possibilities of the language.

Somehow this aspect of making known the benefits of our discipline has been grossly lacking for some time now. We astrologers have instead, unwittingly, tried to inspire others through giving out cursory, and therefore superficial, Sun sign interpretations. Though such descriptions can, of course, be real enough they are essentially insignificant in terms of making any real difference or impact to the listener. Both the public and astrologers have paid a dear price for the error. The worst of which is a great misunderstanding, on the part of the layperson, as to the actual possibilities of the star language. Furthermore, because of all this there now exists an almost inconceivable gulf between those who are knowledgeable in the field and those who are not. There is fortunately a way out of the dilemma. And that is to genuinely share our own personal, in-depth experiences. This, in Astro-Logos, is the heart and soul of our message. It is what we have—it is what we give. It is what is necessary.

Creating a Reality—The Practitioner's Task

Technically speaking, the job of the practitioner of Astro-Logos is to objectively interpret an individual's blueprint of destiny. In practice, when interacting face to face with a client, what this amounts to is creating a reality through language. It is the creating of a probable and potential reality; an experience of life, circumstantial and psychological, likely to occur by virtue of that person's taking his or her most natural course—the individual's "path of least resistance." On the negative side the practitioner advises the person of all the undesirable events and behavioral patterns bound to be encountered if preventative measures are not adopted. And on the positive side of the interpretive process, where more time and attention should generally be placed, the task is to make real as beneficial and fulfilling a scenario as the chart reveals possible. That scenario, being the highest and best possibility for the client, naturally is one which requires effort and persistence. But it is clearly the one most worthy of the person's energies. Hence the interpreter functions as both priest and prophet. In focusing on the more positive aspects of a person's talents and potential accomplishments, the practitioner is more priestly while in advising one of possible dangers and inert or stagnant states of existence, he or she is more the warning prophet.

What is at issue in creating a reality, during the birth-chart interpretive session, is not so much a person's blueprint or the star language itself. It is the interaction between two conscious and intelligent individuals that is essential. Although the reality a practitioner attempts to create for a client is obviously not something pulled out of thin air or one's vivid imagination, the intended state of affairs—the most beneficial conditions of life the practitioner envisions for the client—may not immediately seem a real and attainable possibility to the recipient. Despite the fact that the interpreter expresses the basic truth of what appears in the blueprint, the human condition—replete with its doubts, fears, and pessimism born of past failures—nearly always stands in the way. It is exactly for this reason that there must exist a powerful "working relationship" between the interpreter and the client. This relationship must be one of trust, mutual respect, and understanding.

For it is absolutely the human connection, the interaction between interpreter as experienced guide and client as seeker, that provides the basis for the interpretation of the blueprint to be taken as a body of knowledge worth doing something about. It is the practitioner of the star language who represents why nature's communication is to be utilized as something more than mere entertainment or "pie in the sky" expectations. Therefore the relationship depends, more than anything else, on the *humanity and integrity* of the practitioner. And, successful guidance counseling in this discipline depends quite profoundly upon that person's ability to make real, to translate into earthly experience, the veracity of nature's language of life. For the job of the practitioner, this "creating a reality" business, is really a process of enrolling the client in what the interpreter knows is possible, realistic, and attainable for the client. And at the same time broad enough in its task and commitment to give meaning to the tedious, day-in-and-day-out activities necessary to the success of the ultimate goal. Therefore the interpreter conveys the highest, most desirable, and most *able-to-be-related-to* potential reality to be found within the birthchart.

But clearly mere transmission of information, words alone whether written or spoken, will not likely suffice in terms of moving a person to action. And it is action that the language of life calls for in order to be used to its highest purpose! Ultimately then, whatever the practitioner presents must be intelligently analyzed, discussed with the client, and sensitively delivered such that the person involved can, both mentally and emotionally, perceive that such state of life is not only plausible but in fact destined. Not that any such circumstance is destined by unalterable, unquestionable fate or any other causative agents—namely planets and stars. We are after all not puppets. But it must be gotten that the greatest, most beneficial conditions revealed in the chart are destined in the sense that they are a natural outward extension of one's internal makeup and genetic code. Such specific potential situations are destined in the same way that seeds if properly planted and nourished must mature into fullgrown trees of the exact same variety. Moreover, what shows up in the birthchart is destined because it is that person's self-chosen intention for human existence. And self-chosen intentions (made in the soul realm before birth), because we are made in God's image, do not die easily—if at all. These organic, internal desires, talents, and abilities do not in any way disappear even if ignored or suppressed with lifelong effort. Naturally one may die without realizing many aspects of potential destiny but the human traits and cravings that constitute destiny would simply reappear in future lives if reincarnation is as it is said to be. It is simply part of the design of human beings that our aspirations for achievement, experience, and accomplishment cannot, in the final outcome, go unfulfilled. Astro-Logos exists, if we choose to use it, to aid us in getting on with the process.

And yet interpreters of the heavenly language are neither magicians nor miracle workers in convincing others of their best options or their highest and most natural destinies. We are only evolving human beings ourselves. However, we do have an especially unique advantage, for ourselves, in being able to decipher nature's communiqué. This advantage is not merely the competitive edge of knowing when "the tides are high or low"; when the seasons of our lives are favorable and when they are not, and towards what end. It is much more than this. What we possess is a basic, practical awareness of our connection to the universe and therefore to each other. Our advantage is the ability to identify our tiny individual lives as an integral part of all existence and as purposeful within the entire scheme of evolution.

Whereas so very many people view their lives as occurring quite randomly or at the mercy of some unfathomable God or fate, those who interpret birthcharts based upon nature's language see objective and directed patterns of experience. We perceive through birthchart dictates the reasons for, or what can be gained from, the experience of the different situations encountered in life at any given point in time. Such realities are inevitably passed on to our clients as immediately as they enter our domain and accept (whether they realize it or not) the fundamental premise of the star language—that there is an orderliness about the universe which extends even to the intimate details of our lives.

But in moving clients to make something of their potential destinies, to take their blueprint/map of life as seriously as it deserves to be taken, more—indeed much more—is needed. Of course the entire system of the star language discipline needs to be revamped or at least very well purified. That is what Astro-Logos is about—educating the public, presenting the discipline intelligently, controlling the quality of interpreters and their work, clearly distinguishing the responsibilities of the practitioner and the client, and making known and available what is to be gained from participation in the work. From our side, we the practioners can and must live our lives as embodiments, as living proof of what can be done with the knowledge of our own birthcharts.

Whether and how each particular practitioner cares to elucidate the ways he or she has benefitted from association with Astro-Logos is an individual matter. But the practitioner interested in guiding others must enjoy some discernible measure of success or life dexterity as a direct result of his or her own birthchart knowledge.

Interpretive ability alone is not enough. Astro-Logos is an experiential, not theoretical, discipline and that must be conveyed in every possible way to our clients. Otherwise practitioners remain little more than entertainers and clients the entertained. The heavenly language, because it addresses actual individual lives, is a humanistic discipline. It therefore thrives upon the relationship between the interpreter and the recipient. It is through our humanity, caring, compassion, and sense of inbred connectedness to our clients as fellow human beings that such persons will or will not allow themselves to be affected by our blueprint interpretations. Based upon our presentation and interactions with them as people they will decide whether or not to trust what we have to offer. Our jobs as practitioners being properly done, our lives being the living examples they should be, the important remaining issue is that of the responsibility of the client; how much does that person wish to participate and what must he or she understand about our subject in order to gain benefit. These matters, all but ignored in past centuries, must be made crystal clear.

Positivity

Birthchart interpretations must be uplifting. They must be positive or "something of which an affirmation can be made," as Webster's dictionary defines the word. This is extremely important. For why would people who leave an interpretive session feeling depressed, fearful, or powerless over their destinies ever want to consult with the star language again? Indeed why should they if the outcome is a conversation for negative possibility? They shouldn't. There is a way, however, to describe and discuss the reality of one's fate, as found in the chart, in a positive way no matter how "good" or "bad" the information may seem to our materialistic, comfort loving consciousness. It is not difficult, it does not take any more time or effort to achieve, and requires no greater intellect than any person capable of interpreting the star language possesses anyway. What is needed is a spiritual attitude; a point of view that considers life from a broad, whole, or all-inclusive perspective.

It is obvious to anyone who interprets the heavenly language that life is a growth process, a process of evolving towards realization of the Godhood within ourselves. With this in mind all our experiences on earth can be seen to lead us, ultimately, to that goal. That is the point of karma. If what we reap (what we experience), is what we have sown (caused by previous actions) then even if no one ever explains to us the law of karma, we eventually get the message that there are life supporting and life-damaging ways to be, and we modify our behavior appropriately. Moving towards a God-like (or saintlike, if you prefer) state is also what the choosing of our destinies is about. As spirits or souls we choose our birth time (and therefore the blueprint) in order to confront the experiences and activities necessary to most naturally and rapidly ensure our evolution. In this sense, because all is ultimately moving towards perfection, the universe and our lives and absolutely everything happening at any given point in time are perfect exactly as they are. In this sense nothing exists but positive activity since in the final outcome everyone reaches the desired goal. (Though it may take hundreds or thousands of lifetimes. Perhaps more.)

This does not mean that people do not have problems, which they would love to solve. They certainly do. And it does not mean that a birthchart revealing severe afflictions, perhaps financial hardships, career instability, or marital struggles is not going to produce (coincide with) a painful life. It is. And it most definitely does not suggest that people's dilemmas are to be trivialized or avoided by glibly classifying them as "wonderful opportunities to repay some nasty old karmas." What it means to us that the universe is perfect is that all existence, including humans, is involved in an evolutionary process —a process leading to perfection—and therefore every experience an individual encounters is exactly what is needed and on some level, desired. Therefore people's adversities are their challenges, tests, their opportunities for heroism, and in a certain sense their privileges.

There is a quote by Alfred D'Souza that goes like this: "For a long time it had seemed to me that life was about to begin—real life. But there was always some obstacle

in the way, something to be got through first, some un-
finished business, time still to be served, a debt to be
paid. Then life would begin. At last it dawned on me
that these obstacles were my life." Like this, it is our job
to guide clients to deal with, to directly face, with as
much consciousness as they can muster, whatever difficulties their lives consist of. People's problems are not to
be resisted, judged, or perceived as something *absolutely* requiring change. That is up to the individual to
decide. Of course people nearly always do want relief.
That is not the point. The point is that in order to create a
positive session, to provide a safe space for the recipient
we must not consider and categorize their foibles as ab-
errant, abnormal behavior equivalent to unsightly
warts. Quite simply, people's plights are their
humanity.

The issue of positivity comes into play mainly when
describing particular afflictions that appear in the chart.
And definitely everyone has problems. Problem-free
birthcharts do not exist, neither for the great ones—
Christ, Moses, Krishna, Buddha—nor for celebrities—
Madonna or Michael Jackson—nor for us ordinary folk.
Thus there is no choice but to learn how to deliver what
may be undesirable about a person's life in an acceptable
and useful form. Otherwise the star language is better
left completely ignored. Some years ago, early on in my
work, a man named Freddie came to me whose birthcharts (both Hindu and Western) were so badly afflicted
that I did not know quite how to begin our conversation.
The usual procedure is to ask the exact reason for the
consultation and then interpret the charts beginning
with the more beneficial and uplifting aspects of life that
are revealed. In this way an atmosphere of comfort and
relaxation can be created while confidence in the star
language, as well as my interpretive ability, will be
gained.

However, in Freddie's case nearly all of the typically
enjoyable aspects of life (money, love affairs, marriage,

career success, homes and cars) were badly ruined. Not just afflicted or difficult but denied or devastated. The Hindu chart revealed the sparseness of the man's blessings while the Western chart showed intense inner struggles, as well as behavioral patterns in need of attention. The few benefits that did exist were good intellectual and academic abilities and a strong interest in occult or hidden sciences. But even so, nature, or Freddie's superconscious, had little intention of having the world reward or greatly recognize these talents.

So I decided to feel out the situation by inquiring as to his reaction to life before describing the destiny as seen through his charts. Since I intended to speak candidly about what the blueprints revealed I wanted some idea of his present viewpoint so the reality about to be created with my words would not frighten, depress, or make things worse in any way. It was certainly possible that Freddie was already well accustomed to his situation as it was. If so, then describing his life as being extraordinarily difficult could easily have a negative effect. On the other hand I did not wish to minimize the situation since individuals with painful lives sometimes visit astrologers simply to express their anguish and have it heard by someone who can genuinely appreciate and empathize with the intensity of their suffering. Or they come to determine whether they are somehow at fault; creating problems nature itself did not really intend.

At any rate, communicating delicate or difficult information about a person's life, a life which the person is already quite familiar with, in a positive, non-damaging way is mostly a matter of understanding the recipient's viewpoint and acting accordingly. This means giving out, or framing, the data in a way that is generally compatible with the person's present interpretations of his or her experience (assuming, of course, that those interpretations are in the realm of reasonableness). This creates a starting point of harmony rather than discord no matter how difficult or extreme the particular issues being discussed may be. Thus I attempted to converse with Freddie before explaining my findings.

No such luck. My client politely but firmly insisted that I discuss his blueprint for some time, after which he would, very openly, answer whatever questions were put forth. I appreciated his request and agreed, hesitantly, explaining that his birthchart was a rare one and that our session together might be more delicate than most. Though there was no mincing of words in my description of his apparent hardships I spoke in a decidedly logical manner, with as little emotion, opinion, or judgment in my voice as possible. By doing so a certain kind of neutrality was maintained and the chance of violating his sensibilities lessened. The interpretations were accurate enough and after some time Freddie felt compelled to let me know, with great conviction, how "damned difficult," as he put it, his life was.

Now there was a frame of reference from which to work. This man was miserable and frustrated and wanted relief. Unfortunately he was not seeking to do anything to achieve it. He had tried doing things, all sorts of things—spiritual techniques, self-improvement regimens—for years and wanted no more of that. Even suicide had been a continuing consideration but that was not an option. Aside from the absurdity and horribleness of the act it was not much of a likelihood anyway since the Hindu chart revealed an especially long life. In any case Freddie and I talked for some hours about the situation, life itself, and different religious or spiritual philosophies. We did our best to find the truth and shed as much light on matters as possible.

By the end of our session Freddie's lifelong frustrations were not miraculously resolved. There was no fairy tale ending to our meeting. However, amazingly enough, this session which I so feared because of the seemingly inherent negativity involved turned out to be one of the most positive and memorable experiences of my astrological work. According to Freddie it was the best "reading" of his life (there hàd been many). Because I could so easily understand and empathize with this man's predicament, his intense discontent and explicit unwillingness to take action, I did not in any way resist it. On the contrary I embraced and sought to work with his reality. The more Freddie complained about his difficulties the more I agreed with and acknowledged the scenario he was creating. The more he blamed his stars the more I repeated that his was one of the "roughest" charts I had ever seen, even explaining why I had initially wanted him to speak first.

Finally, after thoroughly indulging ourselves in all the adversities of his life there came a natural end to our griping. And then there was, of course, nothing left to do but face the problem. It was not so difficult, at least in terms of relieving the pressure of Freddie's present depression and resentment. By wholeheartedly agreeing with this man that he was merely a victim of his ill-fated destiny a very real sense of trust had been gained. Incredibly, the rest of our time we spent rigorously analyzing Freddie's responsibility—the reason he himself had chosen his particular birth time (as a soul in the afterlife) and the extraordinarily difficult existence now being lived. Having indulged ourselves to the limit regarding Freddie's helplessness we became perfectly free to focus on a different viewpoint of the situation; what was the possible *value* to be gained in living such a life? What benefits might occur spiritually, emotionally, or characterwise in living an existence so clearly marked by struggle?

Final answers were not determined within our conversation. They were not meant to be. The power of the task did not lie in reaching conclusions but in the process of seeking answers to a question postulating value and benefit to Freddie's life. An alternative way of perceiving his pained existence was already being created in the hour or so we searched Freddie's psyche for insights. The session was exciting—especially for my client who thanked me profusely and left feeling extremely elated. This was, evidently, the first time he had ever realistically viewed his struggle as something other than a completely useless and undesirable experience. With this came a sense of pride, responsibility, and ownership for his life. And a new way of facing future challenges. The key to our success, clearly, was in maintaining a spiritual or broad viewpoint and the position that life, no matter how extraordinarily difficult it can be, is ultimately positive. From my session with Freddie I learned a simple but profound lesson: birthchart sessions can always, if handled sensitively, be uplifting and positive—something of which an affirmation can be made.

A Note to Astrologers

Astro-Logos, as an organization, is not an end in itself. It is a means to an end, the end being the education of society in the ways of the heavenly language. There are many talented, proficient astrologers worldwide whose abilities remain pitifully unused. Until these practitioners can serve the public on a daily basis with respect and appropriate remuneration the purpose of Astro-Logos will not have been achieved. It will only be achieved when the common person has enough understanding of the star language to be able to make appropriate use of nature's great gift. Also, individuals must come to know enough about the subject to be able to discriminate between quality interpretive work and superficial, amateurish, or fraudulent work.

Astrological organizations have been working diligently for decades to train and certify astrologers. The result is a higher standard of practice and better quality birthchart interpretations. This is extremely laudable. There are now certified astrologers throughout the world willing and able to serve the public. However, there is far more work to be done (of a different nature) if these astrologers are to ever practice regularly for a public sufficently knowledgeable about our subject. Astro-Logos' greatest work, then, is educational.

The Astro-Logos organization is autonomous. It will function as its own entity. But our purpose is neither personal nor exclusive. It is broad in vision and scope. By educating the public about the nature and benefits of the star language, Astro-Logos supports the astrological community and is inclusive of all astrologers. In the same way that a few new age movements have made the term meditation—once an occult or mystical word—familiar, Astro-Logos exists to bring the star language back to the people. The public, once informed, can then choose for itself from a variety of astrologers and astrological associations and services which have long been available. Astro-Logos thus works to the benefit of all astrologers.

Astro-Logos endeavors to rectify the main problem in our field today: that the star language has not yet been presented with integrity ("The condition of having no part taken away or wanting. The condition of not being marred or violated." *Oxford English Dictionary*). There can be no integrity of presentation as long as trained astrologers and astrological counselors allow their profound healing work to be called by the same name as newspaper and magazine fortune telling. Nor will there be integrity of presentation until practicing astrologers learn to communicate the real and profound benefits they have gained from their involvement with the star language. Astrologers simply must begin sharing their personal experiences, en masse, in ways the common person can understand and relate to. These are some of the concerns Astro-Logos will address.

There is an ancient Chinese proverb that goes like this: "If you do not change your direction, you are likely to end up where you are headed." At the rate we have been going the gap between astrologers and the public could actually grow wider. The growth and advancement in astrological techniques and practice over the past fifty years has been quite significant. The texts of astrological authors such as Robert Hand, Stephen Arroyo, Alan Oken, and Isabel Hickey to name only a few surpass the older treatises by leaps and bounds. But there has been almost no improvement of public understanding of the subject. Many gifted and sensitive astrologers refuse to practice for the public because of the confused and misguided expectations so many have. The situation demands that we solve the problem of public perception or suffer the consequences of even greater alienation.

While some believe the answer lies in the creation of a "science" of astrology, statistical research, and the licensing of astrologers etc. these are not immediate, and perhaps not essential, concerns. The star language, though not perfectly exact, works powerfully and profoundly when properly understood. If and when people are presented with intelligent, understandable, non-threatening explanations of the ways and benefits of the star language from individuals they can trust the situation will naturally begin to rectify itself. Whatever is required will arise out of the needs of the people. If those needs are predominantly material and financial, a science of astrology with abundant statistical research may be created. If they are emotional, religious, and spiritual astrologers may remain independent practitioners specializing in their own particular methods. And if people's needs are as vast as the nearly infinite varieties of astrological applications now available, we are apt to see little significant change in the *structure* of our field. The present diversity of practice will, appropriately, continue. This is not our concern. Our task is to avail the public of high quality astrological work such that they can make use of their God given birthrights. From there nature will take its course.

We are at a crucial point in the history of this discipline. After centuries of "astrological sleepwalking" the world is beginning to awaken. Let every astrologer do his or her part to educate the public, practice with integrity, remain continuously open to new knowledge, and may we live our lives as examples of what can be gained from our involvement with the star language.

Services

Persons interested in practicing Astro-Logos™ or in attending Astro-Logos™ workshops, classes in the Hindu system, or private birthchart interpretations (please specify your area of interest) please send a stamped, self-addressed envelope to:

ASTRO-LOGOS
P.O. BOX 22-1961
Hollywood, Florida 33022-1961
Name -
Phone -

Please include birth data
DATE—
LOCAL TIME -
PLACE -
SOURCE OF DATA (MOTHER, BIRTH CERTIFI-CATE, ETC.) -

* Copies of *Ancient Hindu Astrology for the Modern Western Astrologer* @ $19.95. Add $1.60 for shipping and handling.
* Copies of *Astro-Logos, Language of Life* @ $12.95. Add $1.00 for shipping and handling.